WORLD
HISTORY SERIES ■ ■ ■

The Roman Empire

Titles in the World History Series

The Roman Empire

by
Don Nardo

Lucent Books, P.O. Box 289011, San Diego, CA 92198-9011

Library of Congress Cataloging-in-Publication Data

Nardo, Don, 1947–
     The Roman Empire / by Don Nardo.
          p.   cm.—(World history series)
     Includes bibliographical references and index.
     Summary: Traces the history of the Roman Empire from
the days of the Republic through the reign of the Caesars and
the influence of Christianity to the fall of Rome.
     ISBN 1-56006-231-2
     1. Rome—History—Empire, 30 B.C.–476 A.D.—Juvenile liter-
ature. [1. Rome—History—Empire, 30 B.C.–476 A.D. 2. Rome—
Civilization.]   I. Title.   II. Series.
DG270.N37   1994
937—dc20   93-6906
                                                                   CIP
                                                                    AC

Contents

Foreword

Each year on the first day of school, nearly every history teacher faces the task of explaining why his or her students should study history. One logical answer to this question is that exploring what happened in our past explains how the things we often take for granted—our customs, ideas, and institutions—came to be. As statesman and historian Winston Churchill put it, "Every nation or group of nations has its own tale to tell. Knowledge of the trials and struggles is necessary to all who would comprehend the problems, perils, challenges, and opportunities which confront us today." Thus, a study of history puts modern ideas and institutions in perspective. For example, though the founders of the United States were talented and creative thinkers, they clearly did not invent the concept of democracy. Instead, they adapted some democratic ideas that had originated in ancient Greece and with which the Romans, the British, and others had experimented. An exploration of these cultures, then, reveals their very real connection to us through institutions that continue to shape our daily lives.

Another reason often given for studying history is the idea that lessons exist in the past from which contemporary societies can benefit and learn. This idea, although controversial, has always been an intriguing one for historians. Those that agree that society can benefit from the past often quote philosopher George Santayana's famous statement, "Those who cannot remember the past are condemned to repeat it." Historians who ascribe to Santayana's philosophy believe that, for example, studying the events that led up to the major world wars or other significant historical events would allow society to chart a different and more favorable course in the future.

Just as difficult as convincing students to realize the importance of studying history is the search for useful and interesting supplementary materials that present historical events in a context that can be easily understood. The volumes in Lucent Books' World History Series attempt to present a broad, balanced, and penetrating view of the march of history. Ancient Egypt's important wars and rulers, for example, are presented against the rich and colorful backdrop of Egyptian religious, social, and cultural developments. The series engages the reader by enhancing historical events with these cultural contexts. For example, in *Ancient Greece,* the text covers the role of women in that society. Slavery is discussed in *The Roman Empire,* as well as how slaves earned their freedom. The numerous and varied aspects of everyday life in these and other societies are explored in each volume of the series. Additionally, the series covers the major political, cultural, and philosophical ideas as the torch of civilization is passed from ancient Mesopotamia and Egypt, through Greece, Rome, Medieval Europe, and other world cultures, to the modern day.

The material in the series is formatted in a thorough, precise, and organized manner. Each volume offers the reader a comprehensive and clearly written overview of an important historical event or period. The topic under discussion is placed in a broad, historical context. For example, *The Italian Renaissance* begins with a discussion of the High Middle Ages and the loss of central control that allowed certain Italian cities to develop artistically. The book ends by looking forward to the Reformation and interpreting the societal changes that grew out of the Renaissance. Thus, students are not only involved in an historical era, but also enveloped by the events leading up to that era and the events following it.

One important and unique feature in the World History Series is the primary and secondary source quotations that richly supplement each volume. These quotes are useful in a number of ways. First, they allow students access to sources they would not normally be exposed to because of the difficulty and obscurity of the original source. The quotations range from interesting anecdotes to far-sighted cultural perspectives and are drawn from historical witnesses both past and present. Second, the quotes demonstrate how and where historians themselves derive their information on the past as they strive to reach a consensus on historical events. Lastly, all of the quotes are footnoted, familiarizing students with the citation process and allowing them to verify quotes and/or look up the original source if the quote piques their interest.

Finally, the books in the World History Series provide a detailed launching point for further research. Each book contains a bibliography specifically geared toward student research. A second, annotated bibliography introduces students to all the sources the author consulted when compiling the book. A chronology of important dates gives students an overview, at a glance, of the topic covered. Where applicable, a glossary of terms is included.

In short, the series is designed not only to acquaint readers with the basics of history, but also to make them aware that their lives are a part of an ongoing human saga. Perhaps they will then come to the same realization as famed historian Arnold Toynbee. In his monumental work, *A Study of History,* he wrote about becoming aware of history flowing through him in a mighty current, and of his own life "welling like a wave in the flow of this vast tide."

Important Dates in the History of the Roman Empire

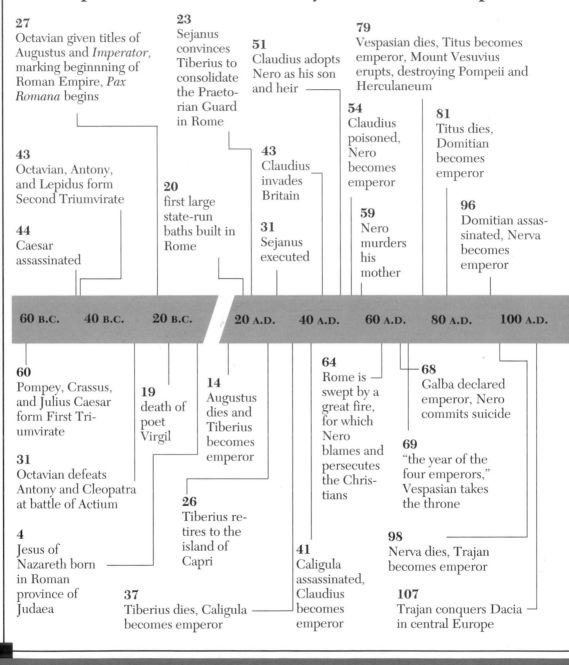

27
Octavian given titles of Augustus and *Imperator,* marking beginnning of Roman Empire, *Pax Romana* begins

23
Sejanus convinces Tiberius to consolidate the Praetorian Guard in Rome

51
Claudius adopts Nero as his son and heir

79
Vespasian dies, Titus becomes emperor, Mount Vesuvius erupts, destroying Pompeii and Herculaneum

54
Claudius poisoned, Nero becomes emperor

81
Titus dies, Domitian becomes emperor

43
Octavian, Antony, and Lepidus form Second Triumvirate

20
first large state-run baths built in Rome

43
Claudius invades Britain

44
Caesar assassinated

31
Sejanus executed

59
Nero murders his mother

96
Domitian assassinated, Nerva becomes emperor

60 B.C.   40 B.C.   20 B.C.   20 A.D.   40 A.D.   60 A.D.   80 A.D.   100 A.D.

60
Pompey, Crassus, and Julius Caesar form First Triumvirate

19
death of poet Virgil

14
Augustus dies and Tiberius becomes emperor

64
Rome is swept by a great fire, for which Nero blames and persecutes the Christians

68
Galba declared emperor, Nero commits suicide

31
Octavian defeats Antony and Cleopatra at battle of Actium

26
Tiberius retires to the island of Capri

69
"the year of the four emperors," Vespasian takes the throne

4
Jesus of Nazareth born in Roman province of Judaea

41
Caligula assassinated, Claudius becomes emperor

98
Nerva dies, Trajan becomes emperor

37
Tiberius dies, Caligula becomes emperor

107
Trajan conquers Dacia in central Europe

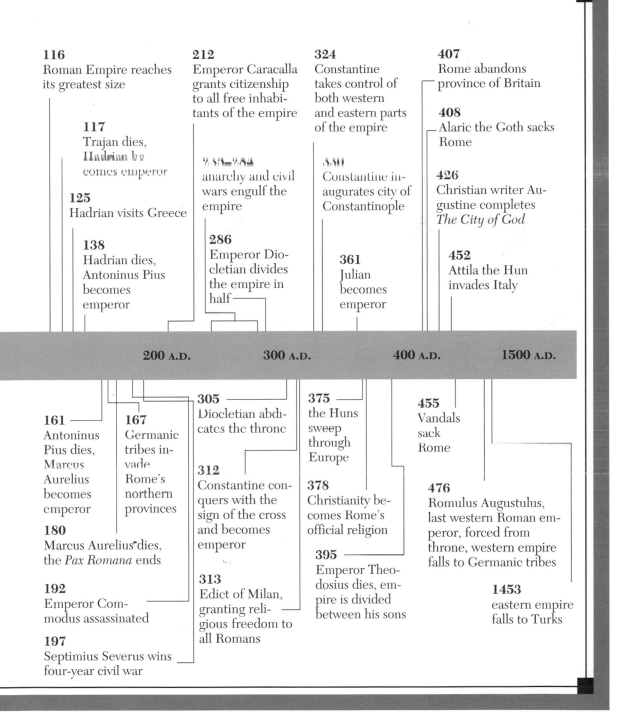

116 Roman Empire reaches its greatest size

117 Trajan dies, Hadrian becomes emperor

125 Hadrian visits Greece

138 Hadrian dies, Antoninus Pius becomes emperor

161 Antoninus Pius dies, Marcus Aurelius becomes emperor

167 Germanic tribes invade Rome's northern provinces

180 Marcus Aurelius dies, the *Pax Romana* ends

192 Emperor Commodus assassinated

197 Septimius Severus wins four-year civil war

212 Emperor Caracalla grants citizenship to all free inhabitants of the empire

235–284 anarchy and civil wars engulf the empire

286 Emperor Diocletian divides the empire in half

305 Diocletian abdicates the throne

312 Constantine conquers with the sign of the cross and becomes emperor

313 Edict of Milan, granting religious freedom to all Romans

324 Constantine takes control of both western and eastern parts of the empire

330 Constantine inaugurates city of Constantinople

361 Julian becomes emperor

375 the Huns sweep through Europe

378 Christianity becomes Rome's official religion

395 Emperor Theodosius dies, empire is divided between his sons

407 Rome abandons province of Britain

408 Alaric the Goth sacks Rome

426 Christian writer Augustine completes *The City of God*

452 Attila the Hun invades Italy

455 Vandals sack Rome

476 Romulus Augustulus, last western Roman emperor, forced from throne, western empire falls to Germanic tribes

1453 eastern empire falls to Turks

200 A.D.   300 A.D.   400 A.D.   1500 A.D.

The Evidence from the Ashes

On August 24 in A.D. 79 a large-scale natural disaster struck suddenly on the western coast of Italy about 120 miles south of Rome. At the time, this thriving city of more than a million people was the capital of the Roman Empire. Consisting of all the lands surrounding the Mediterranean Sea, the empire was the largest and strongest military and political power on earth. But while Roman might had conquered the known world, it could not stand up to nature's unleashed fury. The towering volcano called Vesuvius awakened after thousands of years of dormancy and began spewing out enormous quantities of poisonous gases, volcanic ash, and red-hot lava. This eruption was an event of great significance, not only in a direct way for the people who lived near the volcano, but also indirectly for people today.

Mount Vesuvius, the volcano located seven miles southeast of the modern Italian city of Naples, erupted in A.D. 79, burying the Roman towns of Pompeii and Herculaneum.

The immediate effects of the catastrophe were most severe for the inhabitants of Pompeii and Herculaneum—two Roman towns situated only a few miles from the volcano. The Roman historian Pliny the Younger was visiting Pompeii at the time and he later recalled:

> By now it was dawn, but the light was still dim and faint. The buildings round us were already tottering. . . . We also saw the sea sucked away and apparently forced back by the earthquake. . . . On the landward side a fearful black cloud was rent by forked and quivering bursts of flame, and parted to reveal great tongues of fire, like flashes of lightning magnified in size. . . . Many [people] besought the aid of the gods, but still more imagined there were no gods left, and that the universe was plunged into eternal darkness evermore.[1]

Although a number of people escaped the disaster, many died, and a thick layer of volcanic ash buried the two towns. Believing the eruption to be a punishment sent by the gods, the Romans abandoned the site, and in time Pompeii and Herculaneum were forgotten.

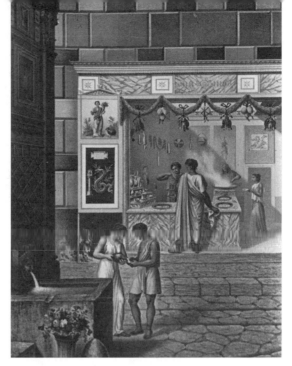

A tavern near the Fountain of Mercurius in Pompeii as it probably appeared before the eruption.

But the towns were destined for a rebirth of a different sort. The Pompeiians' tragedy later became the modern world's good fortune when archaeologists in the 1800s and 1900s began to unearth the remains of the buried cities. Luckily, the hardened ash had preserved nearly everything.

A plaster cast of one of the eruption's victims, lying in the exact position he was in at the moment of death.

The ruins of Pompeii include the public square, or forum, the temples of Jupiter and Apollo, and many houses and shops. Nearly half of the city remains unexcavated.

As a result, visiting Pompeii today is like stepping into the past. The ruins afford us a glimpse of a town of the Roman Empire at its height. As historian James Henry Breasted remarked:

> We can look down long streets where the chariot wheels have worn deep ruts in the pavement; we can enter dining rooms with charming paintings still on the walls; we can look into the bakers' shops with the charred bread still in the ovens. . . . The very life of the people in the early Roman Empire seems to rise before us as we tread the now silent streets of this wonderfully preserved place.[2]

The ruins of Pompeii and Herculaneum reveal some of the habits, likes and dislikes, and overall character of a remarkable people. The layout of the streets, the design of the houses, and the kinds and quality of personal effects show that the Romans were highly practical, industrious, and resourceful. According to the evidence from beneath the ashes, they were also supremely confident in their own institutions and way of life. They strongly believed that they had the best and most logical system yet devised, and they methodically and aggressively imposed that system on others. It is no wonder then that for hundreds of years they held sway over a huge empire of diverse lands and peoples spanning most of the known world. Until Roman civilization eventually declined and thousands of towns like Pompeii crumbled and vanished, the saying "All roads lead to Rome" was a literal fact. Thanks to a random act of nature, Pompeii, located on one of those ancient highways, remains to testify to the greatness of its builders.

Chapter

1 From Republic to Empire: The Augustan Age

January 16, 27 B.C., was a special day for the people of Rome. Large crowds gathered in the Forum, the city's central square, and surrounded an imposing building known as the Senate House. Few knew exactly what was happening inside. But they waited patiently because the government had announced that on this day a new ruler would be named.

A marble statue of Augustus, carved during his reign by an unknown sculptor.

In a large chamber inside the building, the senators, dressed in togas of white and purple, sat in tiers of seats facing a semicircular speaker's platform. At a given signal, a young man named Octavian, a military leader recognized as the most powerful man in Rome, entered and stood on the platform. He was sandy-haired, thin, and walked with a slight limp. Though physically unassuming, he bore an air of great intelligence and self-assurance.

A solemn and elaborate ceremony followed in which the senators heaped praises on Octavian and thanked him for his military exploits, which, they said, had "saved the country." They presented him with a laurel wreath, a symbol of honor and glory, and a golden shield inscribed with his new name, Augustus, or "the great and exalted one." At the same time, he retained the family name of Caesar, handed down from his great uncle, Julius Caesar. In Augustus's honor, the senators changed the name of the Roman month of Sextilis to August and ordered the minting of special coins bearing his image. They also gave him the title of *Imperator,* or "supreme commander," from which the modern word emperor is derived. Augustus Caesar then walked outside and acknowledged the cheers and applause of the Roman people.

A Long and Turbulent History

Although this event marked the beginning of what came to be called the Roman Empire, it was not the beginning of the Roman nation. When Augustus's reign began, Rome was already a large and powerful empire with a long and turbulent history. The use of the word "Empire" with a capital E became a convenience to differentiate the new Rome, a dictatorial state ruled by Augustus and his successors, from the Rome of the past, a more democratic state known as "the Republic."

The Romans were descended from primitive tribes who had migrated from central Europe into the fertile plains of Italy about 1000 B.C. They called themselves Latins and spoke a language of the same name. Initially, they established farming villages on seven hills near a bend in the Tiber River about fifteen miles inland from the western Italian coast. About 750 B.C., these villages combined into the then-small city of Rome, which at the time

Made up of well-to-do patricians, the Senate was the Roman Republic's most respected and powerful political institution.

controlled only a tiny section of central Italy. The Romans were surrounded by other Latin tribes, as well as by more advanced peoples such as the Etruscans in the north, and the Greeks, who had recently colonized southern Italy.

At first, kings ruled Rome. In time, however, some Roman landholders became rich and powerful and challenged the power of the kings. About 509 B.C., the Romans threw out their king and established a republic, a government run by elected representatives. The Romans defined "the people" rather narrowly however, allowing only free adult males, a relatively small portion of the population, to become citizens and take part in government. Periodically, a large group of citizens met in a body called the Assembly, proposed and voted on laws, and once a

This silver coin, minted in Antioch, Syria, bears Augustus's image.

Questioning Greek Honesty

During the century encompassing the late republic and early empire, many Greeks came to Rome, either as slaves or as free workers. Many Romans distrusted Greeks, whom they considered to be inferior, and anti-Greek prejudice was common. Cicero, the great orator and writer of the late republic, put this feeling into words in his speech entitled Pro Flacco.

"This I can say of the whole race of Greeks. I grant them literature, I grant them a knowledge of many arts, I do not deny the charm of their speech, the keenness of their intellects, the richness of their diction; finally, if they make other claims I do not deny them. But truth and honor in giving testimony [in court] that nation [Greece] has never cherished: the meaning, the importance, the value of this whole matter they know not. Whence comes that saying, "Testify for me and I'll testify for you"? It isn't thought to be Gallic, is it? Or Spanish? It is so entirely Greek that even those who do not understand Greek know the Greek words for this expression. . . . And Greeks never bother to prove what they say but only to make a display of themselves by talking. A Greek witness takes the stand with the intention of doing harm, he does not think of the worth of his oath but of words that may injure; to be beaten, to be refuted, to be worsted in an argument, he regards as a disgrace; he protects himself against this and cares for nothing else. So the witnesses selected are in each case not the best and most influential men but the most pert [impudent] and most talkative."

year elected officials called consuls to run the government. The Senate, made up exclusively of wealthy landholders known as patricians, advised the consuls. In the beginning, the patricians totally controlled the government. But eventually the common people, called plebeians, or plebs, won the right to have their own assembly and make laws. The plebs also elected officials known as tribunes, who had the power to veto any law.

The Roman Republic proved to be both flexible and popular and was a source of pride and patriotism for the people. Practical, hard-working, and used to hardships, they came to believe that their system and ways were superior and that they were destined to rule others. This attitude, revealed in their speeches and writings, was strengthened by the Romans' belief that the gods favored their nation above all other nations.

The defeat of Carthage at Mulae in the First Punic War was Rome's first important naval victory. Rome fought and won three wars against Carthage.

Under the republic's banners, and with the blessing of the gods, Roman armies marched outward in the fifth century B.C. and began conquering neighboring peoples. A long series of bloody wars ensued during which Rome subdued the Etruscans, many Italian tribes, and finally the Greeks in the south. By 264 B.C., the Romans controlled all of Italy. They then pushed outward across the Mediterranean Sea and conquered the rich trading nation of Carthage, centered in northern Africa. The large islands of Sicily, Corsica, and Sardinia, as well as most of what are now Spain and southern France, were in Roman hands by the dawn of the second century B.C. Then Rome turned eastward and conquered Greece and most of Asia Minor, what is now Turkey. By the beginning of the first century B.C. the Mediterranean had become almost literally a Roman lake and Rome was the most powerful nation on earth.

One reason the Romans were so successful was that they borrowed the best aspects of the civilizations they encountered. They lacked inventiveness but made up for it by skillfully adapting others' ideas to their own needs. As the Roman historian Sallust put it, "Whatever [the Romans] found suitable among allies or foes, they put in practice at home with the greatest enthusiasm, preferring to imitate rather than envy the successful."[3] The Romans imitated the Greeks the most, basing much of their art, architecture, and literature on Greek models.

The Fall of the Republic

But Rome's phenomenal success came at a price. As the empire grew, the Romans found it increasingly difficult to administer so many diverse lands and peoples. Also, conquest and rule required large, well-trained armies and able generals. Some generals gained great wealth and power and could be counted on to secure pensions and land for their men upon re-

A bust of Pompey (106–48 B.C.), one of Rome's greatest military heroes.

tirement. Consequently, in time the soldiers began to show more allegiance to their generals than to the government. From the beginning of the first century B.C. onward, control of Rome's armies shifted steadily away from the Senate and the consuls to the generals. Repeated power struggles among military strongmen ignited bloody civil wars and put the republic increasingly in jeopardy.

A major threat to republican rule occurred in 60 B.C. when the three strongest generals of the day—Crassus, Pompey, and Julius Caesar—decided to put aside their rivalry. They formed a coalition known as the First Triumvirate, or "rule of three," with the goal of wielding dictatorial powers. At first they were successful. But eventually they fought among themselves in renewed civil wars, and Caesar emerged

triumphant. He realized that Rome's republican government had become ineffective and believed that one-man rule would be more orderly and efficient. But Caesar became unpopular when he imposed restrictions on the Senate and Assembly and proclaimed himself dictator for life. Rumors abounded that he would also make himself king, a title the Romans despised. To prevent this from happening, on March 15, 44 B.C, a group of angry senators assassinated Caesar.

The power vacuum left by Caesar's death was filled by two able generals, Mark Antony and Lepidus, and by Octavian, Caesar's eighteen-year-old grand-nephew and adopted son. The three formed the Second Triumvirate in 43 B.C. and used the army to force the government to recognize their power. But the alliance did not last. More than a decade of brutal civil wars and power struggles followed, eventually leaving Octavian the undisputed victor and strongest man in Rome.

Rome's Sole Master

After nearly a century of political unrest and civil wars, Rome's government was in shambles and its people frustrated and warweary. Like Caesar, Octavian believed that Rome needed the order, guidance, and stability of one able and well-meaning ruler. But he wisely avoided openly declaring himself dictator, so as not to suffer Caesar's fate. Instead, Octavian announced his intention to restore the republic to its former authority. "May it be mine to build firm and lasting foundations for the government of Rome," he said. "May I also attain the reward for which I hope, and be known as the author of the best possible

*After murdering Julius Caesar, the conspirators rush outside shouting
"Liberty!" Their joy is short-lived, for Octavian and Antony soon defeat them.*

constitution, taking with me when I die the hope that these foundations will endure."[4] Octavian made a great show of his respect for the Senate and other republican institutions. He encouraged the Assembly to go on electing public officials and even turned down senatorial offers to give him various government positions with special privileges. "I refused every office offered me which was contrary to the customs of our ancestors," he later wrote.[5]

But all this was mere show. In reality, Octavian was sole master of Rome, mainly because he completely controlled the armies both in Italy and in the Roman provinces. Without an army to enforce its wishes, the Senate was powerless. Octavian also solidified his power by increasing his popularity. Among a number of government-funded public programs he sponsored were large-scale distributions of free food to the poor. In addition, because he had already eliminated all powerful political and military opponents, his reign was peaceful. And with peace came economic prosperity. Octavian's rule won the praises of a populace used to the food shortages and economic disruptions caused by decades of war. Octavian, according to the Roman historian Tacitus:

> won over the soldiers with gifts, the populace with cheap corn, and all men with the sweets of repose [peace], and so grew greater by degrees, while he concentrated in himself the functions of the Senate, the magistrates [government officials] and the laws. He was wholly unopposed, for the boldest spirits had fallen in battle . . . while the remaining nobles . . . preferred the safety of the present to the dangerous past.[6]

Because of his military power, his popularity, and his willingness to allow the old government to keep functioning, Octavian won the respect of the senators. They now believed as he did, that a benign dictator could bring order and prosperity to the country. So they happily went through the fiction of publicly granting him powers he either already possessed or easily could have taken by force. After the ceremony on January 16, 27 B.C., he not only bore the titles of Augustus and *Imperator*, but also exercised direct control over most of the important provinces, including Egypt. He was also granted the powers of tribune for life. This meant that he could instantly veto any law passed by the government. Although the Assembly went on electing local officials, they were almost always the ruler's nominees. Augustus held so many diverse powers that he was, in fact, an emperor. However, to retain his popularity he prudently refrained from calling himself emperor or king and instead used the title of *princeps*, meaning "first citizen." To further bolster his image as a man of the people, he and his wife Livia lived in a modest house and shunned the usual lavish lifestyle of the wealthy.

Peace and Prosperity

Unlike many other dictators in history, Augustus ruled fairly, wisely, and constructively. His peaceful and prosperous forty-two-year reign, the Augustan Age, was the beginning of a long era of prosperity known as the *Pax Romana,* or "great Roman peace." This was a period of economic and cultural growth and stability that would last some 200 years. Thus Augustus kept his promise to build a firm and lasting foundation for the country and the empire. As the generation with firsthand memories of the republic died out, most people looked back on the republican years as a time of trouble and chaos. They were thankful for the order and good times Augustus had brought. Tacitus wrote:

> In the capital the situation was calm. . . . Even most of the older generation had come into a world of civil wars. Practically no one had ever seen truly Republican government. The country had been transformed. . . . Political equality was a thing of the past: all eyes watched for imperial [the emperor's] commands. Nobody had any immediate worries as long as Augustus retained his physical powers, and kept himself going, and his House [his heirs], and the peace of the Empire.[7]

Among other social reforms, Augustus granted citizenship to freed slaves.

The changes Augustus's new order brought to Rome affected many institutions besides the government. First, he reorganized the army. In republican days, there had been more than thirty legions, or groups of about 5,000 soldiers. For the sake of efficiency, Augustus reduced the number of legions to twenty-five. He also raised the troops' pay and instituted regular government pensions, consisting of money and land, thus reducing the old threat of the soldiers giving their allegiance to wealthy generals instead of the state. In addition, he created an elite force of about 9,000 specially trained soldiers known as the Praetorian Guard. Swearing oaths to lay down their lives if need be, the Praetorians acted as Augustus's bodyguards and made sure that his policies were carried out. Augustus also recruited another 1,500 men to act as a police force for the city of Rome, which at the time had a population exceeding one million. This measure significantly reduced the crime rate and the number of public riots, both of which had become serious problems during the chaotic last years of the republic.

Augustus also reformed the administration of the provinces. Under the republic, the provincial governors, appointed by the Senate and consuls, served short terms. Many of these governors, having attained their positions as political favors, were inexperienced, so corruption and mismanagement were common. Augustus improved the system by appointing all governors himself from a pool of capable administrators. He allowed them to serve for a period of several years so that they could carry out long-term policies. He rewarded those who did well and demoted those who ruled poorly.

Augustus reformed the tax system by ordering a census of each province, to find out how many people should pay taxes. And he made sure that the tax money went for building roads and other public works in those provinces rather than ending up in tax collectors' pockets. Overall, his system of running the provinces was fair and efficient and continued in the reigns of his immediate successors.

With just and stable governments in both Italy and the provinces, transporting goods became easier, safer, and more profitable. So trade increased significantly all over the empire, and living standards rose for the middle and upper classes. Rome's vast trading network was supported not only by huge fleets of cargo ships, but also by a complex system of roads. Augustus built many new roads and improved the old ones. He also greatly increased the number of *mansiones,* large guest houses for travelers located about every fifteen miles along the roadways.

Builder and Patron of the Arts

In addition to roads, Augustus constructed many artificial harbors and aqueducts—stone structures housing water pipelines—across the empire. The harbors increased the number of trading centers, and the aqueducts allowed towns and farms to flourish in arid regions. Augustus erected dozens of fine public buildings in Rome, all of marble, including a new forum he named the Forum of Caesar in honor of his great-uncle. He also ordered the construction of the magnificent stone Theater

The ruins of the Theater of Marcellus, where Roman crowds once enjoyed the comedies of Terence, Plautus, and other playwrights.

of Marcellus and the first large public baths in the city, located in an area known as the *Campus Martius,* or Field of Mars. He built several new temples in an effort to promote the traditional Roman gods. One of the finest of these temples was that of Apollo, god of the sun and music, located near Augustus's residence. The building housed a large private library that the *princeps* and his family used often. Describing the new Augustan Rome, the Greek traveler and geographer Strabo wrote:

> The ancients of Republican times bestowed little attention upon the beautifying of Rome. But their successors, and especially . . . Augustus . . . have surpassed all others. . . . The greater number of these [improvements] may be seen in the *Campus Martius*. . . . The structures that surround the *Campus* . . . the summit of the hills beyond the Tiber, extending from its banks with panoramic effect, present a spectacle which the eye abandons with regret. . . . If thence you proceed to visit the ancient forum . . . you will there behold the Capitol [hill], the Palatine [hill], and the noble works that adorn them . . . each successive work causing you to forget that which you have seen before. Such then was Rome![8]

Everywhere in Rome, and in many other cities as well, new buildings sprang up, most of them copying Greek architectural styles.

Augustus also championed the arts, especially literature, and his reign became

An Ode to Rome's Prince

Horace's poetry was nearly as popular in Rome as Virgil's. In the poem titled To Augustus, *Horace extolled the virtues of the ruler he called Rome's "Prince" and expressed how unhappy people were when Augustus was away from the city.*

Sprung from Gods, best guard of Rome,
Long, too long, thou leav'st thy homc.
Thou didst promise shorter stay;
Ah! return, the Fathers pray.

Ah! return, thy country cries,
Like the spring-time to our skies;
Days shall glide more sweetly o'er,
Suns come brighter to our shore. . . .

Long they reign, good Prince, we pray,
Grace by many a festal [festival] day;
This our prayer at sober morn,
This, at cheerful eve's return.

The Roman poets Virgil, Horace, and Varius meet at the home of wealthy literary patron Gaius Maecenas. After Virgil's death, his friend Varius edited The Aeneid.

Many of the poet Ovid's (43 B.C.–A.D. 18) works were based on ancient myths.

one of history's literary golden ages. He and his friends patronized, or supported, many writers and poets, the most famous being Virgil. In addition to the *Georgics*, a group of poems praising country life, Virgil composed the long epic poem *The Aeneid*. Depicting the chief legend of Rome's founding, this work became Rome's national patriotic epic, and in time every Roman schoolboy could recite long passages of the text from memory.

Two other renowned poets patronized by Augustus and other influential Romans were Horace and Ovid. Horace, a friend of both Virgil and Augustus, wrote the *Odes*, a group of poems depicting everyday themes in a humorous, mellow style. Ovid wrote mainly love poetry that, for its day, was considered to be somewhat racy. A part of his work *The Art of Love* proclaims:

> All the stars in the sky are less than the
> girls Rome can offer:
> Venus [goddess of love] is mother and
> queen here in the town of her son.
> If you are fond of them young, you will
> find them here by the thousands,
> Maids in their teens from whom you
> will have trouble to choose.[9]

The Augustan Age's greatest prose writer was Livy, whom Augustus befriended and patronized. At Augustus's request, Livy wrote a huge, 142 volume history of Rome, covering events from the legendary founding up to about 9 B.C. Although only thirty-five of these volumes have survived, they have proved invaluable to modern historians. Livy's descriptions of Roman leaders, battles, customs, and institutions are the only detailed sources available about many periods of Roman history.

A Part Well Played

In A.D. 13, at the age of seventy-six, Augustus sensed that he did not have long to live. He had no surviving male children of his own, so he entrusted the care of the empire to Tiberius, Livia's son from an earlier marriage. Augustus was leaving behind an enormous realm. It included all the lands bordering the Mediterranean, as

Tiberius (43 B.C.– A.D. 37) served as tribune, consul, and general before becoming emperor.

Augustus Lists His Accomplishments

Shortly before his death in A.D. 14, Augustus completed the Res gestae divi Augusti, *a brief summary of his own deeds, which included a number of impressive military and domestic accomplishments.*

"When I was nineteen I collected an army on my own account and at my own expense, by the help of which I restored the republic to liberty. . . . Those who killed my father [Julius Caesar] I drove into exile after a legal trial in punishment of their crime, and afterwards, when these same men rose in arms against the republic, I conquered them twice in a pitched battle. . . . I cleared the sea of pirates. In that war I captured about 30,000 slaves who had run away from their masters and had borne arms against the republic, and handed them back to their owners. . . . The whole of Italy took the oath to me spontaneously and demanded that I should be the leader in the war in which I won the victory off Actium. . . . I extended the frontiers of all the provinces of the Roman people which were bordered by tribes that had not submitted to our Empire. The provinces of the Gauls [later the French] and Spain and Germany . . . I reduced to a peaceful state. The Alps, from the district near the Adriatic [the sea bordering eastern Italy] to the Tuscan sea [the section of the Mediterranean directly west of Italy], I forced to remain peaceful without waging unprovoked war with any tribe. . . . I added Egypt to the Empire of the Roman people. . . . I settled colonies of soldiers in Africa, Sicily, Macedonia [Greece], both the Spains . . . Asia, Syria. Italy has twenty-eight colonies established under my auspices [rule], which have in my lifetime become very densely inhabited and places of great resort. . . . The Senate . . . and the Roman people with one consent greeted me as FATHER OF MY COUNTRY, and decreed that it should be inscribed in . . . the Senate house and in the Forum Augustum. . . . When I wrote this I was in my seventy-sixth year."

well as parts of central Europe and most of Gaul, what is now France—some 3,340,000 square miles in all—an area larger than the continental United States. Augustus urged his stepson to make no more attempts to expand Rome's borders. Instead, Tiberius was advised to use his energies to rule the existing empire wisely and efficiently.

Augustus's health steadily declined until on August 19 in the year 14 he lay on his deathbed surrounded by family and friends. Reportedly, his last words repeated the line often used to end Roman comedies in the theater. "Since well I've played my part," he said, "clap now your hands, and with applause dismiss me from the stage." He then embraced his wife and whispered, "Remember our long union, Livia; farewell."[10] A few seconds later he was dead.

In the days that followed, millions across the empire mourned the loss of the leader they had come to view as a father-figure. Many wept openly as a group of senators carried the fallen *princeps* through the streets of Rome to the *Campus Martius*. There, he was cremated while a choir of children sang a sacred hymn for the dead. It was a fitting end for one of the world's best and most beloved rulers, a man who had indeed played his part well.

Chapter

2 Rome of the Caesars: The First Century of Peace

The first century A.D. was largely a peaceful and prosperous era for the Roman Empire. Because Augustus had ruled so efficiently and benevolently, nearly all ambitions and desires to bring back the republic had died out during his long reign. Under his guidance, the chaos and instability of the civil wars had become distant memories. All over the empire trade flourished, new towns sprang up, and living standards rose. Even many of the poor benefited, thanks to government-sponsored food distribution programs and new temples, theaters, and other public buildings. The vast majority of people were satisfied with this situation. So, few opposed the continuation of one-

Merchants sell their wares in an outdoor market-place in the Roman Forum.

man rule after Augustus's death. In accordance with Augustus's wishes, the Senate bestowed all his titles and powers, including *Imperator* and tribune, on the fifty-five-year-old Tiberius.

Like Augustus, Tiberius retained the family name of Caesar. The new emperor and his three successors, all related to Augustus, formed the empire's first dynasty, or ruling family. In time, the name Caesar became an imperial title, given to all emperors regardless of heritage. Under Augustus's dynasty and the Flavian dynasty that followed, the Caesars continued to operate the political and economic systems Augustus had put in place. Some of these rulers were much less effective and just than others. But overall, the *Pax Romana* begun by Augustus remained in effect. Enjoying what Pliny the Younger called *Immensa Romanae pacis maiestas,* "the boundless majesty of the Roman peace," the empire thrived.

An Able but Unpopular Ruler

From the beginning, Tiberius recognized that to keep the government and economy running smoothly, he had to perpetuate

A View of the Sea and Distant Hills

From the first century B.C. on, most well-to-do Romans owned villas, luxurious homes usually located in the countryside or near the seashore, to which they could go to escape the hustle and bustle of city life. In a letter to a friend, Pliny the Younger described his own villa, located near a Mediterranean beach about seventeen miles from Rome.

"The villa is large enough for all requirements, and is not expensive to keep in repair. At its entrance there is a modest . . . hall; then come the cloisters [covered walkways], which are rounded into the likeness of the letter D, and these enclose a smallish but handsome courtyard. . . . Facing the middle of the cloisters is a cheerful inner court, then comes a dining-room running down toward the shore . . . and when the sea is disturbed by the southwest wind the room is just flecked by the spray of the spent waves. There are folding doors on all sides of it . . . [and] at the back one can see through the inner court, the cloisters, the courtyard . . . and through them the woods and the distant hills. . . . Adjoining one of the rooms is a chamber with one wall rounded like a bay. . . . In the wall of this room I have had shelves placed like a library, which contains the volumes I not only read, but read over and over again. Next to it is a sleeping chamber. . . . Close by is the tennis court, which receives the warmest rays of the afternoon sun; on one side a tower has been built with two sitting rooms on the ground-floor commanding [a view of] a wide expanse of the sea. . . . There is also a second tower. . . . It looks out upon an exercise ground, which runs round the garden."

Augustus's policies. So the new emperor allowed the Senate, the courts, and many other institutions to continue functioning normally. According to Tacitus:

The consuls and the praetors [court judges] enjoyed the ancient honors of their rank. The subordinate officials exercised their functions free from imperial control. The laws . . . flowed in their regular channel. . . . The [tax] revenues were administered by men of distinguished probity [honesty]. . . . In the provinces no new burdens were imposed, and the old duties [taxes] were collected without cruelty or extortion [threats and force]. . . . In all questions of right between the emperor and individuals the courts of justice were open, and the law decided.[11]

Like his stepfather, Tiberius governed efficiently and wisely. He administered the provinces well, and the army remained

Tiberius was well-meaning and efficient but lacked Augustus's gift for winning friends and supporters.

disciplined and loyal under his rule. And his management of the economy was so honest and thoughtful that the government saved a great deal of money. During his reign, the number of *sesterces,* or standard Roman monetary units, in Rome's treasury expanded from 100 million to 2.7 billion—

Tiberius portrayed on a silver denarius. *This common Roman coin weighed 1/8 ounce and equalled four* sesterces.

an increase of twenty-seven times! Tiberius was able to accomplish this partly because he, like Augustus, did not waste the state's money on personal luxuries. Tiberius preferred to live modestly and quietly and disliked the ceremony and flattery so often aimed at him. For example, when the Senate offered to name a month after him, as it had named July and August after his relatives Julius Caesar and Augustus, Tiberius politely refused the honor. "What will you do if there should be thirteen Caesars?" he asked.[12]

But despite his abilities and good intent, Tiberius eventually became unpopular with both the Senate and the people. Many ordinary citizens resented him for his decision to dissolve the two assemblies that proposed laws and elected government officials. Augustus had allowed these republican bodies to continue functioning even though they did nothing more than rubber-stamp the laws and officials he himself had chosen. Tiberius decided that this process had become meaningless and wasteful. Thus even the outward appearance of a government run by the common people passed away for good. The people also disliked Tiberius because, unlike Augustus, he refused to spend large sums on public games and amusements such as chariot races, gladiatorial contests, and theatrical performances.

The senators came to dislike Tiberius after he began delegating many of his governing duties to an ambitious younger man, Lucius Sejanus, head of the Praetorian Guard. Sejanus convinced Tiberius that if the widespread contingents of the Guard were moved to a barracks in Rome, he (Sejanus) could better protect the emperor. But in reality, Sejanus was trying to consolidate his own power by concentrating many troops loyal to himself in one place. In 26, the aging Tiberius decided that life would be safer and more pleasant away from the senators and public who disliked him. So he moved his residence to the island of Capri, about 100 miles south of Rome, and left Sejanus to run the government.

Sejanus became more and more powerful. He installed a network of spies in the capital and began executing for treason senators and other officials who had merely spoken out against the emperor. Eventually, Tiberius discovered that Sejanus was plotting to kill him and seize total power. In 31, the emperor executed Sejanus. But it was too late to undo the damage Sejanus had done. Tiberius remained an unpopular leader, and the Praetorian Guard was now a powerful military presence that would prove dangerous to future emperors. Tiberius, one of Rome's ablest rulers, died a lonely and hated man in 37 after reigning twenty-three years.

Corrupted by Power

Tiberius had no living sons, so Augustus's only living great-grandson, twenty-five-year-old Gaius Caesar, became the next emperor. Because his father had been a general, Gaius had spent much of his childhood in army camps, where the soldiers affectionately nicknamed him Caligula, or "Little Boots." Although Caligula hated it in later life, the name stuck. What also stuck to the successor to Tiberius was a well-deserved reputation for extravagance, cruelty, and sexual perversion.

Caligula did not earn his wild reputation immediately, however. At first, because his youth, energy, and outgoing personality contrasted sharply with Tiberius's retiring character, the senators liked him. And because the new emperor quickly began spending large sums of money on public

A Roman charioteer leads his horses around the spina, *a structure with three pillars at each end that ran down the center of the racing arena, or* circus.

Seneca's Suicide

In the year 65, a group of senators, Praetorian guardsmen, and other important Romans led by a senator named Piso, plotted to kill Nero. Among the conspirators was Seneca, a well-known writer and philosopher, hated by the emperor. Nero discovered the plot and brutally tortured and executed the conspirators. As Tacitus described it in his Roman history The Annals, *Seneca chose to cheat Nero of his revenge by committing suicide.*

"He embraced his wife; then softening awhile from the stern resolution of the hour, he begged and implored her to spare herself the burden of perpetual sorrow, and . . . to endure a husband's loss with honorable consolations. She declared, in answer, that she too had decided to die, and claimed for herself the blow of the executioner. . . . Then by one and the same stroke they sundered [broke] with a dagger the arteries of their arms. Seneca, as his aged frame, attenuated [thin] by frugal diet, allowed the blood to escape but slowly, severed also the veins of his legs and knees. . . . Afraid too that his sufferings might break his wife's spirit, and that, as he looked on her tortures, he might himself sink into irresolution [change his mind], he persuaded her to retire to another chamber. . . . Seneca meantime, as the tedious process of death lingered on, begged [a friend] . . . to produce a poison with which he had some time before provided himself. . . . It was brought to him and he drank it in vain. . . . He was then carried into a bath, with the steam of which he was suffocated, and he was burnt without any of the usual funeral rites."

games, the people also liked him. Caligula started a number of large building projects, took a keen interest in maintaining Roman roads, and initially showed every sign of administering the empire in the tradition of his two illustrious predecessors.

But Caligula's popularity did not last long. The reasons for his descent into what most Romans considered to be immoral and deranged behavior remain uncertain. Some historians point out that he became seriously ill in 38, six months after becoming emperor. They maintain that the unknown sickness may have left his mind unbalanced.

Others feel that Caligula was weak-willed and could not resist the temptation to abuse his great position, that wielding absolute power had corrupted him absolutely.

Whatever the cause, Caligula's rule became a disgrace to the Roman people and to the empire. The emperor became convinced that his own whims were law. According to the Roman historian Suetonius, when Caligula's grandmother tried to give him some advice, he told her, "Remember that I have the right to do anything to anybody."[13] And he often put this belief into practice, disregarding the public good. In

Caligula (A.D. 12–41), described by the writer Suetonius as arrogant and cruel.

replace those of Jupiter in temples. Considering these excesses, it is hardly surprising that there were a number of plots to assassinate him. In 41, one of these succeeded. High-ranking members of the Praetorian Guard cornered Caligula in a palace corridor and stabbed him to death. On that day, according to the Greek historian Dio Cassius, Caligula learned that he was not a god.

Luckily for the empire, during the four years in which Caligula had indulged himself, many of Tiberius's competent generals and administrators were still in office. So, Roman borders remained well guarded, widespread trade continued, and the provinces were well run. Except for the depletion of the imperial treasury, there was no significant interruption in the prosperity of the *Pax Romana*. Had Caligula ruled longer, the situation might have been different.

Expansion Under Claudius

The man who replaced Caligula as emperor, his uncle Claudius, ensured continued prosperity by bringing competent, effective leadership back to Rome. This surprised many people because for years Claudius had appeared to be quiet, timid, and sickly, a bookworm who seemed to lack the ability to rule. Certainly he himself never expected to become emperor of the world's mightiest nation. As Suetonius describes it:

He came at last to the empire [as emperor] in the fiftieth year of his age by a very surprising turn of fortune. . . . Prevented from approaching Gaius

less than two years, he spent the entire treasury surplus that Augustus and Tiberius had built up. Along with his spending on public games, Caligula built himself a palace and huge pleasure barges equipped with baths, banquet halls, and gardens. Reportedly, he spent ten million *sesterces*, equivalent to more than one million dollars today, on a single banquet. To raise the money to continue his extravagant spending, he ordered many wealthy Romans to present him with gifts and to name him in their wills. He also imposed heavy and unfair taxes on everything he could think of.

Caligula became increasingly corrupt. Even though he was married, he took many lovers, both male and female, shocking ordinary Romans who believed strongly in the sacredness of marriage and family. And in what most saw as a final insult to Rome, Caligula demanded to be worshiped as a living god and to have statues of himself

This fanciful depiction done long after his death shows Claudius with European-style clothes and mustache.

[Caligula] by the conspirators . . . he retired into an apartment [in the palace] called the Hermaeum; and soon afterwards, terrified by the report of Gaius being slain, he crept into an adjoining balcony, where he hid himself behind the hangings of the door. A common soldier who happened to pass that way, spying his feet and desirous to discover who he was, pulled him out; . . . immediately recognizing him, he threw himself in a great fright at his feet and saluted him by the title of emperor. He then conducted him to his fellow soldiers, who . . . brought him into [their] camp. . . . He continued all night with sentries on guard, recovered somewhat from his fright. . . . The day afterwards . . . he suffered the soldiers assembled under arms to swear allegiance to him, promising them 15,000 *sesterces* a man; he being the first of the Caesars who purchased the submission of the soldiers with money.[14]

Enjoying the support of the army, Claudius, like Augustus and Tiberius, encountered no serious opposition in assuming power. And in the years that followed, Rome's fourth emperor proved himself so able a ruler that he became very popular with the people. Claudius built hundreds of roads, aqueducts, temples, and other public works. He also greatly expanded the civil service in the provinces, appointing many new officials to handle the everyday business of governing these territories. To coordinate the administration of both Italy and the provinces, Claudius appointed four men as his personal assistants. Acting as treasurer, secretary of state, and so on, these men were equivalent to a modern president's cabinet members.

Claudius's most important achievement was the expansion of Rome's frontiers. The empire's borders had remained about the same under his three predecessors and he felt it was time for new growth. In 43 and 46, he made Lycia, in Asia Minor, and Thrace, south of the Black Sea, new provinces.

Also in 43, Claudius ordered the invasion of Britain. His ancestor Julius Caesar had led troops into Britain a century before, but the Romans, preoccupied with incessant civil wars, had not followed up on this campaign. Claudius did so. Proving himself far from timid, he even traveled to Britain and rode at the head of the troops. Britain subsequently became a Roman province. Claudius's accomplishments helped make up for Caligula's misrule, and the empire continued to thrive.

A Corrupt and Infamous Reign

Unfortunately for Claudius, he was not so accomplished in managing the affairs of his own family. His third wife Messalina eventually plotted to kill Claudius and place one of her several secret lovers on the throne. In 48, Claudius discovered the plot and executed her. Next he married Agrippina, Caligula's sister, and his own niece, an ambitious, scheming woman. It was a common custom to give new male members of the ruling family impressive names. So Domitius, Agrippina's son by an

The emperor Nero (A.D. 37–68) is best remembered for the fictitious tale that he played his lyre while Rome burned.

Julius Caesar, Claudius's illustrious ancestor, landing with his troops on the southern shore of Britain in 55 B.C.

earlier marriage, and the great-great-grandson of Augustus, became Nero Claudius Caesar Drusus Germanicus. But everyone referred to him simply as Nero. In 51, Agrippina persuaded Claudius to adopt Nero formally as his son and heir. Three years later, she poisoned her husband and bribed the Praetorian Guard to recognize sixteen-year-old Nero as the new emperor. Afterward, the soldiers took Nero to the Senate House, where the senators had no choice but to confer on him all of the imperial titles. "Of all the honors that were heaped upon him," Suetonius recalled, "he refused only one, the title of Father of his Country, and that because of his youth."[15]

Nero's reign was one of the most corrupt and infamous in history. Like Caligula, Nero respected no one but himself. He instituted a reign of terror, often torturing and executing people simply because they had said or written something that displeased him. He wasted public monies on lavish banquets and parties and, fancying himself a great poet and actor, he often performed in public. Fearing his wrath, the audiences applauded him wildly, further inflating his ego. One of Nero's favorite pastimes was to disguise himself and, with a gang of friends, visit prostitutes and mug innocent bystanders. So brutal was the new emperor that by the age of twenty-two he had had both his wife and his mother murdered, claiming falsely that they were plotting against him.

Perhaps Nero's greatest outrage occurred in 64, after a disastrous fire destroyed nearly two-thirds of the city of Rome. To his credit, Nero helped organize shelters for the homeless and encouraged rebuilding projects. But when rumors circulated that he himself had set the fire, a charge that is almost certainly false, he searched for someone to blame. He chose the followers of Jesus of Nazareth. Jesus had been born about the year 4 B.C. in the eastern Roman province of Judaea, what had once been the kingdom of Israel. He had grown up in Augustan days, preaching and dying in Tiberius's reign, and his followers, who maintained that Jesus was the son of the one and only god, had been growing in number ever since. Because they openly rejected all other gods, the followers of Jesus were very unpopular with the Romans and other peoples of the day who worshiped many gods.

Also, most Romans believed that the followers of Jesus, who by then had become known as Christians, were unsociable and that they looked down on non-Christians. Since so many people distrusted or disliked the Christians already, Nero found them an easy scapegoat and accused them of starting the fire. Thus began the first of several terrible persecutions. According to Tacitus:

> A number of Christians were convicted, not indeed on clear evidence of having set the city on fire, but rather on account of their sullen hatred of the whole human race. They were put to death with exquisite cruelty, and to their sufferings Nero added mockery and derision. Some were covered with skins of wild beasts, and left to be devoured by dogs; others were nailed to crosses; numbers of them were burned alive; many, covered with inflammable matter, were set on fire to serve as torches during the night.[16]

After the fire and persecutions, Nero's thoughtless extravagance continued. He built himself a magnificent new palace, which he named the Golden House. Suetonius wrote that its vestibule [lobby]

> was large enough to contain a colossal statue of the emperor 120 feet high; and it was so extensive that it had a triple colonnade [row of columns] a mile long. There was a pond, too, like a sea, surrounded with buildings to

Jesus of Nazareth teaching at the shore of the Sea of Galilee in Palestine.

A Roman crowd watches as Nero burns Christians as torches on the grounds of his Golden House.

represent cities. . . . In the rest of the house all parts were overlaid with gold and adorned with gems and mother-of-pearl. When the edifice was finished . . . [Nero said] "Now at last I have a dwelling fit for a man."[17]

The Honest and Efficient Flavians

Eventually, Nero's misrule prompted the army to act. In 68, the Roman legions in Spain proclaimed Galba, their commanding general, as emperor. The Praetorian Guard and the Senate accepted this and declared Nero an enemy of the people. Rather than face execution, he stabbed himself and, according to tradition, as he died he shouted, "What an artist the world is losing!"

In reality, the world had lost one of its worst tyrants. Yet, though Nero was corrupt and brutal, his death created a crisis

the like of which Rome had not faced since the end of the civil wars. Galba was old and feeble. And when he became emperor he made the mistake of refusing to pay the bonuses he had promised to the soldiers of the Praetorian Guard. So the guards murdered him. A power struggle ensued, during which two other important generals, Otho and Vitellius, each received a share of army backing. Each one, then, declared himself emperor. Eventually, late in 69, a general named Vespasian challenged them and emerged victorious. Because he was the fourth man to sit on the throne in a little more than a year, 69 became known as "the year of the four emperors."

Since one of his family names was Flavius, Vespasian and his sons became known

Vespasian (A.D. 9–79) served as a general in Britain, Germany, Africa, and Palestine before becoming emperor in A.D. 70.

A Terrible and Hideous Sight

When Vespasian marched his army into Rome in the year 69 and attacked the forces of Vitellius, who had claimed the throne, the fighting in the streets was fierce and bloody. This excerpt describing that day is from The Annals *of* Tacitus.

"Numerous engagements [battles] . . . took place before the walls [of the city], but they generally ended in favor of the Flavianists [Vespasian's troops], who had the advantage of more skilled generalship. . . . The Vitellianists, taking their stand on the garden-walls, kept off the assailants with stones and javelins till late in the day, when they were taken [overrun] in the rear by the cavalry, which had then forced an entrance by the Colline gate. In the *Campus Martius* also the hostile armies met, the Flavianists with all the prestige of fortune and repeated victory, the Vitellianists rushing on in sheer despair. Though defeated, they rallied again in the city. The populace stood by and watched the combatants; and, as though it had been a mimic [pretend] conflict, encouraged first one party and then the other by their shouts and plaudits [praises]. . . . It was a terrible and hideous sight that presented itself throughout the city."

After his son Titus conquered Jerusalem in A.D. 70 Vespasian issued this commemorative coin.

as the Flavian dynasty. Unwilling for the empire to sink into a new and destructive cycle of civil wars, Vespasian made sure to appoint his own followers as commanders of key legions and thereby quickly won the backing of all factions of the army. He gained control of the Praetorian Guard by appointing his son Titus as its head. The Praetorians felt it a compliment to have a possible future emperor as their leader. Vespasian also established good relations with the Senate. Seeing himself as a new Augustus, he ruled wisely and well and in the next ten years managed to reverse the economic problems Nero had created. This ensured a continuation of the *Pax Romana's* prosperity. Vespasian reinforced his popularity by tearing down Nero's Golden House and beginning construction of the Colosseum, a large amphitheater, or arena for public games, in its place.

Vespasian died in 79, and his sons continued his honest and efficient policies. Titus, who succeeded first, ruled wisely and completed work on the Colosseum. When he died suddenly at age forty after reigning only two years, his younger brother Domitian became emperor. Domitian was also an able ruler. He administered the economy and the provinces well and constructed many public buildings, including temples and libraries. But unlike his father and brother, he was moody and trusted few people. He also hated the Senate and treated its members with disrespect. Eventually, he made so many enemies in the capital that in 96 a palace plot to assassinate him succeeded. Thus ended the Flavian line of rulers.

Titus (c. A.D. 41–81), whose public generosity earned him the nickname "Delight of Mankind."

A relief from the Arch of Titus, erected by Domitian in A.D. 81 to celebrate Titus's victory over the Jews in A.D. 70. Note the Jewish menorah, or candlestick, carried as part of the spoils.

The *Pax Romana's* Fruits

Domitian (A.D. 51–96), last of the Flavian line, raised the yearly pay of Roman soldiers from 225 to 300 denarii.

For more than a century, the new imperial system established by Augustus had served Rome well. The empire's trading network, its economy, its armies, and its provincial administration had proven strong and flexible. Even the neglect and abuses of Caligula and Nero had not significantly dented Roman prosperity. The entire Mediterranean world, made up of so many different lands and peoples, seemed to thrive and operate almost as a single nation. And the fruits of the *Pax Romana* had only begun to be harvested. Under Domitian's five successors, the empire would reach new heights of power and influence, fulfilling Augustus's goal of bringing peace and order to a troubled world.

Chapter

3 Bread and Circuses: The Task of Controlling the Masses

The number one concern of the Roman emperors was maintaining their great power over the state and the people. The army's backing was essential to this task, and each emperor made sure he had the soldiers' allegiance. But controlling the military was not enough. Appeasing the "mob," as many Roman leaders arrogantly called the people, was also important. Rome and other cities had large populations, including many poor and unemployed people who could not adequately support themselves. And because slaves did most of the everyday menial tasks for the middle and upper classes, large numbers of people had a great deal of free time on their hands. There was always the danger that the people, if hungry or idle, might riot or even rebel. Using the army to quell such uprisings was an option. But even corrupt emperors like Nero knew that controlling the populace at the point of a sword was expensive and would only lead to more discontent and rebellion.

The emperors found that it was far easier, cheaper, and safer to keep the masses fed, busy, and reasonably happy. Every emperor sponsored regular large-scale distributions of bread and other foodstuffs to the poor. And most of these rulers also spent huge sums on public festivals, shows, and games. Historian Jerome Carcopino explains:

> The Caesars had in fact shouldered the dual task of feeding and amusing Rome. Their monthly [food] distributions . . . assured the populace its daily bread. By the shows and spectacles they provided in various public places, religious and secular [nonreligious], in the Forum, at the theaters, in the Stadium [also called the arena or the circus] . . . they occupied and disciplined its [the city's] leisure hours.[18]

The strategy worked. Many Romans eventually came to care about little but being fed and entertained. This prompted the Roman writer Juvenal to remark with contempt that the mob "limits its anxious longings to two things only—bread, and the games of the circus!"[19]

A Dirty, Noisy City

Nearly every city in Italy and many in the provinces had generous facilities for public gatherings, relaxation, and entertainment. Pompeii, for example, with a population of only 20,000, had a forum, public baths, a

Part of the emperor Hadrian's villa at Tivoli, a vast, luxurious compound that covered 180 acres and included two theaters, three bath complexes, and several libraries.

theater, and an arena, all of them large. Not surprisingly, Rome, a much more populous city, had many dozens of public areas and buildings. These facilities offered people a diversion from the rat race of city life.

In the middle of the first century A.D., Rome was a sprawling, dirty, noisy metropolis of about 1.2 million people. Even at night, the city did not sleep. Juvenal complained: "What sleep is possible in a lodging [house]? The crossing of wagons in the narrow, winding streets, the swearing of drovers [drivers] brought to a standstill would snatch sleep from a sea-calf or the emperor Claudius himself."[20] Most streets were also choked with filth and foul odors. Adding to everyday dirt and litter, many Romans emptied their chamber pots directly into the streets. The problem was es-

pecially bad in the poorer sections of the city, where tens of thousands lived in crowded, multistoried, badly constructed apartment buildings called *insulae*.

A street in Pompeii. The raised sidewalks and stepping stones helped pedestrians avoid puddles.

Like many modern cities, ancient Rome was often a dangerous place to live. The police force Augustus had installed had helped to reduce the crime rate, but muggings, thefts, and murders still occurred frequently at night. And there were other dangers. "Think," wrote Juvenal, "of the number of times cracked or broken [flower] pots fall out of windows. . . . Anyone who goes out to dinner without making a will, is a fool . . . you can suffer as many deaths as there are open windows to pass under."[21]

People of all ages and social status looked forward to escaping, at least temporarily, from the sober realities of city life. They regularly flocked to such public diversions as plays, chariot races, and religious celebrations. Rich and poor and young and old attended. It is important to note that women and often even slaves attended, too. This was possible because the status of women and slaves had improved considerably since the days of the republic.

Women and Slaves

In early Roman times, women had no rights. They could not inherit property or take part in politics and, in general, had to do the bidding of their husbands. This situation gradually changed, however. During the last two centuries of the republic, women won the right to divorce their husbands, and they became increasingly independent. Women also received better educations, as evidenced by the ancient writer Plutarch's description of Pompey's second wife, Cornelia: "She was highly educated, played well upon the lute [a stringed instrument like a guitar], and understood geome-

Assisted by two slaves, a well-to-do Roman woman gets dressed. A typical wealthy family owned well over 100 slaves.

try, and had been accustomed to listen . . . to lectures on philosophy."[22]

By the mid-first century A.D., Roman women, rich and poor, were, socially speaking, nearly equal to men. The philosopher Musonius Rufus, who wrote during Flavian times, spoke for many when he argued that women were intellectually and morally equal to men. Women not only attended public baths, festivals, and games whenever they wanted, but also engaged in "manly" pursuits such as discussing and writing about politics. A few women even competed in men's sports such as hunting, fencing, and wrestling.

Slaves also fared better during the empire. In republican days, most slaves had been captives taken in Rome's many aggressive foreign wars. Many were treated as objects, beaten, and even killed by their owners. But in the early empire, though

Pliny's Love Letter

The strong love bond between so many Roman husbands and wives is illustrated in this letter written by Pliny the Younger to his wife Calpurnia (translated by Betty Radice in Pliny: Letters and Panegyricus). *Calpurnia, being sick, had traveled to the country for a rest, but Pliny's work kept him from going with her.*

"Never have I complained so much about my public duties as I do now. They would not let me come with you to Campania in search of better health, and they still prevent me from following hard on your heels. This is a time when I particularly want to be with you, to see with my own eyes whether you are gaining in strength and weight, and if the pleasures of your holiday and the luxuries of the district are doing you no harm. Indeed, I should worry when you are away even if you were well, for there are always anxious moments without news of anyone one loves dearly, and, as things are, I have the thought of your health as well as your absence to alarm me. . . . I am full of forebodings of every imaginable disaster, and like all nervous people dwell most on what I pray fervently will not happen. So do please think of my anxiety and write to me once or even twice a day—I shall worry less while I am reading your letters, but my fears will return as soon as I have finished them."

some slaves still suffered cruelties, most owners treated their slaves more humanely. Some slaves lived and worked on farms, especially the *latifundia,* large plantations in the countryside. Many more dwelled in the cities, where they performed numerous jobs and often enjoyed relatively comfortable lives. As historian R. H. Barrow pointed out:

> It was discovered that, the nearer the lot of a slave approached to that of a free man, the more useful he was. The Romans disliked retail trade and the routine of business, and slaves performed these tasks for them; the slaves themselves were often more skilled than their masters. Slaves had always been allowed to have property of their own, and in the early Empire this property was often considerable. . . . Slaves owned land, property, ships, interests in business concerns, even slaves of their own, and . . . their rights were protected by law. . . . Many a slave was the trusted friend of his master. Indeed, slavery comes nearest to its justification in the early Roman Empire.[23]

The slaves who sometimes went to the public games and festivals were among the few working Romans in attendance. A large proportion of free Romans, rich and poor, did not have full-time jobs in the modern sense. Ironically, the institution of slavery itself was one of the chief causes of the mob's idleness. Because slaves took care of most of their business and chores, most slave owners worked only a few hours a day or did no work at all. But while slavery was a convenience for some, it was a hindrance to many others. Slaves did so many jobs on farms, in homes, and in the cities that hundreds of thousands of free Romans could not find work. Having neither opportunity nor reason to learn a trade, whole generations found themselves locked permanently into a state of poverty. Without government handouts of bread, many would have starved. Thus, slavery weakened Roman society by perpetuating poverty and helping to create large numbers of idle persons of all classes.

Holidays and Feasts

The many and various public games, plays, and festivals the people attended to fill their leisure time were collectively referred to as *ludi*. Some ludi were religious celebrations honoring specific gods. For instance, the *Vestalia*, celebrated on June 9, honored Vesta, goddess of the hearth. In early republican times, Rome's traditional gods were the only deities so honored. Eventually, however, the influence of foreign gods worshiped in some of Rome's distant provinces began to be felt in Italy. In the early empire, cults of foreign gods were quite popular in Rome. Some of the more important of these were the goddess Isis, from Egypt, seen as ruler of heaven and

earth; Cybele, from Asia Minor, a goddess of nature and healing; and Mithras, a Persian god whose followers advocated treating everyone with kindness and respect. A few of these deities had their own public festivals—for example, the *Ludi Megalenses,* honoring Cybele from April 4 to 10.

The Romans had many other ludi. Some were secular, such as the Parentalia, celebrated from February 13 to 21 to honor the memory of deceased parents. Still other ludi began as religious ceremonies but later became more secular. The most notable example was the *Ludi Romani.* In earlier centuries, this fifteen-day festival, observed from September 5 to 19, honored Rome's head god Jupiter in his own temple. By the first century A.D., however, much of the religious significance of this celebration had disappeared. Senators and other public officials met in the temple for a party and banquet, and other people

Upper-class Romans enjoying a holiday feast. It was customary to dine in a reclining position.

The Training of an Orator

Well-to-do Romans hired tutors, who taught their children reading, writing, and ultimately oratory. In his book The Training of an Orator, *the writer and teacher Quintilian explained his belief that most children had the intelligence to become orators.*

"Upon the birth of a son, the father should entertain the highest hopes of him from the start. If he does so, he will be more careful of the boy's elementary training. For unfounded is the complaint that to very few persons is there granted the power of learning what is presented to them, but that most of them waste through their dullness of native mentality the effort and time spent on them. For on the contrary you will find the majority [. . . full of] facile invention and quick to grasp an idea. Obviously this is natural to mankind; and, just as birds are born for flying, horses for running, wild beasts for ferocity, so mental activity and cleverness are characteristic of us. . . . No one is found who has attained nothing by study. If one has accepted this view, as soon as he becomes a father let him expend the utmost eager care on the prospects of the coming orator."

had feasts in their homes. Thus, the *Ludi Romani* became just another holiday among many others. During Augustus's reign, the Romans had some 115 separate holidays. By the end of the first century A.D. that number had risen to 132, and some later emperors recognized as many as 200 holidays. Nearly all these occasions were accompanied by feasts and often races, contests, and dramatic presentations.

Roman feasts differed in size and extravagance according to social status. Not surprisingly, the wealthy classes enjoyed the most varied and elaborate menus, usually accompanied by entertainment. Describing one of his own feasts in a letter to an invited guest who did not show up, Pliny the Younger wrote good-naturedly:

Who are you to accept my invitation to dinner and never come? . . . It was all laid out, one lettuce each, three snails, two eggs, wheat-cake, and wine with honey chilled with snow . . . besides olives, beetroots, gherkins, onions, and any number of similar delicacies. You would have heard a comic play, a reader or singer, or all three if I felt generous. Instead you chose to go where you could have oysters, sow's innards, sea-urchins, and Spanish dancing-girls. You will suffer for this—I won't say how.[24]

Members of the middle and lower classes ate more humbly but still managed to put together appetizing holiday dinners. Typical was the following simple feast Juvenal proposed to a friend:

> And now hear my feast, which no meat market shall provide. From my . . . farm there will come a plump kid [young goat] . . . that has . . . more milk in him than blood; some wild asparagus . . . and some lordly eggs warm in their wisps of hay together with the hens that laid them. There will be grapes too . . . pears . . . and in the same basket fresh-smelling apples.[23]

"We who are about to die salute you!"

Rome's public games were as varied as its feasts. Chariot races took place in the city's circuses, long rectangular structures that could accommodate many thousands of spectators. The oldest and largest of these was the Circus Maximus, first erected in early republican times. Over the centuries, various rulers, including Julius Caesar, Augustus, Claudius, and Nero, enlarged and improved it until it became one of the marvels of the ancient world. By the early second century A.D., the "great Circus," as many called it, was more than 2,000 feet long and 700 feet wide, seating more than 250,000 people. In Augustan days, the crowds watched as many as twelve races a day, each race averaging about five miles. Caligula increased the number of races to twenty-four a day, which then became standard. The chariots were usually drawn by four horses, although teams of two, three, six, and even ten were sometimes used. Sitting on cushions and eating snacks sold to them by vendors, the crowds loudly cheered and applauded their favorites, creating a din that often could be heard from one end of the city to the other. In his *Georgics,* Virgil captured some of the excitement of the races, writing:

> Seest how the chariots in mad rivalry
> Poured from the barrier [starting gate], grip the course and go,
> When youthful hope is highest, and every heart
> Drained with each wild pulsation?
> How they ply [use]

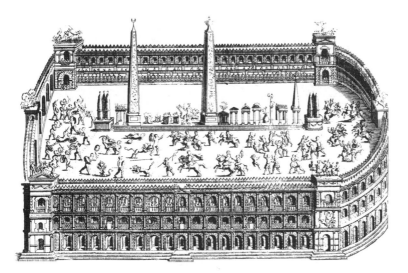

An engraving of the Circus Maximus, in which as many as twelve chariots completed seven laps around the central spina *in each of twenty-four daily races.*

The circling lash [whip], and reaching
forward let
The reins hang free! Swift spins the
glowing [chariot] wheel:
And now they [the drivers] stoop, and
now erect in air
Seem borne through space and towering to the sky:
No stop, no stay; the dun sand whirls
aloft;
They [the horses] reek with foam-
flakes [sweat and saliva] and pursu-
ing breath;
So sweet is fame, so prized the victor's
palm.[26]

Equally exciting for the crowds were
the gladiatorial combats, fights between
men or between men and animals. The
gladiators were variously convicts, slaves,
or paid volunteers. Prisoners and slaves
who fought well sometimes earned their
freedom. The gladiators entered the arena
accompanied by musicians, dancers, and
jugglers, then raised their weapons in a
salute to the emperor or whatever impor-

Only the class of gladiators called murmillos
wore helmets of this style.

tant official was present. After reciting the
phrase, *"Morituri te salutamus!"* or "We who
are about to die salute you!" the gladiators
usually fought to the death. Also common
were fights between wild animals, most
often bears, panthers, and bulls. In a single
day in Titus's reign, more than 5,000 animals died. In all these fights, the arena sand
was often dyed dark orange to conceal the
blood stains. The Roman writer Seneca
penned the following description of the
games, which he found needlessly brutal:

*A gladiator awaits the crowd's decision to kill or
spare his opponent.*

> I've happened to drop in upon the
> midday entertainment of the arena in
> hope of . . . a touch of relief in which
> men's eyes may find rest after a glut of
> human blood. No, no: far from it. . . .
> Now for butchery plain and simple!
> The combatants have nothing to pro-
> tect them: their bodies are utterly open

Practical Means to Practical Ends

The Romans constructed their theaters, baths, and other great public buildings to be useful rather than beautiful. That was because nearly everything they did served some practical or realistic purpose. As the famous classical scholar Edith Hamilton pointed out in her book The Roman Way, *even their sculptors tried to capture the realism rather than the beauty of life.*

"Roman genius was called into action by the enormous practical needs of a world empire. Rome met them magnificently. Buildings tremendous . . . amphitheaters where eighty thousand could watch a spectacle, baths where three thousand could bathe at the same time. . . . Bridges and aqueducts that spanned wide rivers. . . . That is true of the art of Rome, the spontaneous expression of the Roman spirit, its keen realization of the adaptation of practical means to practical ends, its will-power and enduring effort, its tremendous energy and audacity and pride. . . . The conscious art of such a people would be, so anyone would reason, sternly realistic, revealing life as pitiless fact, with no desire to express anything except implacable truth. And such is the case with the peculiarly Roman achievement in sculpture, the portrait-bust. These heads are all implacably true with the external truth of accuracy. An exact likeness was all the sculptor sought. . . . The more faithful the portrait, the greater the artist's success in the eyes of his patron. This is as true of the women as of the men."

The remains of the inner courtyard of a Roman bath complex that accommodated over 1,000 people. By A.D. *284, the city of Rome alone had 11 public baths and over 1,000 private ones.*

to every blow: never a thrust but finds its mark.... What good is armor? What good is swordsmanship? All these things only put off death a little. In the morning men are matched with lions and bears.... Death is the fighter's only exit.

Seneca then records some of the crowd's remarks, making the point that the spectators were more bloodthirsty than the fighters.

"Kill! Flog! Burn! Why does he jib at cold steel? Why die so squeamishly? ... Let them have at each other in the nude.... Cut a few throats in the meanwhile to keep things going!" Come now [said Seneca], can't you people see even this much—that bad examples recoil on [end up hurting] those who set them?[27]

At first, these games took place in the circuses or in temporary wooden enclosures set up in town squares. The first permanent stone stadium for gladiatorial events was erected in 29 B.C. south of the

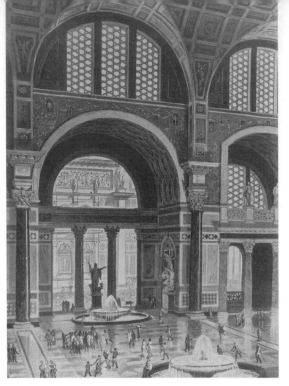

The magnificent lobby of the baths built by the emperor Caracalla.

Campus Martius. After the great fire in A.D. 64 destroyed the structure, Vespasian and Titus built the Colosseum to replace it. The well-preserved ruins of this famous stadium, some 1,800 feet in circumference and seating 50,000 spectators, still stand in modern Rome.

Theaters and Baths

Visits to the theaters and baths were relaxing and popular pastimes. The first stone theaters in Rome, designed after Greek models, appeared in late republican times. The Theater of Pompey, built in 55 B.C., sat about 27,000 people, while the Theater of Marcellus, completed by Augustus, could accommodate about 14,000. Like their Greek counterparts, Roman actors

Actors on a Roman stage, or pulpitum, *wore masks identifying them as specific traditional characters.*

usually wore brilliantly decorated masks so that spectators in the back rows could better recognize the characters. At first, the plays had complicated plots and dialogue, also in the Greek tradition. But beginning in the first century A.D. many theatrical presentations evolved into more visual spectacles with little dialogue. These resembled elaborate ballets or pantomimes, complete with dancing, musical accompaniment, and striking special effects such as simulated battles and rainstorms. The Roman writer Quintilian marveled at the breadth of emotions the actors could convey without words:

> Their hands demand and promise. . . . They translate horror, fear, joy, sorrow, hesitation, confession . . . restraint, abandonment, time, and number. They excite and they calm. They implore and they approve. They possess a power of imitation that replaces words.[28]

Roman theatergoers were boisterous, often applauding and cheering their favorite characters and booing and jeering at performers they did not like.

The Roman baths, or *thermae,* began in the second century B.C. as small, simple washing facilities for men. But in time these structures grew in size, complexity, and beauty and admitted women, too. Not until the second century A.D. did rules forbidding mixed bathing take effect. It became common for many Romans to visit the baths at least once a day, and increasingly fewer people bathed at home. In Augustus's reign, to meet public demand, the city of Rome alone had about 170 privately owned *thermae.* Shortly afterward, in A.D. 20, the first large state-run baths appeared.

A Roman Boxing Match

In addition to gladiatorial contests, wrestling and boxing matches were popular in Roman arenas. This account of two boxers in action from Virgil's Aeneid *shows that the ancient and modern versions of the sport are strikingly similar.*

"Then the son of Anchises [Aeneas, Virgil's hero] brought out hide gloves of equal weight, and bound the hands of the antagonists [opponents]. . . . Each took his stand, poised on tiptoe and raising one arm. . . . Drawing their heads back from the blows they spar, hand against hand. They aim many hard blows, wildly pummeling each other's sides and chests, ears and brows and cheeks, making the air resound with their strokes. . . . Entellus puts forth his right; Dares slips aside in a nimble dodge. . . . Entellus furiously drives Dares headlong over the arena, redoubling his blows, now with the right hand, now with the left. . . . Then [at the end of the match] Dares's mates led him to the ships with his knees shaking, his head swaying from side to side, his mouth spitting teeth and blood."

Almost every subsequent emperor built a public bath complex, usually trying to outdo in size and splendor those erected by his predecessors. Some of the largest *thermae* bore the names of the emperors Nero, Titus, Trajan, and Caracalla. These structures had both hot and cold pools, steam rooms, and exercise areas where people could do calisthenics, play ball, and even wrestle. The larger baths were also equipped with massage parlors, hair-cutting salons, libraries, reading rooms, various shops, and fast-food vendors. Combining many features of modern malls and social clubs, the *thermae* were places in which Romans of all walks of life could spend a pleasant hour or an entire day.

The baths, the theaters, the games, the races, the festivals, and the food hand-outs—all these kept the Roman populace busy and content. The emperors learned that government sponsorship of these diversions was essential in maintaining control of the mob. But the social system of bread and circuses was more than a political and managerial tool. It became an integral part of everyday Roman life, as important and natural to people as institutions like the family and religion. And so it reflected the new Roman character. The early Romans had been conservative and austere, with a dislike for luxury. In stark contrast, the inhabitants of the empire lived by the words expressed by an unknown author of the second century A.D. Into the pavement in the forum of the Roman town of Thamugadi in northern Africa he carved: "To hunt, bathe, play, and laugh, this is to live."[29]

Chapter 4

The Five Good Emperors: Rome Reaches Its Zenith

Beginning in the year 96 after the assassination of Domitian, last of the Flavians, Rome entered a long period during which five extremely capable emperors ruled. They were Nerva, Trajan, Hadrian, Antoninus Pius, and Marcus Aurelius. Known to history as the five "good" emperors, they brought Roman civilization to its economic and cultural zenith. Their achievements were impressive. Although they did not attempt to restore republican government, they reestablished an efficient working relationship with the Senate. Senators received a degree of respect they had not known since pre-Augustan days. The five good emperors also instituted many social reforms and laws designed to protect the poor, the underprivileged, and even slaves. In addition, these rulers increased the empire's size to its largest extent, a vast territory covering much of the known world. Most important, they ensured a healthy economy by extending the *Pax Romana* for almost another century. There were defensive and offensive

---

Investing in Land

During the Pax Romana, *wealthy individuals often invested their money in land. In this excerpt from a letter to a friend, quoted in Lionel Casson's* Daily Life in Ancient Rome, *Pliny the Younger described his desire to buy some property:*

"As usual, I am asking your advice on a matter of business. There are now for sale some landed properties that border on mine and, as a matter of fact, run into them. They have many points that tempt me. . . . First, the gain in beauty by rounding off my holdings; then, the pleasure—to say nothing of the economy—of making one trip and expense serve for a visit to both properties and of keeping both under the same agent and practically the same managers. . . . It is 3,000,000 *sesterces* [about $300,000] . . . . True, I've [got] practically all my funds tied up in land, but I have some cash [owed me] and borrowing presents no problem."

border wars during this period, to be sure. But the many lands within the empire's borders remained peaceful, safe, and prosperous. The great historian Edward Gibbon wrote:

> If a man were called upon to fix the period in the history of the world during which the condition of the human race was most happy and prosperous, he would without hesitation name that which elapsed from the accession of Nerva to the death of Aurelius. Their united reigns are possibly the only period of history in which the happiness of a great people was the sole object of government.[30]

A Sincere and Able Ruler

The first of the good emperors, Marcus Cocceius Nerva, was a senator in his sixties when he ascended to the throne in 96. Unlike his predecessors, he neither sought nor even dreamed of attaining imperial power. The conspirators who eliminated Domitian gained the backing of most senators, who had come to hate the emperor for treating them with disrespect. No one wanted a rerun of the violent rivalries among army generals that had followed Nero's demise. So the Senate chose as emperor the surprised Nerva, a civilian and one of the most capable and respected lawmakers in Rome. A large bonus temporarily quieted opposition from the Praetorian Guard.

Nerva quickly established himself as a sincere and able ruler. Having been a senator, he realized that good relations between the emperor and the Senate would benefit everyone. So he returned to Augustus's wise policy of treating the Senate with respect. Nerva promised never to execute a senator and, although he was firmly in control, he allowed the Senate the appearance of running the government. He also began a series of social reforms, similar to modern welfare systems, which his successors would continue and enlarge. Among these reforms was a law that provided some 60 million *sesterces* worth of government-owned land to needy people. In addition, Nerva established a fund for orphans and poor children and eliminated a number of taxes he felt were unfair.

Nerva realized that despite his good works, he would not be able to hold onto power without the support of the Praetorian Guard and the army. Less than a year into his reign, however, that support began to weaken. So to appease the soldiers, the emperor decided to name a respected military man as his successor. He proclaimed as his heir Marcus Ulpius Trajanus, known as

Nerva (A.D. 30–98) had already completed a long career as a respected lawyer and senator before being appointed emperor.

Trajan, who was not a blood relative, giving him the title of Caesar along with several imperial powers. Nerva retained the title of Augustus. The practice of a reigning emperor deciding who would succeed him was to continue. The new custom was significant in that it was an open admission that neither the emperor nor the Senate wielded the true power. As historian Michael Grant explains:

> It meant that the Senate's legal right to nominate emperors, long since eroded, had now been openly shattered. . . . In order to avert [the soldiers'] wrath Nerva had been compelled to appoint a general as his successor. So now, even more than ever before, the imperial regime was a military monarchy, dependent upon the troops. All other considerations were secondary. . . . The army was the master—and the best an emperor could achieve was to share and guide its exploitation of the mastery.[31]

The emperor Trajan (c. A.D. *53–117) took the title* Imperator Caesar Nerva Trajanus Augustus.

Conquest and Expansion

Nerva's timing in choosing a successor had been fortunate. In January 98, three months after naming Trajan as his heir, Nerva died of natural causes. The planned succession proceeded in an orderly fashion, and the forty-two-year-old Trajan became emperor with both the army's and the Senate's blessing. Hailing from Spain, he was the first emperor born outside of Italy. This indicated that the old image of the provinces as foreign territories ruled by and inferior in status to Italy was rapidly disappearing. From the second century A.D. onward, most Romans viewed the empire more as a single political unit composed of many diverse regions.

Like Nerva, Trajan was an able ruler whose primary interest was the welfare of the empire and its people. Describing Trajan's generous character, his friend Pliny the Younger wrote, "He regarded nothing as his own unless his friends possessed it."[32] The new emperor showed the Senate every courtesy, often socializing with its members and asking their advice. He also carried on his predecessor's domestic policies, increasing state funds for poor children and other needy individuals. Trajan's economic administration was extremely honest and sound. As a result, he found the money to launch the largest public building program since Augustan days. All over the empire Trajan built aqueducts,

An aqueduct near Rome. Pipes set into the arched bridges carried water for many miles.

harbors, canals, and many fine roads. One of his largest projects was the *Via Traiana,* a wide stone highway nearly 150 miles long, linking the southern Italian cities of Beneventum and Brundisium.

Trajan's most important accomplishment was expansion of the empire. Most of his predecessors had followed Augustus's policy of being content with existing Roman borders. But Trajan wanted to match or even surpass his personal hero, Julius Caesar, by aggressively expanding Rome's horizons. Like many other Romans, Trajan believed he was doing "barbarians" a favor by subduing and "civilizing" them. In a series of brilliant military campaigns between the years 101 and 107, he conquered Dacia, now Romania, located west of the Black Sea. He then made the area a province. Immediately began the process of "Romanizing" Dacia—building Roman

colonies, towns, and roads, as well as spreading Roman customs and the Latin language. To celebrate these deeds, Trajan erected a 110-foot-high column in Rome. Covered

In this relief from Trajan's victory column, Roman soldiers attack a German fortress in Dacia.

with magnificent sculptures depicting his campaigns, the column still stands. Trajan also celebrated by proclaiming 123 days of *ludi* and staging arena combats involving some 10,000 gladiators.

Trajan was not content with his Dacian conquests. Between 114 and 116, he marched his legions into the lands of Armenia and Mesopotamia, located east and southeast of the Black Sea, and made them Roman provinces. The empire was now larger than it had ever been or ever would be. It stretched from the Atlantic Ocean in the west to the Persian Gulf in the east, and from northern Africa in the south to central Britain in the north. In total, this colossal political unit encompassed 3.5 million square miles and 100 million people.

Trajan and the Christians

While Trajan was an aggressive conqueror, he was a fair and compassionate ruler. His lenient treatment of the Christians was a typical example. Because the Christians swore allegiance to Jesus rather than to the emperor, the Romans branded them criminals. Periodic Christian persecutions had occurred since Nero's time, but these had failed to stop the sect from slowly but steadily gaining new members. Converts were attracted by the religion's promises of salvation in the afterlife as a reward for following the teachings of Jesus. Trajan did not understand or sympathize with Christian views. But unlike earlier emperors, he did not consider these views to be a

A Soldier Writes Home

By the second century A.D., the Roman army was made up of soldiers from every province. This letter, quoted in James Henry Breasted's Ancient Times, *was composed by a young Egyptian recruit named Apion. As was the custom, he adopted a Roman name and then wrote to his father.*

"Apion to Epimachos his father and lord, many good wishes! First of all I hope that you are in good health, and that all goes well with you and with my sister and her daughter and my brother always. . . . When I arrived at Misenum, I received from the emperor three gold pieces [about fifteen dollars] as road money, and I am getting on fine. I beg of you, my lord father, write me a line, first about your own well-being, second about that of my brother and sister, and third in order that I may devotedly greet your hand, because you brought me up well and I may therefore hope for rapid promotion, the gods willing. Give my regards to Caption [a friend]. . . . My [new Roman] name is Antonius Maximus. I hope that it may go well with you."

The Nature of the Soul

Gentle, fleeing little soul,
My body's guest and comrade,
Where do you go now,
Pale, cold and naked,
And not, as is your custom, giving joy?

■   ■   ■   ■

"The properties of the rational soul: it is conscious of itself, it molds itself, makes of itself whatever it will . . . it achieves its proper end, wherever the close of life comes upon it. . . . Moreover, it goes over the whole Universe, and the surrounding void and surveys its shape, reaches out into the boundless extent of time, embraces and ponders the periodic rebirth of the Whole, and understands that those who come after us will behold nothing new nor did those who came before us behold anything greater. . . . A property too of the rational soul is love of one's neighbor, truth, self-reverence, and to honor nothing more than itself."

dangerous threat to the empire. In 112 Trajan received a report concerning the Christians from Pliny, whom he had sent to investigate domestic affairs in the province of Bithynia in northern Asia Minor. Pliny wrote to Trajan:

Having never been present at any trials concerning those who profess Christianity, I am unacquainted not only with the nature of their crimes . . . but how far it is proper to enter into an examination concerning them. . . . They affirmed that the whole of their guilt or their error was that they . . . addressed themselves in a form of prayer to Christ as to some God, binding themselves by a solemn oath, not for the purposes of any wicked design, but never to commit any fraud, theft, or adultery, never to falsify their word. . . . I thought proper therefore to adjourn all farther proceedings in this affair in order to consult with you. . . . From hence it is easy to imagine what numbers might be reclaimed from this error [made to give up Christianity] if a pardon were granted to those who repent.

Trajan answered Pliny:

> The method you have pursued, my dear Pliny, in the proceedings against those Christians . . . is entirely proper. . . . But I would not have you [officially] enter into any enquiries concerning them. If indeed they should be brought before you and the crime is proved, they must be punished; with this restriction, however, that where the party denies himself to be a Christian . . . let him . . . be pardoned upon his repentance.[33]

Trajan's treatment of the Christians was significant. Although he did not openly tolerate them, by allowing some to be pardoned rather than punished he helped open the way for future toleration of the sect.

Hadrian (A.D. 76–138) was a scholar. As emperor, he built a library in Athens.

The Distinguished Traveler

Trajan ensured that his fair policies would continue after his death by choosing as his heir Hadrian, an honest, intelligent man who was a distinguished military officer. When Trajan died in 117, Hadrian, then forty-one, ascended to the throne. Fulfilling his mentor's expectations, the new emperor immediately devoted all his energies to running a fair and efficient government. Among Hadrian's many reforms was a requirement that all senators and many other public officials receive training in government administration. There was no pretense that anyone but the emperor made the really important decisions. But Hadrian wisely built up a large pool of well-trained officials to carry out his policies. He also expanded the Roman welfare system, opening free schools for poor children and strengthening laws protecting slaves from abuse. Hadrian's only major difference of opinion with his predecessor concerned the size of the empire. Hadrian felt that it had become too large to administer efficiently. So he decided to pull back the eastern borders Trajan had established by giving up the new provinces of Armenia and Mesopotamia.

Hadrian based his provincial policies on firsthand information. Unlike other emperors, he traveled extensively to all the provinces, actually spending more of his reign abroad than in Rome. In 121, he visited Gaul and Britain. At the time, the Romans controlled the southern section of Britain while what is now Scotland remained independent. In keeping with his desire to maintain rather than expand, Hadrian refrained from invading Scotland and built a long defensive wall separating it

This stone relief depicts a Roman secondary school called a grammaticus, *where boys eleven and older learned history, philosophy, geography, music, and astronomy.*

from Roman territory. In 125 and then again in 129, Hadrian visited Greece. He was fascinated by Greek culture and history and generously restored many fine Greek buildings that had fallen into disrepair.

During his travels, the emperor paid special attention to the army and its problems. Often, he personally inspected military camps in remote areas, listening to the soldiers' complaints and praising their achievements, however small. For example, he told a cavalry regiment in Pannonia, a province lying northeast of Italy:

> You have done everything in order. You have filled the parade ground with your charges, you have thrown the javelin in a stylish manner. . . . You

A Roman general gives his troops a pep talk. Rising above the men are the silver eagle, the aquila, *and other army emblems which the soldiers carried into battle.*

Part of Hadrian's Wall, built between A.D. *122 and 129, which stretched nearly eighty miles across northern Britain.*

have jumped with speed and agility the other day. If there had been any fault, I would have noted it. . . . You are uniformly good throughout the whole maneuver. . . . Your commander appears to look after you carefully. You will receive a bonus.[34]

It is no wonder that Hadrian was closer to his soldiers than any other emperor.

Rome's Potential Fulfilled

Shortly before his death from illness in 138, Hadrian named as his Caesar and heir fifty-one-year-old Titus Aurelius Antoninus, a former provincial governor. Antoninus was one of the ablest and perhaps the most humane of all Roman rulers. He was so ethical, honest, and sincere that the Senate bestowed on him the titles of *Pius,* or "devout," and *Optimus Princeps,* "the best of princes." His successor Marcus Aurelius later said of him:

Remember his constancy in every reasonable act, his evenness in all things, his piety . . . and his disregard of empty fame . . . with how little he was satisfied; how laborious and patient, how religious without superstition.[35]

Antoninus lived up to the name of *Optimus Princeps,* and under his enlightened rule the empire reached the height of its prosperity. His first act as emperor was to donate his large personal fortune to the public treasury. And he made sure the treasury was never depleted. He ran the economy so well, in fact, that at the end of his reign he left a surplus of 2.7 billion *sesterces*. Antoninus carried on his predecessors' social welfare programs and showed an unprecedented degree of sympathy for oppressed groups. For example, he provided severe punishments for any owner who killed a slave. And he openly tolerated the Christians and their religious views. Possibly no other leader in history ruled so large an empire so fairly and efficiently. During Antoninus's twenty-three-year reign, Roman civilization most fulfilled its great potential for creating order and justice. Describing the great benefits of the *Pax Romana* at its height, the Greek writer Aelius Aristides stated:

> Only those, if there are any, who are outside your Empire are to be pitied for the blessings they are denied. Better than all others you have demonstrated the universal saying, that the earth is the mother of all and the common fatherland of all. Greek and barbarian [non-Greek], with his property or without it, can go with ease wherever he likes, just as though going from one homeland to another. . . . You have measured the whole world, spanned rivers with bridges . . . cut through mountains to make level roads for traffic . . . filled desolate places with farmsteads, and made life easier by supplying its necessities amid law and order. Everywhere are gymnasia, fountains, gateways, temples, factories, schools. . . . Cities are radiant in their splendor and their grace, and the whole earth is as trim as a garden.[36]

The Philosopher Emperor

But unknown to anyone at the time, Rome's great age of peace and plenty would not last much longer. In the years following Antoninus's death in 161, Rome began to experience serious problems. Shortly after becoming emperor at the age of forty, Antoninus's successor, Marcus Aurelius, had to defend the empire's borders. The Parthians, who dwelled in the lands north of the Persian Gulf, invaded some of Rome's eastern provinces. Between 161 and 166, the Romans defeated the Parthians and restored order, but during the campaign some of the soldiers caught a deadly disease, possibly smallpox. Returning veterans spread the illness across the

This well-preserved statue of Marcus Aurelius (A.D. 121–180) looks much as it did when carved in the second century.

The Roman army lays siege to a fortress. A defensive testudo, *or "turtle," (left) repels rocks, while an offensive* scorpione, *or catapult, (right) and siege tower (in distance) press the attack.*

empire and millions died. The city of Rome itself was so devastated by the plague that it did not regain its former population of more than a million until the twentieth century. Many frightened people blamed the Christians for the plague and attacked members of the sect. The emperor disapproved of these new persecutions, but he could not control angry mobs all over the empire.

Marcus Aurelius also had no control over or even knowledge of the mass migrations of tribal peoples that had been occurring for decades in northern Europe. Tribes from the lands north and east of the Black Sea had been steadily pushing westward. In the process, they displaced several Germanic peoples who lived north of the Danube River, the empire's northernmost European border. In 167, the

Germans, whom the Romans looked upon as barbarians, spilled into the northern provinces. For the next fifteen years, Marcus Aurelius personally led his armies in defensive campaigns against the invaders.

During these troubled times, the emperor, an honest, just, and hard-working man, did his best to rule his vast domain efficiently. A scholar and thinker as well as a statesman, he tried to govern according to the tenets of Stoicism, a school of thought advocated by the first century A.D. Greek philosopher Epictetus. The Stoics believed that restraining their passions and emotions and viewing life logically and seriously would bring them wisdom and happiness. Marcus Aurelius believed strongly in the basic stoic principle of "live and let live" and treated his subjects fairly and tolerantly. A talented writer, he recorded his

This bronze coin bears the image of Marcus Aurelius on the front and the god Neptune on the back.

everyday thoughts in a book titled *Meditations*. In describing his view of a good ruler, he inadvertently summed up the admirable qualities he and his four predecessors shared:

> Take heed not to be transformed into a Caesar [here meaning an extravagant ruler], not to be dipped into purple dye [the traditional color of royalty]. . . . Keep yourself therefore simple, good, pure, grave, unaffected [modest], the friend of justice, religious, kind, affectionate, strong for your proper work. . . . Reverence the gods, save men. Life is brief; there is one harvest of earthly existence, a holy disposition [nature] and neighborly acts.[37]

With Marcus Aurelius's death in 180, the 200-year-long *Pax Romana* initiated by Augustus came to an end. Although Aurelius had managed to keep the barbarians out, the peace he gained was temporary. In time, more and larger invasions from the north would threaten the security and very survival of Rome's vast empire. Ironically, the great size of this domain ensured that the prosperity enjoyed under the good emperors could not last. The state could not afford to administer and defend so large a territory indefinitely, especially with invaders crowding its borders. Eventually, economic problems would take as large a toll on the empire as its defensive wars. The passing of the last good emperor was accompanied by a marked change of attitude among the Roman people. For the first time in living memory, many realized that Rome might not be invincible. And they were afraid.

Chapter

5 The Century of Crisis: Rome on the Brink of Collapse

After the passing of Marcus Aurelius, last of the "good" emperors, Rome's political and economic problems rapidly increased. More than a century of severe crisis followed, during which peace and prosperity were shattered and the empire approached the brink of total collapse. The crisis had several dimensions and causes. First, it was a crisis of leadership. In contrast to the honest and able rulers of the second century, most of those that followed were ambitious, brutal, and/or incompetent men. They had little or no concept of how to deal with the serious problems the empire faced. The period also witnessed a military crisis. In the face of large-scale invasions from the north and east that threatened to rip the empire apart, the army proved weak, disorganized, and sometimes even disloyal. Often the army and the Praetorian Guard ran amok, choosing and disposing of emperors at will. Another dimension of the crisis was economic. War and political instability disrupted trade, and the decline of farming, which had been going on for some time, began to take its toll. The government also spent too much money and overtaxed the populace to make up its losses.

As a result of these and other problems, law and order often broke down, poverty increased sharply, and life in the empire became miserable, dangerous, and uncertain. Eventually, Rome managed to recover somewhat from the disasters of this period. But it did so at the price of radically reorganizing both government and society. The Roman Empire that emerged after the century of crisis was more unstable and far less prosperous and happy than the one that had thrived during the *Pax Romana*.

The Need for Strong Leadership

Rome's leadership crisis began when Marcus Aurelius broke the tradition begun by Nerva of naming a competent and experienced general or administrator as heir to the throne. Instead, Aurelius chose his own son Commodus, and the empire suffered for the mistake. Commodus, who became emperor in 180 at the age of nineteen, had a character almost exactly opposite that of his father and other recent emperors. Vain, selfish, spoiled, and lazy, Commodus cared little for the welfare of the empire or the people. Like Caligula and Nero, he neglected his governmental responsibilities and spent large sums of public money on his own luxuries and pleasures. Describing

The mad emperor Commodus with the headdress and club of Hercules.

Commodus's favorite pastimes, historian Will Durant wrote:

> He hunted beasts on the imperial estates and developed such skill with sword and bow that he decided to perform publicly. For a time he left the palace and lived in the gladiator's school; he drove chariots in the races, and fought in the arena against animals and men. Presumably the men who opposed him took care to let him win; but he thought nothing of fighting, unaided and before breakfast, a hippopotamus, an elephant, and a tiger. . . . He was so perfect a bowman that with a hundred arrows he killed a hundred tigers in one exhibition. . . . Commodus drank and gambled, [and] wasted the public funds.[38]

Commodus also showed great cruelty, sometimes gathering cripples and other defenseless people together and killing them with clubs and arrows merely for his own amusement.

In many ways indeed Commodus's corrupt reign seemed reminiscent of those of Caligula and Nero. But there was an important difference. These earlier emperors had ruled during the beginning decades of the *Pax Romana,* when Rome's economic, social, and military institutions were stable. So their brief periods of poor leadership had little effect on overall prosperity.

By contrast, when Commodus came to power the empire faced many serious problems. The plague of the 160s had significantly decreased the population. With fewer consumers needing and buying goods, the volume of trade had shrunk and the economy had grown weaker. Making economic matters worse, by the end of the second century, most of Rome's gold and silver mines around the Mediterranean had been depleted. The lack of precious metals forced the government to mint coins containing cheaper alloys, and this made money worth less. For example, a common coin called a *denarius* had been worth about twenty cents in Augustan days. By Marcus Aurelius's time, this coin was worth only half a cent.

The economy also suffered because of declining agriculture. More and more small farmers, unable to compete with the large *latifundia* owned by wealthy Romans, abandoned their fields. Many of these fields remained unused for decades or even centuries. The *latifundia* by themselves could not supply all the food the population needed, so food shortages began to occur and food prices in cities

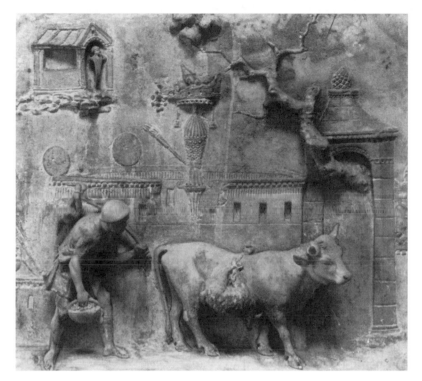

A Roman peasant carries produce to market. Many poor farm workers became so dependent on their employers that they earned the nickname "slaves of the soil."

rose sharply. At the same time, the out-of-work farmers became part of a growing class of agrarian poor. Some migrated to the cities and lived on government bread. Others became *coloni,* low paid workers on the larger farms. Desperate for work, they became financially dependent on their employers, who often took advantage of legal procedures to bind the *coloni* and their descendants to the same jobs for generations. Historian Arthur Boak explains:

> The status of the *coloni* became hereditary. . . . Their condition was halfway between that of freemen [freed slaves] and that of slaves, for while they were bound to the estate upon which they resided and passed with it from one owner to another, they were not absolutely under the power of the owner and could not be disposed of [sold] by

him apart from the land. They had also other rights which slaves lacked, yet as time went on their condition tended to approximate more and more to servitude. "Slaves of the soil," they were [later] called.[39]

The rich Roman landowners and their *coloni* formed the basis for the system of lords and serfs that would later dominate medieval Europe.

Commodus also faced grave military threats and problems. As they had during his father's reign, large and powerful Germanic tribes posed a formidable threat to the empire's northern borders. And the Roman army charged with defending those borders was less disciplined and reliable than it had been in the past. Originally, most of the soldiers had been Roman citizens and of Italian birth. Over the years, however, the army ranks increasingly filled with men from the provinces, a large proportion of them noncitizens from northern border areas. Most were poor, uneducated, and had enlisted only for the money. They had little motivation to risk their lives for Rome, a faraway city few had seen. The Praetorian Guard presented another military problem. It had grown powerful and selfish, caring more for its own needs and desires than for the good of the state. Now more than ever, Rome needed strong leadership to control the army and the Guard, as well as to deal with a worsening economy and other problems.

A Disgrace Unworthy of Rome

Commodus did not provide the leadership the empire needed. In addition to squandering public money on himself, he reversed his father's policy of resisting the influx of barbarian tribes into the northern provinces. Unwilling to interrupt his pleasures in Rome with time-consuming military campaigns, Commodus struck a deal with the tribes. In exchange for peace, he allowed many foreigners to settle in the provinces and even encouraged some 13,000 barbarians to enlist in the Roman army. This angered most generals, who felt that Rome needed to ensure its future safety by keeping the barbarians out. Commodus also created enemies by maintaining a reign of terror in the capital. His spies were everywhere and he executed hundreds of people, some for offenses as slight as mere suspicion of disloyalty to the emperor. No one was surprised or sorry

when a palace plot to assassinate Commodus succeeded in 192.

Commodus's reign marked only the beginning of Rome's downward spiral into more unstable and troubled times. The empire's worsening leadership and military problems are perhaps nowhere better illustrated than in the events that followed his death. Commodus's murderers, among them the leader of the Praetorian Guard, chose as emperor Pertinax, a respected public official. It soon became clear that the new ruler wanted to make up for Commodus's excesses by tightening the public budget. Many Guard members worried that the economic cutbacks might include their own bonuses, so they assassinated Pertinax after a reign of only three months. The episode that followed made it painfully clear to all Romans just how powerful and self-serving the Guard and other military elements had become. The Guard leaders put the imperial throne up for bid. According to Dio Cassius:

> There ensued a most disgraceful business and one unworthy of Rome. For, just as if it had been in some market or auction-room, both the city and its entire empire were auctioned off. The

This coin bears the image of Pertinax (A.D. 126–193), who reigned only three months.

sellers were the ones who had slain their emperor, and the would-be buyers were Sulpicianus and Julianus [two wealthy Romans], who vied to outbid each other.... They gradually raised their bids up to five thousand *denarii* per soldier.... Sulpicianus would have won the day, being ... the first to name the figure of five thousand, had not Julianus raised his own bid ... by one thousand two hundred and fifty *denarii* at one time, both shouting it in a loud voice and also indicating the amount with his fingers. So the soldiers, captivated by this excessive bid ... received Julianus inside the camp and declared him emperor.[40]

But other military factions refused to accept Julianus as emperor. As had happened in 69 after Nero's death, various army generals in Syria, Britain, and the northern provinces now claimed the throne and received the backing of their troops. One of these was Septimius Severus, who marched on Rome in June 193. Facing superior forces, the Praetorian Guard changed its mind once more and, with Severus's and the Senate's blessing, Julianus was executed after ruling a mere sixty-six days. The crisis was far from over, however. Severus spent the next four years fighting a bloody civil war against the competing generals. Finally, in 197, Severus emerged as Rome's undisputed master.

Building an Army Camp

Most Roman military weapons and practices remained unchanged throughout the history of the empire. In his military manual titled Epitome of Military Science, *the Roman writer Vegetius described the three standard methods of building an army camp in the field.*

"1. If danger is not too pressing, turves [wads of earth] are dug from the earth all around, and from them a kind of wall is built, three feet high above the ground, in such a way that there is a ditch in front ... and then an emergency ditch is dug, nine feet wide and seven deep. 2. If the enemy force is rather more threatening, then it is worthwhile to fortify the circuit of the camp with a full-scale ditch. This should be twelve feet wide and nine feet deep.... Above this, placing supports on both sides, a mound is raised to a height of four feet.... On top of this mound the soldiers fix the stakes of stout wood which they always carry with them.... 3. But if the enemy is pressing, then the whole of the cavalry and half of the infantry are drawn up in a line to repel an attack, while behind them the remainder of the men fortify the camp by digging ditches.... Afterwards the ditch is inspected by the centurions, and measured. Men whose work is found to have been negligent are punished."

Enriching the Soldiers

Severus was a strong and able general who managed to restore order and keep the barbarians on the northern borders at bay. But he did not understand or even care to deal with the many economic and social problems the empire faced. His major concern was the army and maintaining order and power through military dictatorship, as evidenced by his well-known remark, "Enrich the soldiers, despise the rest."[41] Ruling by this motto, Severus increased the soldiers' pay. He also expanded the army's size to thirty-six legions, plus auxiliary troops, so that by the early third century Roman military forces numbered some 400,000. But no matter how big an emperor's army, Severus realized, the Praetorian Guard still posed a threat to the throne. The ancient writer Herodian recorded the clever way the emperor dealt with this problem:

> Severus used a trick to seize and hold prisoner the Praetorian Guard. . . . He quietly sent private letters to the Guard's tribunes and centurions, promising them rich rewards. . . . He also sent an open letter to the Praetorian camp, directing the soldiers to leave their weapons behind . . . as was the custom when they escorted the emperor . . . to the celebration of a festival. . . . Trusting these orders . . . the Praetorians left their arms behind and appeared from the camp in holiday uniform . . . [and] moved towards the emperor. . . . At a given signal, while cheering him in unison, they were all seized. . . . When he had them netted like fish in his circle of weapons, like

An able general, Septimius Severus (A.D. 146–211) waged a successful war against Parthia.

prisoners of war, the enraged emperor shouted in a loud voice. "You see by what has happened that we are superior to you in intelligence. . . . Surely you were easily trapped, captured without a struggle. It is in my power to do with you what I wish when I wish."[42]

Severus replaced the imprisoned guards with his own loyal Praetorian Guard recruited from the non-Italian northern legions.

But though he was a powerful and feared figure, Severus failed to help Rome's ailing economy. In fact, he made things worse. He further devalued the coinage, decreasing the amount of silver and increasing the proportion of worthless metals in coins. He also introduced many new and burdensome taxes to support his military expenditures. People across the empire, overtaxed and uncertain about the future, and still suffering from the effects of plague, civil war, and declining trade, began to feel the strain.

The situation did not improve under Severus's successors. His son Caracalla, who became emperor in 211, kept the army strong and the borders intact, but he was a poor administrator and often treated his subjects cruelly. In 212, to bolster his image, he made a huge show of granting citizenship to all free inhabitants of the empire. But this move was designed mainly to increase the number of people he could tax. And anyway, since the people had no say in government, as they had had in republican days, citizenship was no longer a boon or an honor. As historian Donald R. Dudley put it, "What seems clear is that Roman citizenship became universal when it was no longer a privilege but a burden."[43] Caracalla was murdered by one of his officers in 217. He was succeeded by a series of incompetent and/or ineffective emperors, including Macrinus, Elagabalus, and Alexander Severus. They all ended up being removed from power or assassinated by the army or the new Praetorian Guard. During their reigns, the empire became increasingly unstable, both politically and economically.

The Anarchy

Eventually Rome faced a crisis of epic proportions. By the early 230s its government was in a state of turmoil, trade was on the decline, money was nearly worthless, and poverty and crime were widespread. Seeing the empire so weakened from within, foreign enemies felt bold enough to begin violating Roman borders. The Neo-Persian Empire, a new and powerful realm centered in the Middle East near the Persian Gulf, suddenly invaded several eastern Roman provinces. Soon afterward, several Germanic tribes poured into Gaul. Unable to deal with so many internal and external problems and threats at once, Rome's once mighty military and administrative structure began to buckle.

The result was a period of anarchy, nearly fifty years of chaos and civil war that brought the Roman Empire to the verge of complete collapse. A major cause of this disorder was a lack of central military leadership and organization. Without a strong emperor in Rome, legions in various parts of the empire swore allegiance to individual generals. These men then tried to fight one another while defending the empire against invaders—a foolhardy and self-defeating endeavor. Between 235 and 284, more than fifty rulers claimed the throne. About half were actually acknowledged as emperors, and all but one died by assassination or other violent means. Although

Caracalla (A.D. 188–217) was a cruel, self-indulgent, and ineffective ruler.

Roman armies sometimes won victories over the foreign invaders, Rome's constant civil strife undermined its defensive capabilities. This allowed one German tribe, the Goths, to overrun the province of Dacia, which the empire eventually had to abandon. Another German group, the Franks, invaded both Gaul and Spain.

In the meantime, Roman public works and commerce came to a near standstill. Many areas suffered from sporadic famine, as well as from looting and rape at the hands of invaders. Many people also endured theft and cruelties meted out by undisciplined Roman troops and officials. Some of the common citizens' plight was recorded in a petition sent to Rome from a province in Asia Minor:

> We are most atrociously oppressed and squeezed by those whose duty it is to protect the people. . . . Officers, soldiers, city magistrates, and imperial agents come to our village and take us away from our work and requisition [seize] our oxen; they exact [take] what is not due and we suffer outrageous injustice and extortion [obtaining money and goods by threats and force].[44]

Heightening the human-made chaos and misery of the period, a series of earthquakes and disease epidemics ravaged many sections of the empire.

A Miraculous Recovery

By the 260s, there seemed to be little hope that the empire would recover from its troubles. In addition to destructive invasions, civil turmoil, and natural disasters, the realm had split into three parts: a western, a central, and an eastern region. Each had a leader claiming to be the rightful emperor. This disunity appeared to spell the end of the old Roman world. Fortunately for Rome, however, beginning in the year 268 a series of strong military leaders took control of the empire's central region, which included Italy and Greece. In the span of about sixteen years, Claudius II, Aurelian, Probus, and Carus managed what many at the time regarded as a superhuman task. They not only pushed back the Persians and Germans, but also defeated the imperial claimants in the western and eastern regions. Rome was once more a single entity and, generally speaking, at peace. To a generation of Romans exhausted by the turmoils of the anarchy, it seemed like a miracle.

With the empire reunited and minimal order restored, a remarkably intelligent and able ruler took the throne. He was Diocletian, born of a poor peasant family, a soldier who had risen in the ranks. Like Augustus, Diocletian took on the task of completely reorganizing the Roman state after a long period of disorder. Immediately after becoming emperor in 284, Diocletian instituted a plan designed to protect the emperor from assassination and at the same time restore the government's prestige. He established an "eastern"-style monarchy similar to those in ancient Egypt and Persia. In these lands, the rulers were kings, absolute monarchs usually looked upon as living gods. There was no more pretense about Rome's emperor being first citizen and a man of the people. Diocletian dropped the title of *princeps* and called himself *dominus,* or

Diocletian's Economic Edict

As part of his ambitious economic reorganization, Diocletian attempted to regulate prices and wages. He believed that this would keep inflation down and help the economy to thrive. The move was unpopular, mainly because people did not like the government telling them what they could earn or charge for goods, and it ultimately failed. In 301, Diocletian ordered the regulations in his "Edict of Diocletian," (quoted in The Ancient World: To 300 A.D.). *Like politicians in all ages, including our own, he justified an unpopular action in a statement filled with lofty rhetoric and patriotic slogans.*

"We, who by the gracious favor of the gods have repressed the former tide of ravages of barbarian nations by destroying them, must guard by the due defenses of justice a peace which was established for eternity. If, indeed, any self-restraint might check the excesses with which limitless and furious avarice [greed] rages . . . there would perhaps be some room for . . . silence [inaction]. . . . Since, however, it is the sole desire of unrestrained madness to have no thought for the common need . . . we—the protectors of the human race—viewing the situation, have agreed that justice should intervene . . . so that the long-hoped-for solution which mankind itself could not supply might . . . be applied to the general betterment of all. . . . We, therefore, hasten to apply the remedies long demanded by the situation, satisfied that there can be no complaints. . . . For who is so insensitive and devoid of human feeling that he cannot know . . . that in the commerce carried on in the markets . . . immoderate prices are so widespread. . . . Aroused justly and rightfully by all the facts which are detailed above, and with mankind itself now appearing to be praying for release [from economic misery], we have decreed that there be established . . . a maximum [ceiling for prices and wages], so that when the violence of high prices appears anywhere—may the gods avert such a calamity! . . . It is our pleasure, therefore, that the prices listed in the subjoined [attached] summary be observed in the whole of our empire. . . . We . . . urge upon the loyalty of all our people that a law constituted for the public good may be observed with willing obedience and due care."

Diocletian (A.D. 245–313) introduced an atmosphere of lavish pomp and ceremony into the court.

"lord." He filled the Roman court with elaborate ceremony, ordering that trumpets be sounded when he entered and that people bow deeply when approaching him. Like the eastern monarchs, he declared himself a kind of living god. Thus he created around himself an air of awe and superstition that made would-be assassins and rebels fearful and established the first stable government Rome had seen in generations.

Diocletian also drastically reordered the Roman economy. To pay for his new government and maintain a strong army, he taxed everyone heavily. Because money was almost worthless, his agents often collected goods such as jewelry, livestock, and foodstuffs as payment. And to make sure that goods and services continued uninter-

rupted, the emperor ordered that all workers remain in their professions for life. This command served its purpose but also significantly changed how people lived. It restricted most Romans from moving freely from place to place, made life more regimented, and locked many into permanent poverty. It also reinforced and expanded the system of *coloni* working in hereditary servitude on large estates.

Diocletian's most important change was a reorganization of the empire itself. Realizing that administering so vast a realm was too difficult for one man, he divided the empire in half in 286. He himself took charge of the eastern empire, ruling from the city of Nicodemia in northern Asia Minor, and appointed a general named Maximian as ruler of the western empire. Later, in 293, Diocletian further divided power. He and Maximian each retained the title of Augustus and appointed an assistant emperor who took the title of Caesar. The prominent military leaders Galerius and Constantius became Caesars to Diocletian and Maximian, respectively. This four-man combination, often referred to as the Tetrarchy, was really one-man rule because Diocletian dominated and controlled the others. But in delegating duties to his colleagues, he ensured a smoothly running and efficient government.

But though well-managed, the new Roman world was harsher and less hospitable than the empire of the *Pax Romana* era. With few personal freedoms and little to look forward to, many people were bored, depressed, and unhappy. Most came to accept their downtrodden lives as inevitable, and some looked forward to death as an escape. This made Christianity, which promised eternal salvation and happiness in an afterlife, increasingly popular.

In this painting by French artist Jean Gerome, Christian martyrs face death in the Circus Maximus.

All through the turmoil and miseries of the century of crisis, the Christians grew in numbers. But whereas some emperors had tolerated the followers of Jesus, Diocletian considered them to be a threat. Because they refused to recognize the emperor as a god, he reasoned, they might upset his new order. So in 303 he began a systematic and harsh persecution of the Christians in which many were harassed, threatened, tortured, and killed. This cruel and useless action was to be the last state-sponsored attack on the sect. In sweeping changes that Diocletian and his fellow-rulers could not foresee, Christianity would soon create its own new order in the troubled empire.

Chapter

6 Sword and Cross: Christianity and the Late Empire

Thanks to Diocletian's sweeping reforms, as the fourth century opened the Roman Empire enjoyed some measure of economic and political stability. But the foundations of that stability were far shakier than in earlier Roman times. The government could not completely erase the terrible toll taken by the anarchy, civil strife, plagues, and foreign invasions of the preceding century. So trade volume, living standards, and prosperity in general remained low, and the bread lines stayed long. And while the Persians and Germans had been driven back, these invaders still posed a potential threat to Rome's borders. Many Romans feared that new attacks might come at any time. For most citizens of the empire, then, poverty, fear, and uncertainty about the future had become facts of life.

As a result of the century of crisis and the uncertain times that followed, the Roman populace underwent a significant change of attitude. The old belief that Rome had been chosen by the gods to rule the world forever steadily disappeared. Taking its place were widespread feelings of hopelessness, despair, and apathy. Many felt that the gods had abandoned them, accepting the idea that misery and unhappiness were inevitable. Others came to believe that the traditional gods did not exist and,

searching for comfort, embraced other gods and faiths. Of these other faiths, Christianity grew the fastest. Its promise of happiness in the life to come was only one of the things that made it so appealing. The faith also preached a doctrine of love, the idea that in the eyes of its god everyone, from the loftiest king to the lowliest slave, was equally worthy. In the fourth century Christianity spread rapidly until it became Rome's official state religion.

An engraving based on a fanciful second-century painting of Jesus playing a lyre.

But while the new faith filled the spiritual needs of many, it could not halt the empire's economic decline. It could not stop the increasing attacks and ravages of foreign invaders. Throughout the century, the empire would continue to decay, and the period in which Christianity triumphed would mark the beginning of the end of Roman power.

A Message of Hope

No one at the beginning of the fourth century expected that the small and traditionally unpopular sect of Christianity would become accepted so quickly and so overwhelmingly. In the past, the new faith, enjoying only marginal appeal, had grown

Looking Hideous and Leaping like Maniacs

Christianity was not the only new religion to pique the interest of the Roman populace during imperial times. Many cults and sects flourished. In the following excerpt from his prose work The Golden Ass, *the Roman writer Apuleius described the colorful worship of the Syrian goddess Atargatis, pictured by her followers as half-woman and half-fish. As in many ancient religions, the priests of the cult were eunuchs, men who had shown their devotion to their god by having their sexual organs removed.*

"The eunuch priests prepared to go out on their rounds, all dressed in different colors and looking absolutely hideous, their faces daubed [dabbed] with rouge and their eyesockets painted to bring out the brightness of their eyes. They wore mitre-shaped birettas [pointed hats], saffron-colored chasubles [orange-yellow robes] . . . girdles [wide belts] and yellow shoes. . . . They covered the Goddess with a silk mantle [cloth] and set her on my back, the hornplayer struck up [began playing] and they started brandishing enormous swords and maces [clubs], leaping about like maniacs. . . . After passing through several [towns] we reached a large country house where, raising a yell at the gate, they rushed frantically in and danced again. . . . Every now and then they would bite themselves savagely and as a climax cut their arms with the sharp knives that they carried. One of them let himself go . . . more than the rest. Heaving deep sighs from the very bottom of his lungs, as if filled with the spirit of the Goddess, he pretended to go stark mad. . . . He began by making a bogus confession of guilt, crying out . . . that he had in some way offended against the holy laws of his religion. Then he [used] his own hands to inflict the necessary punishment and snatching up one of the whips [they] always carry . . . gave himself a terrific flogging."

very slowly. In the year 300, more than two-and-a-half centuries after the death of Jesus, the Christians still made up only about 10 percent of the empire's population. And many people continued to view Christians as odd, demented, or dangerous. These factors apparently convinced Diocletian that a large-scale persecution would succeed in stamping out Christianity once and for all. As in the earlier persecutions, the government played up public suspicions about the sect and accused its members of offenses against both society and the state. Historian Mortimer Chambers explains:

> First, they were a secret group, unsociable and self-contained. Tacitus reports that the Romans thought the Christians "hated mankind," and by their own profession [admission] they ate the flesh and drank the blood of their savior [in the ritual of communion]. . . . Christians publicly defied the traditional gods of Rome and refused to sacrifice to the health of the emperor. . . . The Christian church set itself up as a state within a state. The members distinguished sharply between the community of the faithful and the general community. . . . Worse than that, the Church developed a network of bishops communicating with and assisting each other. A Roman might have described this movement as a Christian secession [breaking away from the state]; and it seemed especially intolerable [unacceptable] during the third century when invasion and anarchy had already attacked the Empire at its foundations.[45]

Despite all these motivations for disliking the Christians, the persecutions Diocletian had begun in 303 failed, and the sect

Roman soldiers break up a Christian service in the catacombs beneath Rome.

continued to grow. One reason for this pair of results was that increasing numbers of Christians openly and vigorously spoke out in defense of their faith. By doing so they eliminated misconceptions such as the ideas that they were disloyal to the state and hated humanity. With its image thus improved, the sect gained more converts. In a work titled *Apology*, the Christian writer Tertullian told why the Christians refused to worship the emperor as a god:

> Why should I say more about the respect and the loyalty of Christians toward the emperor? We are under obligation to look up to him as one whom our Lord has chosen. So, I might well say: "Caesar belongs to us, since he has been appointed by our God." . . . I will not call the emperor

The Cruelty of the Persecutions

The persecutions conducted by the Roman government against Christians were cruel and deprived many citizens of their property, their reputations, and sometimes even their lives. The persecution ordered by the emperor Valerian in the year 257, typical of the others before and after, is here described in a letter (quoted in The Ancient World: To 300 A.D.) *written by a Christian bishop named Cyprian.*

"Cyprian to his brother Successus, greeting. The reason why I could not write to you immediately, dearest brother, was that all the clergy . . . were unable in any way to depart [because of the current persecutions]. . . . The truth concerning them is as follows, that Valerian had sent [an order] that bishops . . . should immediately be punished; but that senators and men of importance and Roman knights [if found to be Christians] should lose their dignity and moreover be deprived of their property; and if, when their means were taken away, they should persist in being Christians, then they should also lose their heads; but that matrons [women] should be deprived of their property and sent into banishment. Moreover, people of Caesar's household, whoever of them had either confessed before [to being Christians] or should now confess, should have their property confiscated, and should be sent in chains . . . to Caesar's estates. . . . I beg that these things may be known . . . to the rest of your colleagues. . . . Wherein they know that the soldiers of God and Christ are not slain [defeated], but crowned [blessed for their courage]. I bid you, dearest brother, ever heartily farewell in the Lord."

God, either because I do not know how to lie, or because I dare not make fun of him, or because even he himself does not want to be called God. If he is a man, it is to his interest as a man to yield precedence [importance] to God. Let him consider it enough to be called emperor. That, indeed, is a title of dignity which God has given him.[46]

Another reason Christianity continued to grow was that its central message was one of love. The Christians emphasized God's love for humanity and also people's love for one another. This theme appealed especially to members of the lowest classes, poor people and slaves, who often felt unloved and abandoned by both their rulers and the traditional gods. According to the *Gospel of Luke,* one of the earliest Christian writings, Jesus had preached:

Blessed are you poor, for yours is the kingdom of God. Blessed are you that hunger now, for you shall be satisfied. Blessed are you that weep now, for you shall laugh. Blessed are you when men hate you, and when they exclude you and revile [curse] you, and cast out your name as evil. . . . Rejoice in that day, and leap for joy, for behold, your reward is great in heaven.[47]

This message of hope inspired growing numbers of Romans, especially in the increasingly uncertain times that followed the disruptions of the third century.

The Sign of the Cross

Also contributing to the failure of Diocletian's persecutions of Christians was a diversion of the government's attention and energies to pressing political and military events. In 305, tired of his duties as emperor, Diocletian became the first Roman ruler voluntarily to give up the throne. He forced Maximian, still in charge of the western half of the realm, to step down also. The plan was for the two Caesars of the Tetrarchy, Galerius and Constantius, to assume power in an orderly fashion and rule together. To Diocletian's dismay, however, the events that followed were anything but orderly. In the next few years, a power struggle among Maximian, Galerius, Constantius, and several of their sons developed into a new and bloody civil war. Many different men proclaimed themselves emperor while fighting major battles all over the empire.

An important turning point in the civil war occurred in 312. In that year, Constantine, son of Constantius, invaded Italy in an effort to defeat Maxentius, Maximian's son, who controlled the city of Rome and most of the peninsula. After destroying

Maxentius's armies in the Po Valley, Constantine marched on Rome. Outside the city, Constantine camped near the Mulvian Bridge, a major route over the Tiber River. There, on the eve of battle, an event reportedly occurred that would significantly affect the future of both the empire and Christianity. In his *Life of Constantine*, the Christian bishop Eusebius reported Constantine's own claim:

> A most marvelous sign appeared to [Constantine] from heaven. . . . He said that about noon, when the day was already beginning to decline, he saw with his own eyes the trophy [image] of a cross of light in the heavens, above the sun, and bearing the inscription, CONQUER BY THIS [*In hoc signo vinces*]. At this sight he himself was struck with amazement, and his whole army also, which followed him on this expedition,

This image of Constantine I, "the Great," (c. A.D. 274–337), was taken from a gold coin.

and witnessed the miracle. . . . And while he continued to ponder and reason on its meaning, night suddenly came on; then in his sleep the Christ of God appeared to him with the same sign which he had seen in the heavens, and commanded him to make a likeness of that sign . . . and to use it as a safeguard in all engagements with his enemies.[48]

The truth of this story remains uncertain. What *is* certain is that the next day Constantine ordered his soldiers to paint crosses on their shields and attack Maxentius's forces at the Mulvian Bridge. Constantine's men shattered the opposing army, and Maxentius was slain.

Constantine's Achievements

Constantine's victory gave him control of the western half of the empire. At the time, a ruler named Licinius held sway in the east. Trying to reach an accord, the two men met in 313 at Milan in northern Italy, and each agreed to respect the other's right to govern his own territory. The meeting's most important product, however, was a proclamation guaranteeing religious freedom to all inhabitants of the empire. Usually referred to as the Edict of Milan, this document said in part:

> No man should be denied leave [permission] of attaching himself to the rites of Christians or to whatever other religion his mind directed him. . . . The open and free exercise of their respective religions is granted to all others, as well as to the Christians.[49]

Constantine and his army see a shining cross in the sky before the battle at the Mulvian Bridge.

Constantine seemed to believe that his military successes had been orchestrated by the Christian's god and wanted to show his appreciation. He may, in fact, have already become a believer. But he was not yet ready publicly to declare himself a Christian. Members of the sect were still in the minority, and most Romans were not ready to accept a Christian emperor. However, over the years Constantine increasingly took an interest in the church's affairs and supported its leaders. As a result, large numbers of Romans converted to Christianity during his twenty-five-year reign.

A Message of Brotherhood

One of the most popular of the early Christian writings was the Letter to the Romans *of Paul, an early apostle, or leader, of the faith. Chapter 12 (verses 9, 10, 14–21) sets forth standards of Christian behavior.*

"Let love be genuine; hate what is evil, hold fast to what is good; love one another with brotherly affection; outdo one another in showing honor. . . . Bless those who persecute you; bless and do not curse them. Rejoice with those who rejoice, weep with those who weep. Live in harmony with one another. . . . Repay no one evil for evil. . . . If possible . . . live peaceably with all. Beloved, never avenge yourselves, but leave it [revenge] to the wrath of God; for it is written, "Vengeance is mine, I will repay, says the Lord." No, "if your enemy is hungry, feed him; if he is thirsty, give him drink". . . . Do not be overcome by evil, but overcome evil with good."

Constantine's rule was marked by other important achievements. Shortly after their meeting in Milan, he and Licinius quarreled and a long war ensued. In 324, Constantine emerged victorious and became the first emperor since 286 to rule over both western and eastern sections of the empire. One of his most important acts was to use the power of the army to disband the Praetorian Guard altogether, thus eliminating a dangerous force that had done in many an emperor. He also recognized an important geographical change that had been reshaping the empire for some time. During the Persian wars of the third century, the balance of trade and population had begun to shift toward the eastern section of the realm. This is why Diocletian had established court at Nicodemia. The shift had continued, and by the early fourth century the empire's eastern half was more prosperous and politically important than its western half. Nicodemia was a small and very old town. So Constantine decided to build a completely new eastern capital, one befitting the mighty Roman Empire in size and splendor.

As a site for the new city, Constantine chose Byzantium, an ancient Greek town located along the Bosporus Strait, the narrow waterway separating the Black and Mediterranean seas. Edward Gibbon described the location's many advantages, saying that it

appears to have been formed by nature for the center and capital of a great monarchy. Situated in the forty-first degree of latitude [on a map], the Imperial city commanded [overlooked] . . . the opposite shores of Europe and Asia; the climate was healthy and temperate, the soil fertile, the harbor secure and capacious [roomy]. . . . When the passages of the straits were thrown

Hagia Sophia in Constantinople (modern Istanbul) was the largest church in the world when built by the Eastern emperor Justinian in A.D. 537. The main dome is 185 feet high and 107 wide.

Carved symbols of the western (left) and eastern halves of the Roman Empire.

open for trade, they alternately admitted the natural and artificial riches of the North and South, of the Euxine [Black Sea] and of the Mediterranean. . . . The corn of Egypt, and the gems and spices of the farthest India, were brought by the varying winds into the port.[50]

Workmen began construction in 325, and Constantine officially inaugurated the magnificent new city on May 11, 330. He first called it *Nova Roma,* or New Rome, but it soon became known as Constantinople, the city of Constantine. The emperor dedicated the city to the Virgin Mary and the Holy Trinity, the Christian concept of God as Father, Son, and Holy Ghost. Thus, Constantinople, which would remain a seat of Roman power for many centuries, was, from the outset, a Christian city. This did much to legitimize Christianity in the empire.

A Sinking Ship

Constantine gave Christianity a further boost when, in 337, on his deathbed, he converted to the faith. But the events that followed his passing showed that it mattered little what faith was strongest in the empire. The major problems of the preceding century persisted. As the economy continued to decline, poverty increased and the building of new cities and public works virtually ceased. Also, both Persians and northern barbarians once more pressed the borders. In addition to the Germanic tribes, other groups of invaders threatened from the north. Chief among these were the Huns, a nomadic people who had originated in central Asia. In 375, their armies, consisting solely of horsemen, swept into Europe, forcing the Germans and other tribes into Roman territories. And many Romans were disturbed about the makeup of the armies that defended them against these invaders. The trend of recruiting barbarians into the Roman army, begun in the late second century, had continued. By the mid-fourth century, most Roman soldiers were either foreigners or descended from the empire's former enemies. And by 380, the legions were composed almost entirely of Germans, Gauls, Britons, and Huns. Serving only for the pay, these troops felt no concern or loyalty for the inhabitants of Rome, Alexandria, or Constantinople.

The Huns were ferocious warriors whose armies invaded Europe in A.D. *375, displacing the Ostrogoths, Visigoths, Vandals, and other barbarian tribes.*

All these problems had become so serious that the leaders that followed Constantine, even the strongest, were unable to eliminate them. Some rulers were too preoccupied with enhancing their own power to deal effectively with the empire's troubles. For instance, Constantine had ordered that his sons—Constantine II, Constantius II, and Constans—divide the imperial power equally after his death. But almost immediately a bloody power struggle erupted among these brothers. The ensuing civil strife did not end until 351, when Constantius II, after weeding out potential rivals by killing nearly everyone in his own family, emerged the winner. Constantius II died of sickness in 361, and Julian, a distant relative who had been spared in the family purge, became emperor. An able and humane ruler, Julian might have done much for the empire. But he died in battle in 363, before his potential could be realized.

In the next three decades, a series of strong emperors, including Valentinian, Valens, and Theodosius, ruled Rome. All were devout Christians and under Theodosius, Christianity, which had grown steadily since Constantine's time, became the official state religion. In 378, Theodosius forbade worship of the old Roman gods and converted their temples into museums. He also revised the calendar, eliminating the non-Christian holidays and celebrations. Theodosius, like Valentinian and Valens, also tried his best to stem the tide of foreign invasions and to reverse the trend of economic decay.

But these tasks had become superhuman. In 395, the year of Theodosius's death, the empire was noticeably worse off than it had been a century before. In fact, all the emperors since Diocletian had barely managed to keep its borders intact, its soldiers paid, and its aging roads and buildings repaired. As writer Isaac Asimov commented in his book *The Roman Empire:*

> On the whole . . . the Imperial ship was sinking and with every decade, the Empire's fight to remain barely afloat drained it of a bit more strength—its population declined a bit more, its cities fell a little farther into impoverishment and ruin, its administration sank a bit deeper into corruption and ineffectiveness.[51]

As has happened so often in the history of human affairs, the beginning of a new order signaled the end of an old one. Christianity had triumphed, but Rome was doomed.

7 Eagle in the Dust: The Fall of Rome

Rome fell in the latter part of the fifth century. But the word "fall," so often used to describe this important event, is misleading and often misunderstood. First, it was only the western portion of the empire, encompassing Italy, northern Africa, and western Europe, that ceased to exist. The eastern empire, with its capital at Constantinople, endured until 1453. Second, Rome's fall was not a sudden event. It was instead a slow disintegration, beginning in the late second century, as economic decay, civil war, and foreign invasions steadily took their toll. Over the course of nearly three centuries, Roman social institutions, values, and religion changed under the influence of foreign peoples. All the while, Rome's military and administrative structure grew weaker, less organized, and more corrupt. In short, the Roman world's structure gradually rotted away from within, leaving the empire open to attack by outsiders. Eventually western Rome, as an organized political entity, ceased to exist. Yet its cities, ideas, laws, and institutions did not simply and abruptly disappear. They were slowly absorbed by the "barbarian" cultures that had overcome the western empire, the societies that would later evolve into the kingdoms of medieval Europe.

A Dying Society

Rome suffered a crisis of leadership in the fifth century. For the most part, its emperors, in both the east and west, were corrupt and inefficient. Government was no longer responsive to the needs of the people, but this by itself was not the cause of Rome's fall. Poor leadership was just one symptom among many of a sick and dying society, one more negative result of centuries of overall decline.

Economic decay had begun in the late second century during the reign of Commodus. The financial costs of the civil strife and anarchy that followed soon afterward were enormous, and the governments of later emperors were never able to make up the shortfall. While the government debts became huge, so too did private debts. As a result, many wealthy and middle-class families lost their money and property and joined the growing ranks of the poor. In fact, by the end of the fourth century, the Roman middle class had almost entirely disappeared. At the same time, the volume of trade across the empire gradually decreased, weakened by shrinking markets, piracy, and a lower supply of manufactured goods. In addition,

This carved relief depicts settlers in a Roman-occupied Germanic province paying taxes in the third century.

the system of large estates worked by *coloni* turned free Roman farmers into poor serfs, and agriculture steadily declined. Historian W. L. Westermann explains:

> As the Roman Empire passed from its small estates, worked by slave and free labor, to its great imperial and private domains, the number of free agricultural "production units" [land acreage producing crops and livestock] declined enormously. Consequent upon [this decline] came a great decrease in productivity and the tax-paying power of a given acreage of land.[52]

Thus, as the empire grew increasingly less able to feed itself, the government also lost vital tax revenue and sank farther into debt. Often desperate for money, the state overtaxed everyone, especially the poor. About the year 450, the Christian priest and writer Salvian complained:

> Who can find words to describe the enormity of our present situation? Now, when the Roman commonwealth [empire], already extinct or at least drawing its last breath . . . is dying, strangled by the cords of taxation as if by the hands of brigands [bandits] . . . the poor must endure the frequent, even continuous, ruin of state requisitions [seizures of property and goods], always menaced by severe . . . proscription [threats and physical force]; they desert their homes to avoid being tortured in them, and go into voluntary exile to avoid heavy punishment [for not paying].[53]

Rome showed other symptoms of decay. The population had been severely diminished by the plagues of the second and third centuries. Because of relentless wars, the ravages of poverty, and a general tendency toward having fewer children,

Shame on You Romans

"In [the games] the greatest pleasure is to have men die, or, what is worse and more cruel than death, to have them torn to pieces, to have the bellies of wild beasts gorged [filled] with human flesh; to have men eaten, to the great joy of the bystanders and the delight of onlookers, so that the victims seem devoured almost as much by the eyes of the audience as by the teeth of beasts. . . . They [the Romans] reclined at feasts, forgetful of their honor, forgetting justice, forgetting their faith and the name they bore. There were the leaders of the state, gorged with food, dissolute [lacking restraint] from winebibbing [drinking], wild with shouting, giddy [silly] with revelry [partying], completely out of their senses, or rather, since this was their usual condition, precisely in their senses. If my human frailty [weakness] permitted, I should wish to shout beyond my strength, to make my voice ring through the whole world: Be ashamed, ye Roman people everywhere, be ashamed of the lives you lead. No cities are free of evil haunts [places], no cities anywhere are free from indecency, except those in which barbarians have begun to live."

depopulation of the empire continued in the fourth and fifth centuries. On the national and local levels alike, administrative inefficiency, neglect, and corruption also took a toll. As the government gradually lost both respect and control, law and order frequently broke down, and rebellions, riots, and crime plagued town and countryside. Also, the army, badly disorganized and manned primarily by foreigners, was no longer the mighty military machine of the early Caesars. From the mid-fourth century on, Roman troops were increasingly ineffective in defending the empire's borders.

A Flood over the Borders

It was this sick and weakened empire, this mere shell of the thriving happy Rome of the *Pax Romana* era, that faced the fifth century's great foreign invasions. These were similar to but much larger than those of the two preceding centuries. As Donald Dudley put it, "Central and northern Europe were seething with the turmoil of the greatest folk migrations of history." In addition to the Goths and Huns, tribes including the Vandals, Burgundians, Franks, Angles, Swabians, Alani, Saxons, and Jutes

Frankish warriors ride a barge across a river during their invasion of Gaul. The Franks' influence was so strong that the area still bears their name—France.

spread across the continent. These peoples were largely illiterate and less technically and culturally advanced than the Romans. But they were hardy, bold, often fiercely warlike, and in desperate need of new lands to settle in. The fertile valleys of Roman Italy, Gaul, and Spain beckoned to them. In Dudley's words: "The Empire was like a great whale, slowed down and stopped by a school of killers, the barbarians, who were now closing in to tear it to pieces."[54]

A ring bearing the name and image of Alaric the Goth.

Theodosius was the last emperor to rule the empire's western and eastern portions as a united realm. Shortly after his death in 395, the flood of invaders broke over the northern borders. Each of the two sons of Theodosius took a portion, dividing and further weakening the government just when a united front should have been presented to the barbarians. Arcadius, aged seventeen, became emperor in the east, while Honorius, aged eleven, sat on the western throne. Both youths were weak and incapable rulers, surrounded by greedy and self-serving advisers. One whose advice they did not seek was Alaric, a Christian Goth who had been one of Theodosius's most capable generals. Angered at being passed over for an important government post, Alaric sought revenge. Combining troops loyal to him with Goths from the north, he successfully invaded Greece in 396. The emboldened Alaric then marched into Italy in 400. But Honorius's armies managed to mount a credible defense, and the Goths temporarily retreated in 403.

Alaric's actions had indirect effects that proved more disruptive and dangerous for the empire than his own attacks. To meet the Gothic threat, Honorius had to call back some of the legions from Britain. Almost immediately, the tribal Picts

Social Breakdown and More Lost Territory

Fear and despair grip Rome as the Vandals sack the city in A.D. 455.

of Scotland began raiding southward, while several Germanic tribes crossed the North Sea and pillaged British towns. At the same time, encouraged by Alaric's partial success, a tribe from the lands north of the Danube River, the Swabians, invaded northern Italy. And in 406, fierce Vandal and Alani armies swept through Gaul and into Spain. The Romans managed to drive the Swabians out of Italy. But in 407 they had to recall their last legions from Britain, and the island fell under the control of native and Germanic peoples. And because the Romans lacked the resources to stop them, the barbarians in Gaul and Spain stayed permanently.

Yet the invaders were no mere destroyers. They settled and farmed the land and took advantage of Roman roads and public works. And in many areas they encountered little resistance from the local inhabitants. Often, Romans in these conquered areas preferred being ruled by foreigners who did not tax and brutalize them than by Roman officials who did. Seeing that this loss of allegiance to the state was contributing to the breakdown of Roman society, Salvian wrote:

> All the Romans under [barbarian] rule have but one desire, that they may never have to return to the Roman jurisdiction [authority]. It is the unanimous prayer of the Roman people in [those districts] that they may be permitted to continue to lead their present life among the barbarian. Hence the name of Roman citizen, once not only much valued but dearly bought, is now voluntarily . . . shunned, and is thought not merely valueless, but even almost abhorrent [hated].[55]

The Vandals and Alani were followed by other invaders. In 408, Alaric regrouped his forces and once more entered Italy. This time, as a result of widespread fear and military disorganization, he was able to march straight to Rome almost unopposed, boldly camping near the city. Many Romans were embarrassed and grief-stricken. It was the first time a foreign army had stood outside Rome's walls since Hannibal of Carthage had invaded Italy more than 600 years before. After a two-year siege, Alaric took the city. This major blow to Roman prestige made the western empire look weaker than ever and encouraged other foreigners to challenge Roman power. In 418, the Visigoths, led by Theodoric I, invaded Gaul and set up an independent kingdom just north of the Spanish border. The Romans, pressed by dangers on all sides, had to accept this loss of territory and were obliged to treat Theodoric as an equal.

Searching for Explanations

As the empire continued to fall apart, fear was widespread. Many people wondered if these dire events might be divinely inspired. Pagans, or non-Christians, began to argue that the old Roman gods were punishing the empire for accepting Christianity. In contrast, Christian leaders maintained that Rome's troubles were God's revenge for the sins of the long pagan era. According to this view, advocated by the Christian writer Augustine (later Saint Augustine), Christianity's mission was to save what was left after Rome's fall. Other people looked to ancient prophecy for an explanation of this impending fall. According to legend, before establishing Rome in 753 B.C., Romulus had seen twelve eagles flying together. The eagle became Rome's national symbol. All through the city's history, a superstition lingered, interpreting Romulus's eagles as a prediction of how long Rome would exist. Each eagle represented a century of that existence. In A.D. 447, the 1200 years of the prophecy would be up. Did this mean that Rome's end was near?

Succeeding events convinced many that it was. Honorius died in 423 and was succeeded by a series of rulers as inept and ineffective as himself. In 428, the Vandals overran the province of Africa and set up their own kingdom, similar to that of the Visigoths in Gaul. And in 433, a war chief named Attila, whose ferocity earned him the nickname "the scourge [destroyer] of God," became leader of the European Huns. His armies swept into Germany, forcing the Burgundians, Franks, Angles, Saxons, and Jutes to move into Gaul and Britain. Then, in 451, Attila invaded Gaul.

The barbarian horsemen who conquered Gaul were skilled and fearless warriors.

Attila, known as the "Scourge of God," leads his fearsome Huns into Italy.

The Last Emperor

The demise of the Huns set the barbarian migrations and invasions in motion again. Several Germanic tribes attacked their neighbors as well as Roman borders. In 455, the African Vandals launched a raiding fleet, sailed up the Tiber, and sacked Rome, the second time the city had been taken in less than half a century. The Vandals mostly looted gold and other valuables, leaving the city intact. But after they departed, many of the survivors fled permanently to other areas. The city's administrative and public services broke down, bringing on chaos and famine, and its population quickly shrank from one million to about 20,000. Many people gloomily noted that this dark event had occurred a mere eight years after the 1200th year of the ancient prophecy.

Romulus Augustulus, the last Roman emperor, signifies his submission to the German Odoacer.

This action was unsuccessful, so he turned south in the following year and entered Italy.

As Attila marched on Rome, the emperor Valentinian III hid in terror in a faraway town. The only man in the capital with the courage to face the Huns was Leo, the bishop of Rome, the Christian leader whose title today would be pope. The word "pope" comes from "papa," or father, a title given to priests. Leo traveled to the Po River in northern Italy, met with Attila, and somehow, perhaps by bribing him with gold, convinced the invader to leave Italy. Not long after this departure Attila died, and his short-lived Hunnish empire fell apart.

Inspired by Cicero

Augustine was a Christian teacher and writer of the fifth century. His works, including The City of God *and* Confessions, *are still widely read and discussed. In this excerpt from* Confessions, *Augustine tells how as a young man he read* Hortensius *by the Roman writer and orator Cicero. This work inspired Augustine to study many other philosophical and religious ideas, including those of Christianity.*

"In that unsettled age of mine, learned I books of eloquence [oratory], wherein I desired to be eminent [skillfull], out of . . . a joy in human vanity. In the ordinary course of study, I fell upon [found] a certain book of Cicero, whose speech almost all admire. . . . This book of his contains an exhortation to [strong recommendation to read] philosophy, and is called *Hortensius*. But this book altered my affections [interests] and turned my prayers to Thyself, O Lord; and made me have other purposes and desires. [After finding Christianity] every vain hope at once became worthless to me; and I longed with an incredibly burning desire for an immortality of wisdom. . . . How did I burn then, my God, how did I burn then to re-mount [turn away] from earthly things to Thee, nor knew I what Thou wouldest do with me? For with Thee is wisdom. But the love of wisdom is in Greek called "philosophy," with which that book inflamed me. . . . I resolved then to bend my mind to the holy Scriptures [biblical writings], that I might see what they were."

The western empire now consisted only of the Italian peninsula and portions of a few nearby provinces. The rest of the former realm—Britain, Gaul, Spain, Africa, and central Europe—was in barbarian hands. It was a pitiful realm indeed that the last Roman emperor, Romulus Augustus, an inexperienced boy of fourteen, inherited in 475. There was great irony in his name. The first Romulus was the founder of the city-state that became the Roman Republic, and Augustus had created the empire. Now an unfortunate boy bearing their names presided over the end of Roman power. Because of his youth, many called him Augustulus, or "little Augustus."

On September 4, 476, an army of paid barbarians led by a German general named Odoacer entered Rome and forced Augustulus from the throne. No emperor took his place. The government, which had been barely functioning for decades, now simply ceased to exist. For that reason, 476 is usually seen as the date of Rome's fall.

A Fatal Mistake?

Modern historians have offered many explanations for the decline and fall of Rome. According to teacher and historian Max Cary, one of Rome's fatal mistakes was to pursue its aggressive policy of foreign conquest in republican times. Cary discussed the fall of Rome in his essay "The Roman Empire: Retrospect and Prospect."

"Was this policy conceived on the wrong lines? It has been suggested that the Roman conquerors overreached themselves by annexing more land than they could profitably or safely hold. The extension of the Roman boundaries across the Danube [River] to Dacia, or across the [English] Channel to Britain, was but a matter of minor moment [importance]; the critical question is whether the Senate of the second century B.C. was well-advised to make conquests in the eastern Mediterranean. It may be contended [argued] that if the Romans had left the Greeks to their own devices [affairs] and had applied themselves to the consolidation [strengthening] of their rule in the west, they might have created a compact and homogeneous [related] *bloc* [group] of Latin-speaking peoples which would have been impregnable to all assailants [too strong to conquer]."

The Prophecy Fulfilled?

The eastern empire, however, was still largely intact and functioning. After the collapse of government in Italy, the eastern rulers considered themselves to be legally in control of the western empire. But they were never able to exercise that control. They lacked the huge amounts of money and troops that would have been needed to retake the conquered western lands. Involved in its own problems and sphere of influence, the eastern empire steadily lost touch with the west.

Rome and Italy continued under German rule for a few decades. Thereafter, Rome was continuously inhabited, but its government and central organization were gone. The great public buildings continued to decay, their ruin aided by people dismantling them to obtain materials from which to build cruder structures. As in the past, Rome's destruction continued to be less the work of invaders and more that of the Roman people themselves. As Edward Gibbon observed:

The spectator who casts a mournful view over the ruins of ancient Rome is tempted to accuse the memory of the Goths and Vandals for the mischief. . . . But the destruction that undermined the foundations [of Rome] was prose-

The Arch of Titus is one of many Roman monuments that have survived nearly intact.

cuted [occurred] slowly and silently over a period of ten centuries. . . . [After Rome's fall] the monuments of . . . Imperial greatness were no longer revered as the immortal glory of the capital; they were only esteemed [looked upon] as an inexhaustible mine of materials, cheaper, and more convenient, than the distant quarry. . . . The fairest forms of architecture were rudely defaced for the sake of some paltry [minor] . . . repairs; and the degenerate [now less-civilized] Romans . . . demolished . . . the labors of their ancestors.[56]

Thus did Rome, the grand city that had overseen the stately republic and the majestic empire, fade into obscurity. Whether by divine intervention or by mere coincidence, its 1229-year reign nearly matched the one predicted in the ancient prophecy. The once proud and mighty Roman eagle lay buried in the dust of ages, never to rise again.

Immortal Rome

After the fall of the western Roman Empire, the European world underwent a gradual transformation. The eastern empire and a number of small kingdoms set up by the western barbarians continued to thrive. Smaller, weaker, and less organized than the Roman Empire had been, these states developed separately, evolving their own cultural personalities and spheres of influence. Where Rome had once been the major center of European civilization, there were now many minor centers scattered over the continent. "As we look out over this . . . world situation," wrote James Henry Breasted, "we see, lying in the middle, the remnant of the Roman Empire ruled by Constantinople . . . while on one side was the lost West, made up of the German kingdoms of the former northern barbarians."[57]

Over the centuries, the eastern empire slowly and steadily declined, losing most of its power and territory. Its culture retained Roman elements, but eventually its customs, language, and religion changed. The Greek language replaced Latin. And the eastern church developed its own ceremonies so that it became distinct from its counterpart in the west. The results of this religious split are the eastern Greek Orthodox Church and the western Roman Catholic Church. Eventually, the eastern empire shrank until it controlled only the region surrounding Constantinople and parts of Greece. In 1453, 977 years after the collapse of the western empire, the eastern empire fell to the Turks.

In the west, the barbarian kingdoms slowly grew into the small European realms of medieval times. Also called the Middle Ages, this was the period beginning with Rome's fall and ending with the European Renaissance nearly a thousand years later. England, settled by the descendants of the Angles and Saxons, was one of these medieval kingdoms. Among the

Merchants and soldiers mingle in a medieval German city.

many others were Lombardy and Tuscany in what is now Italy, Navarre and Aragon in Spain, Burgundy and Aquitaine in France, and Bavaria and Saxony in Germany. After many centuries, as these and other kingdoms rose, fell, and combined, they became the nations of modern Europe.

The Roman legacy passed on to the modern world through the medieval kingdoms was enormous. After Rome fell, European cultures retained many Roman ideas, customs, and institutions, as well as Roman law and language. Historian Solomon Katz has remarked:

> Roman civilization . . . lived on as an integral [essential] element of medieval and modern civilization. Rome's triumphs and successes were canceled by her failure, but what she accomplished in diverse areas of endeavor was not lost. In the long perspective [view] of history, the survival of Roman civilization, the heritage which generation after generation has accepted, is perhaps more significant than the decline of Rome.[58]

Often, medieval cultures modified Roman ideas to suit their own situations. For example, most Europeans in the Middle Ages practiced an agricultural and social system known as feudalism. It developed directly from the Roman farming system, in which poor *coloni* worked for wealthy masters on large farms and estates. Later, medieval feudal lords, presiding over estates called manors, had serfs, tenants who served the lords and were dependent on them. In exchange for raising crops and livestock and fighting the lord's enemies, the serf received a home, a share of what he raised, and the lord's protection.

Ancient Roman walls and modern buildings in London create a stark visual contrast.

The medieval and modern worlds inherited many of Rome's public works. For instance, many Roman roads continued to be used throughout the Middle Ages and some are still in use today. Many Roman cities and towns survived and remained continuously populated. Some, such as Milan, Italy; Toledo, Spain; Paris, France; and London, England, are among the world's great modern cities. Other modern cities around the world are laid out in a grid pattern directly copying that used by the ancient Romans. New York City and Lisbon, Portugal, are two prominent examples.

One of the most important things the Romans left the world was their language. Adapted by different peoples in different areas, Latin gradually developed into French, Spanish, Portuguese, Italian, and Romanian. These are often referred to as the Romance languages in honor of their common Roman heritage. Latin influenced other modern languages as well. The Germanic tongues of the Angles and Saxons eventually mixed with Latin and French to form the English language. More than half the words in English are of Latin origin. Even after it had ceased to be widely spoken, Latin survived for more than a thousand years as the leading language of European literature. And it also remained the official language of the western Catholic church. Latin became a kind of international scholarly language and is still widely taught in high schools and colleges.

The Romans also left behind their laws, developed and refined over the course of more than a thousand years. Their legal system became the basis for those used by later European cultures and also for the one employed by the church. Comments Solomon Katz:

> The Roman law, the instrument and symbol of her unity, was Rome's greatest achievement. The acceptance of this legacy by the Middle Ages gave both church and state a basis for their own systems of law and helped to civilize Europe by spreading widely the principles of equity and humanity which were embodied in the structure of the law. . . . In the East and the West during the Middle Ages the church erected [built] canon law, its own legal system, upon Roman foundations.[59]

One of Rome's greatest legacies was its transmission of Greek ideas and culture to the modern world. The Romans themselves owed much to the Greeks, for much in Roman literature, architecture, and religion was based on Greek models. Without the elements of Greek civilization preserved by the Romans, a great deal of Greece's own magnificent heritage might have been lost forever. For example, many famous Greek sculptures and writings are known only from Roman copies. The ancient Greek and Roman cultures together are often called classical civilization. The classical legacy in art, language, literature, architecture, law, and government remains part of the very fabric of modern society. And in that sense, though the Roman Republic and Empire have passed away, the spirit of the people who built them lives on. As R. H. Barrow put it:

> Rome never fell, she turned into something else. Rome [after disappearing] as a . . . political power, passed into even greater supremacy [importance] as an idea; Rome, with the latin language, had become immortal.[60]

Notes

Introduction: The Evidence from the Ashes

1. Pliny the Younger, *Letter to Cornelius Tacitus.* Translated by Betty Radice, in *Pliny: Letters and Panegyricus.* Cambridge, MA: Harvard University Press, 1969.

2. James Henry Breasted, *Ancient Times: A History of the Early World.* Boston: Ginn and Company, 1944.

Chapter 1: From Republic to Empire: The Augustan Age

3. Sallust, *The War with Cataline.* Quoted in Stringfellow Barr, *The Mask of Jove: A History of Graeco-Roman Civilization from the Death of Alexander to the Death of Constantine.* Philadelphia: J. B. Lippincott, 1966.

4. Suetonius, *Lives of the Twelve Caesars.* Translated by Joseph Gavorse. New York: Modern Library, 1931.

5. Augustus Caesar, *Res gestae divi Augusti.* Quoted in *The Ancient World: To 300 A.D.,* edited by Paul J. Alexander. New York: Macmillan, 1963.

6. Tacitus, *The Annals.* Translated by Alfred John Church, in *Great Books of the Western World,* Volume 15. Chicago: Encyclopaedia Britannica, 1952.

7. Tacitus, *The Annals.*

8. Strabo, *Geography.* Quoted in Dorothy Mills, *The Book of the Ancient Romans.* New York: G. P. Putnam's Sons, 1937.

9. Ovid, *The Art of Love.* Translated by Rolphe Humphries, in *Sources in Western Civilization,* edited by William G. Sinnigen. New York: Macmillan, 1965.

10. Quoted in Will Durant, *Caesar and Christ: A History of Roman Civilization and of Christianity from Their Beginnings to A.D. 325.* New York: Simon & Schuster, 1944.

Chapter 2: Rome of the Caesars: The First Century of Peace

11. Tacitus, *The Annals.*

12. Dio Cassius, *History of Rome.* Quoted in Durant, *Caesar and Christ.*

13. Suetonius, *Lives of the Twelve Caesars.*

14. Suetonius, *Lives of the Twelve Caesars.*

15. Suetonius, *Lives of the Twelve Caesars.*

16. Tacitus, *The Annals.*

17. Suetonius, *Lives of the Twelve Caesars.*

Chapter 3: Bread and Circuses: The Task of Controlling the Masses

18. Jerome Carcopino, *Daily Life in Ancient Rome: The People and the City at the Height of the Empire.* New Haven, CT: Yale University Press, 1940.

19. Juvenal, *Satires.* Quoted in *Latin Literature in Translation,* edited by Kevin Guinagh and Alfred Paul Dorjahn. New York: Longman's Green and Company, 1952.

20. Juvenal, *Satires.*

21. Juvenal, *Satires.*

22. Plutarch, *Life of Pompey.* Quoted in Dorothy Mills, *The Book of the Ancient Romans.* New York: G. P. Putnam's Sons, 1927.

23. R. H. Barrow, *The Romans.* Baltimore: Penguin Books, 1949.

24. Pliny the Younger, *Letter to Septicius Clarus,* in *Letters.*

25. Juvenal, *Satires.*

26. Virgil, *Georgics.* Quoted in Mills, *The Book of the Ancient Romans.*

27. Seneca, *Epistulae morales.* Quoted in Michael Grant, *The World of Rome.* New York: New American Library, 1960.

28. Quintilian, *The Training of an Orator.* Quoted in Carcopino, *Daily Life in Ancient Rome.*

29. Quoted in Durant, *Caesar and Christ.*

Chapter 4: The Five Good Emperors: Rome Reaches Its Zenith

30. Edward Gibbon, *The Decline and Fall of the Roman Empire,* in *Great Books of the Western World.* Chicago: Encyclopaedia Britannica, 1952.

31. Michael Grant, *The Army of the Caesars.* New York: M. Evans & Company, 1974.

32. Pliny the Younger, *Panegyricus.*

33. Pliny the Younger, *Letter to Trajan,* and Trajan, *Letter to Pliny the Younger.* Quoted in *The Ancient World: To 300 A.D.*

34. Hadrian, quoted in Michael Grant, *The Army of the Caesars.*

35. Marcus Aurelius, *Meditations.* Quoted in Durant, *Caesar and Christ.*

36. Aelius Aristides, *Roman Panegyric.* Quoted in Barrow, *The Romans.*

37. Marcus Aurelius, *Meditations.* Quoted in *Sources in Western Civilization.*

Chapter 5: The Century of Crisis: Rome on the Brink of Collapse

38. Will Durant, *Caesar and Christ.*

39. Arthur E. R. Boak, *A History of Rome to 565 A.D.* New York: Macmillan, 1943.

40. Dio Cassius, *History of Rome.*

41. Dio Cassius, *History of Rome.*

42. Herodian, *History of Twenty Caesars.* Quoted in Grant, *The Army of the Caesars.*

43. Donald R. Dudley, *The Civilization of Rome.* New York: New American Library, 1960.

44. Quoted in Barrow, *The Romans.*

Chapter 6: Sword and Cross: Christianity and the Late Empire

45. Mortimer Chambers, "The Crisis of the Third Century," in *The Transformation of the Roman World,* edited by Lynn White Jr. Berkeley: University of California Press, 1966.

46. Tertullian, *Apology.* Quoted in *Sources in Western Civilization.*

47. *Gospel of Luke, 6: 20–23.*

48. Eusebius, *Life of Constantine.* Quoted in *Sources in Western Civilization.*

49. Lactantius, *Death of the Persecutors.* Quoted in Barrow, *The Romans.*

50. Gibbon, *The Decline and Fall of the Roman Empire*.

51. Isaac Asimov, *The Roman Empire*. Boston: Houghton Mifflin, 1967.

Chapter 7: Eagle in the Dust: The Fall of Rome

52. W. L. Westermann, "The Economic Basis of the Decline of Ancient Culture," in Donald Kagan, editor, *Decline and Fall of the Roman Empire. Why Did It Collapse?* Boston: D. C. Heath, 1952.

53. Salvian, *On the Government of God.* Quoted in Chester G. Starr, *The Ancient Romans.* New York: Oxford University Press, 1971.

54. Dudley, *The Civilization of Rome.*

55. Salvian, *On the Government of God.*

56. Gibbon, *Decline and Fall of the Roman Empire.*

Epilogue: Immortal Rome

57. Breasted, *Ancient Times.*

58. Solomon Katz, "The Roman Legacy," in Mortimer Chambers, editor, *The Fall of Rome: Can It Be Explained?* New York: Holt, Rinehart and Winston, 1963.

59. Katz, "The Roman Legacy."

60. Barrow, *The Romans.*

For Further Reading

Ian Andrews, *Pompeii.* Cambridge, England: Cambridge University Press, 1978. An easy-to-read, colorfully illustrated synopsis of the eruption of Mount Vesuvius, the destruction of Pompeii, and the facts learned by archaeologists from excavating that buried city.

Isaac Asimov, *The Roman Empire.* Boston: Houghton Mifflin, 1967. An excellent overview of the empire, well researched and clearly explained.

Lionel Casson, *Daily Life in Ancient Rome.* New York: American Heritage Publishing, 1975. A fascinating presentation of how the Romans lived: their homes, streets, entertainments, eating habits, theaters, religion, slaves, marriage customs, government, tombstone epitaphs, and much more. Aimed at intermediate and advanced readers.

Ron and Nancy Goor, *Pompeii: Exploring a Roman Ghost Town.* New York: Thomas Y. Crowell, 1986. An overview of the excavations at Pompeii, aimed at young readers.

Jill Hughes, *Imperial Rome.* New York: Gloucester Press, 1985. Nicely illustrated introduction to the Roman Empire, covering basic aspects of Roman civilization.

Anthony Marks and Graham Tingay, *The Romans.* London: Usborne Publishing, 1990. Beautifully illustrated summary of Roman history and life.

Author's note: I strongly recommend the following films about the Roman Empire for their accuracy, dramatic impact, or both. All are available on videotape.

Barabbas, (1962) with Anthony Quinn, Arthur Kennedy, and Jack Palance, directed by Richard Fleischer. Based on a best-selling novel about the criminal supposedly freed after Jesus was arrested, this is a well-acted and beautifully photographed film. Although most of the situations are fictional, the depictions of Roman cities and customs, including slavery and dress of the first century A.D. are accurate.

Ben-Hur (1959), with Charlton Heston, Stephen Boyd, and Hugh Griffith, directed by William Wyler. A magnificently mounted spectacle based on the book by Lew Wallace. Traces the faltering relationship between a Jewish prince and a Roman officer who had been friends as boys, depicting Tiberius's reign and Jesus' crucifixion along the way. The detailed settings are accurate, and the chariot race is one of the greatest action scenes in film history. Winner of eleven Oscars, including best film, director, actor, supporting actor, and music. *Note:* The 1926 version, though silent, is also quite good, with a chariot race nearly as spectacular as the newer one.

Cleopatra (1963), with Elizabeth Taylor, Richard Burton, and Rex Harrison, directed by Joseph L. Mankiewicz. Overlong but visually stunning depiction of the affairs Cleopatra had with Julius Caesar and Mark Antony. Contains authentic sets and costumes, an excellent performance by Rex Harrison as Caesar, and spectacular reproductions of Cleopatra's parade into Rome and the sea battle of Actium.

Demetrius and the Gladiators (1954), with Victor Mature, Susan Hayward, and Jay Robinson, directed by Delmer Daves. This sequel, made to capitalize on the popularity of the religious spectacle *The Robe,* is actually a better film. Depicts the court intrigues during Caligula's reign, as well as a number of exciting and amazingly accurate gladiatorial combats. Much of the plot is fictional, but those interested in Rome will love the colorful spectacle and atmosphere. Robinson's portrayal of the psychotic Caligula is a treat.

The Fall of the Roman Empire (1964), with Stephen Boyd, Christopher Plummer, and Alec Guinness, directed by Anthony Mann. Overlong, but an accurate, beautifully produced, and fascinating depiction of the final days of the emperor Marcus Aurelius and the reign of his mad son Commodus, well played by Plummer. Does not show the actual fall of Rome, but makes the point that from Commodus's reign on, the empire steadily decayed. Well acted and scripted, with several exciting action scenes and one of the largest film sets (of the Roman Forum) ever constructed. Famed historian Will Durant was technical adviser.

Quo Vadis? (1951), with Robert Taylor, Peter Ustinov, and Leo Genn, directed by Mervyn LeRoy. A sometimes slow, but colorfully filmed rendition of Henryk Sienkiewicz's novel about Nero's persecution of the Christians. The scenes of death in the arena and the burning of Rome are spectacular, and Ustinov's performance as Nero is wonderful. Genn, as the Roman writer Petronius, is also excellent.

Works Consulted

Paul J. Alexander, editor, *The Ancient World: To 300 A.D.* New York: Macmillan, 1963. A large collection of original ancient writings, including many from Greece and Rome.

Isaac Asimov, *The Roman Empire.* Boston: Houghton Mifflin, 1967.

Stringfellow Barr, *The Mask of Jove: A History of Graeco-Roman Civilization from the Death of Alexander to the Death of Constantine.* Philadelphia: J. B. Lippincott, 1966. Long, well-researched account of classical civilization. Contains a number of long primary source quotes.

Anthony A. Barrett, *Caligula: The Corruption of Power.* New York: Simon & Schuster, 1990. A fascinating and detailed study of one of Rome's worst but most colorful emperors. Barrett takes the view that despite his corrupt practices, Caligula did accomplish some useful works.

R. H. Barrow, *The Romans.* Baltimore: Penguin Books, 1949. Short, but well-written summary of both the Roman Republic and the Roman Empire.

Arthur E. R. Boak, *A History of Rome to 565 A.D.* New York: Macmillan, 1943. A very detailed account of Roman history which pays special attention to political developments and intrigues.

Keith R. Bradley, *Discovering the Roman Family: Studies in Roman Social History.* New York: Oxford University Press, 1991. Well-researched and interesting material about social life in ancient Rome. For those fascinated by Rome, this is the sort of work that should be read along with the usual political history to get a balanced view of Roman life.

James Henry Breasted, *Ancient Times: A History of the Early World.* Boston: Ginn and Company, 1944. One of the best general sources on ancient civilizations, extremely well researched, well organized, and clearly written. Contains more than 200 pages on Rome alone.

Jerome Carcopino, *Daily Life in Ancient Rome: The People and the City at the Height of the Empire.* New Haven, CT: Yale University Press, 1940. Extremely well-researched and entertaining study of Roman imperial customs, people, dress, food, games, religion, and much more.

Lionel Casson, *Daily Life in Ancient Rome.* New York: American Heritage, 1975. A colorful and well-illustrated summary of Roman life and customs.

Mortimer Chambers, editor, *The Fall of Rome: Can It Be Explained?* New York: Holt, Rinehart and Winston, 1963. A collection of essays by noted historians, each considering a cause for Rome's decline. Manpower shortages, economic crises, agricultural exhaustion, barbarian invasions, and other topics are discussed.

Donald R. Dudley, *The Civilization of Rome.* New York: New American Library, 1960. A well-written Roman history with special emphasis on cultural aspects.

J. Wight Duff, *A Literary History of Rome.* New York: Barnes & Noble, 1960. Lists and analyzes the important Roman writers and their works. A valuable reference book for those interested in Latin works.

Will Durant, *Caesar and Christ: A History of Roman Civilization and of Christianity from Their Beginnings to A.D. 325.* New York: Simon & Schuster, 1944. Immense and sometimes ponderous, but brilliantly researched and organized summary of Roman civilization by a great historian.

Donald Earl, *The Age of Augustus.* New York: Crown Publishers, 1968. Nicely written overview of Augustus and his achievements. Includes many fine photos.

Jane F. Gardner, *Women in Roman Law and Society.* Indianapolis: Indiana University Press, 1986. Excellent study of women in Roman times. Highly recommended for those wishing to delve into the details of Roman life.

Edward Gibbon, *The Decline and Fall of the Roman Empire,* in *Great Books of the Western World.* Chicago: Encyclopaedia Britannica, 1952. Even though Gibbon wrote his book more than two centuries ago, it remains a masterful study of Roman history and *the* authoritative source for the collapse of the Roman Empire.

Michael Grant, *The Army of the Caesars.* New York: M. Evans & Company, 1974. Grant's detailed study of the evolution of Roman armies and military customs is first-rate scholarship.

Michael Grant, *The World of Rome.* New York: New American Library, 1960. A fascinating view of Roman culture, including thematic chapters like "Subjects and Slaves," "Fate and the Stars," and "The Great Latin Writers." Contains plenty of primary source quotations revealing much about Roman life.

Kevin Guinagh and Alfred Paul Dorjahn, editors, *Latin Literature in Translation.* New York: Longman's, Green and Company, 1952. Good selection of Roman writings, including works by Plautus, Terence, Caesar, Cato, Cicero, Sallust, Virgil, Horace, Ovid, and many others.

Edith Hamilton, *The Roman Way to Western Civilization.* New York: W. W. Norton, 1932, reprinted by New American Library, 1960. One of Hamilton's three timeless, classic, and beautifully written studies of the foundations of Western culture, the others being *The Greek Way,* and *Mythology.*

The Holy Bible. New York: Thomas Nelson & Sons, 1952.

Donald Kagan, editor, *Decline and Fall of the Roman Empire: Why Did It Collapse?* Boston, D. C. Heath, 1962. This revealing collection of essays by various modern experts explores some of the major reasons for Rome's fall.

Barbara Levick, *Claudius.* New Haven, CT: Yale University Press, 1990. Thoughtful, up-to-date study of Claudius's reign.

Lives of the Later Caesars: The First Part of the Augustan History, with newly compiled lives of Nerva and Trajan. Translated by Anthony Birley. New York: Penguin Books, 1976. A modern translation of the writings of various later imperial writers. (All the names may have been pseudonyms for one man.)

Dorothy Mills, *The Book of the Ancient Romans.* New York: G. P. Putnam's Sons, 1927. Well-researched summary of ancient Roman culture, supported by many long, fascinating primary source quotations.

Betty Radice, editor, *Pliny: Letters and Panegyricus.* Cambridge, MA: Harvard University Press, 1969. An excellent translation of the many surviving letters of Pliny the Younger. These letters afford modern readers an informative and entertaining glimpse into life during the empire.

William G. Sinnegin, editor, *Sources in Western Civilization: Rome.* New York: The Free Press, 1965. A fine collection of Roman writings, including excerpts from works by Livy, Polybius, Appian,

Cicero, Suetonius, Tacitus, Marcus Aurelius, and Tertullian.

Chester G. Starr, *The Ancient Romans*. New York: Oxford University Press, 1971. Well-written short summary of both the Roman Republic and the Roman Empire. Includes several interesting primary source quotations.

Suetonius, *Lives of the Twelve Caesars*. Translated by Joseph Gavorse. New York: Modern Library, 1931. A fine translation of Suetonius's chronicles of the early Roman emperors.

Tacitus, *The Annals*. Translated by Alfred John Church, in *Great Books of the Western World,* Volume 15. Chicago: Encyclopaedia Britannica, 1952. Tacitus's long historical tracts on Rome comprise one of the two or three most important primary sources about the Roman Empire. Very difficult but worthwhile reading.

Lynn White Jr., editor, *The Transformation of the Roman World*. Berkeley: University of California Press, 1966. A collection of essays discussing how the Roman Empire changed and declined and how this transformation affected Western civilization.

Index

Picture Credits

About the Author

Don Nardo is an award-winning writer, composer, and filmmaker. His writing credits include short stories, articles, and more than forty-five books, including *Lasers, Gravity, Germs, The War of 1812, Medical Diagnosis, Eating Disorders, Charles Darwin, H. G. Wells, Thomas Jefferson,* and *Ancient Greece,* as well as *Cleopatra* and the companion volume to this book, *The Roman Republic.* Mr. Nardo has also written an episode for ABC's "Spenser: For Hire" and numerous screenplays. He lives with his wife, Christine, on Cape Cod, Massachusetts.

Oz Clarke's

LET ME TELL YOU
ABOUT WINE

Oz Clarke's
LET ME TELL YOU
ABOUT WINE

STERLING EPICURE
An imprint of Sterling Publishing Co., Inc.

New York / London
www.sterlingpublishing.com

10 9 8 7 6 5 4 3 2 1

First Sterling edition published 2009.
Published by Sterling Publishing Co., Inc.
387 Park Avenue South, New York, NY 10016

Distributed in Canada by Sterling Publishing
c/o Canadian Manda Group, 165 Dufferin Street,
Toronto, Ontario, Canada M6K 3H6

Manufactured in Malaysia

Sterling ISBN 978-1-4027-7123-1

For information about custom editions, special sales, premium and corporate purchases, please contact Sterling Special Sales Department at 800-805-5489 or specialsales@sterlingpublishing.com

www.ozclarke.com

Colour reproduction by Dot Gradations, London
Printed and bound by Times Offset in Malaysia

READER'S NOTE

In **Part One, Discover Grape Varieties** the star symbol ★ next to a grape heading indicates that the grape has been highlighted by Oz as a future star

In **Part Three, The World of Wine**, the price bands for the wines recommended in the *Quick Guide* sections, for example on page 112, correspond to the following dollar prices for a standard 750ml bottle. Prices are intended for guidance only and may vary.

1 under $8   **2** $8–$16   **3** $16–$24

4 $24–$32   **5** over $32

Pages 2–3 Lake Wanaka in Central Otago in New Zealand's South Island is for me one of the world's most beautiful wine regions.

PICTURE ACKNOWLEDGMENTS

Alamy Pat and Chuck Blackley 164; Michael Busselle 99; Lordprice Collection 104; Hans-Peter Siffert 129; Westend 61 GmbH/ Holger Spiering 183
Anova Books Stephen Bartholomew 83 (above), 89, 90; Robert Hall 86, 86–87 (below), 95; Gary Moyes 7, 26, 38, 77, 94, 97; Lucinda Symons 1, 10, 18, 23 (left), 56 (left), 65, 82, 83 (below), 84, 85, 143
Cephas Picture Library 57; Jerry Alexander 161; Kevin Argue 166; Nigel Blythe 27, 68, 109 (left), 124, 151; Karine Bossavy 105; Hervé Champollion 113; Andy Christodolo 2–3, 34 (left), 48, 132 (left), 154 (right), 167; Jeff Drewitz 177; Juan Espi 182; Fresh Food Images 9 (above), 9 (centre), 22; Dario Fusaro 130, 131; Mark Graham 185 (right); Tom Hyland 31; Duncan Johnson 60; Kevin Judd 34 (right), 41 (right), 49 (background), 49 (below), 50, 52, 53, 169, 172, 173, 179; Pierre Lapin 13, 15 (left), 19 (left), 20, 100; Herbert Lehmann 92, 128, 153, 156; Joris Luyten 74; Char Abu Mansoor 185 (left); Diana Mewes 144 (left); Janis Miglavs 46; R & K Muschenetz 160, 168; David Pearce 15 (right); Neil Phillips 138; Alain Proust 117; Graeme Robinson 181; Mick Rock 28, 29, 30, 33, 35, 36, 40, 43, 44 (right), 45 (above), 49 (above), 54, 55 (left), 55 (right), 56 (right), 61 (left), 61 (right), 63, 71, 108, 118, 120–121, 122, 126, 132 (right), 134, 136–137, 139, 141, 144 (right), 145, 146 (left), 146 (right), 148, 152, 162, 163, 174; Ian Shaw 58, 59, 62, 67; Ted Stefanski 4–5, 9 (below), 37 (above), 39; Martin Walls 154 (left); Matt Wilson 32, 170
Bodega y Estancia Colomé Ossian Lindholm 47
Corbis Tom Bean 42; Richard Klune 44 (left), 45 (below); Gunter Marx 165; Swim Ink 2, LLC, poster by Jean d'Ylen 45 (below); **iStockphoto** pages 12, 14, 19 (right), 23 (right), 24, 25

Contents

Next time you walk into a wine shop, stop for a moment and have a good look around. Don't head straight for this month's special offer, don't blinker your vision to everything but your trusty favourites, just have a good gawp at the whole range that's on display. If the shop is big and you're anything like me, your head will start to spin and the overwhelming abundance of different wines will leave you dizzy with delight. Imagine it – there's a unique flavour stoppered up in every one of those bottles. So open your mind, pick a bottle, any bottle, and head off on a lifetime's joyous voyage of discovery.

But is it really worth making the effort to know the difference between all those bottles on the shelf? Oh yes! Yes, yes and yes again. Just a little knowledge will double the pleasure you get from a glass of wine and will give you the key to choosing wines that you like. And if a little knowledge can give you that, does a little more knowledge sound attractive? That's why this book is here, to help you look beyond those special offers and trusty favourites – to help you discover for yourself a world of new, exciting and delicious flavours. Are you ready? Then get reading, get shopping and start enjoying yourself!

PART ONE
THE FLAVOURS OF WINE

When you buy wine, buy it for its flavour. Reputation, packaging and price all vie to influence your choice, but they can't titillate your tastebuds. The grape variety used is the most significant factor in determining the taste of a wine, but everything that happens to the grapes and their juice on the long journey from the vine to the glass in your hand contributes to that wine's unique identity. Read on and start getting the flavour you want.

get the flavour you want

Your chances of walking into a wine shop and coming out with a wine that's enjoyable to drink, whatever the price level, are better now than ever before. The last quarter of the 20th century saw a revolution in wine, in terms of both style and quality.

All wines are cleaner and fresher-tasting than they were; reds are juicier, rounder and softer; whites are snappier, zestier, more appetizing. There are more new oak barrels being used in expensive wines, which in terms of taste means vanilla and buttered toast. But this isn't to say that all wines taste alike. Indeed, there's never been a wider choice. It's just that modern winemaking is rapidly eliminating faults – it's not eliminating individuality.

So how do you choose? How do you tell a wine that's just right for summer lunch in the garden from one that would be better suited to a winter evening in front of a log fire? Well, imagine if you could walk into a wine shop and just pick up a bottle from the 'green, tangy white' shelf or go for a 'spicy, warm-hearted red'. That would make things pretty easy, wouldn't it?

You see, all those thousands of different flavours fall into the 18 broad styles shown here and which I describe in detail over the next few pages. So, even if you don't yet know a thing about grape varieties and wine-producing regions, just choose a style that appeals and I'll point you in the right direction. And come back to these pages whenever you fancy something new – I'll do my best to set you off on a whole new flavour adventure.

1 Juicy, fruity reds

Refreshing, approachable and delicious – Chilean Merlot shows what modern red wine is all about

2 Silky, strawberryish reds

Mellow, perfumed wine with red fruit flavours – Pinot Noir is the classic grape for this

3 Intense, blackcurranty reds

Reds from Cabernet Sauvignon are most likely to give you this traditionalist's thrill

4 Spicy, warm-hearted reds

Gloriously rich flavours of berries, black pepper and chocolate – Aussie Shiraz can't be beaten

5 Mouthwatering, herby reds

Intriguing wines with a rasping herby bite and sweet-sour red fruit flavours – Italian reds do this better than any others

6 Earthy, savoury reds

The classic food wines of Europe, led by France's Bordeaux and Italy's Chianti

7 Delicate rosés

Fragrant, refreshing and dry – an elegant summer apéritif

8 Gutsy rosés

More colour, more fruit flavour, more texture to roll around your mouth. Spain, Chile, Australia and New Zealand do best

9 Sweet rosés

Blush is the usual name, and most of it comes from California as Zinfandel or Grenache. Anjou Rosé is France's version

10 Bone-dry, neutral whites

Crisp, refreshing wines like Muscadet and Pinot Grigio

11 Green, tangy whites

Sharp, gooseberryish Sauvignon Blanc from New Zealand, South Africa and Chile lead the way

12 Intense, nutty whites

Dry yet succulent, subtle and powerful – white Burgundy sets the style

13 Ripe, toasty whites

Upfront flavours of peaches, apricots and tropical fruits with toasty richness – the traditional flavour of Aussie and Chilean Chardonnay

14 Aromatic whites

Perfumy wines with exotic and floral fragrances – Gewürztraminer gets my vote for scent, Viognier and Muscat for exotic fruit

15 Sparkling

Bubbles to make you happy and delicious flavours, too. Smile, you're drinking fun, not just wine

16 Rich, sweet whites

Luscious mouthfuls with intense flavours of peach, pineapple and honey, such as Sauternes

17 Warming, fortified

Sweet fortified wines with rich flavours – ports, madeiras and sweet brown sherries

18 Tangy, fortified

Bone dry with startling sour and nutty flavours – this is real sherry, and I love it

1 Juicy, fruity reds

Lots of fruit flavour makes for tasty, refreshing reds ideal for gulping down with or without food. This is the definitive modern style for the best cheap and not-quite-so-cheap red wines, emphasizing bright fruit flavours and minimizing the gum-drying toughness of tannin.

Chilean Merlot
is bursting with
blackberry, blackcurrant
and plum flavours

This style had its birth in the New World – you'll find it in wines from **Australia**, **California**, **Washington State**, **New Zealand**, **South America** and **South Africa** – but it has spread right through Europe, overturning any lingering ideas that red wine must be aged. You don't age these wines. You buy them and you drink them. And then you buy some more. For juicy, fruity flavours, don't even look at a wine that's more than about two years old.

Chilean Merlot is the benchmark for this worldwide phenomenon: young, well-balanced, and bursting with blackberry, blackcurrant and plum flavours.

Spain produces lots of inexpensive soft, supple reds in the same mould. Anything from **La Mancha**, **Navarra**, **Campo de Borja** or **Calatayud** is worth a try, as are young **Valpolicella** and **Teroldego** from Italy and unoaked reds from Portugal's **Douro** region. **California** does a nice line in young Merlots and Zinfandels and **Argentina** has smooth Tempranillo, ultra-fruity Bonarda and juicy Malbec.

If you want French wine, **Beaujolais** is famous for this style, sometimes so fruity you think you're sucking fruit gums. **Loire Valley** reds have sharper, but very refreshing fruit and **Vin de Pays d'Oc Merlot** can be good.

2 Silky, strawberryish reds

Mellow, perfumed reds with a gentle strawberry, raspberry or cherry fruit fragrance and flavour. Good ones feel silky in your mouth.

Pinot Noir is the grape that produces the supreme examples of this style. Great Pinot Noir has a silkiness of texture no other grape can emulate. Only a few regions make it well and the good stuff is expensive.

Pinot Noir's home territory, and the place where it achieves greatness, is **Burgundy** in France (**Bourgogne** in French). Virtually all red Burgundy is made from Pinot Noir. The best wines mature to develop aromas of truffles, game and decaying autumn leaves – sounds horrible, I know, but just one taste is enough to get some people hooked for life.

Beyond Burgundy the best Pinot Noir comes from **California** – particularly **Carneros**, **Sonoma Coast**, **Russian River** and **Santa Barbara** – from **Oregon** and from **New Zealand**. **Germany** can nowadays hit the spot, too, with its Pinot Noir, locally called Spätburgunder.

Cheap Pinot Noir is rarely good, but **Chile**'s usually have loads of vibrant jellied fruit flavour. **Somontano** in Spain has some tasty budget examples, too.

Red **Rioja** and **Navarra**, also from Spain but made from different grapes, principally Tempranillo, are soft and smooth with a fragrant strawberryish quality. This also appears in the lightest **Côtes du Rhône-Villages** from France. None of these wines, however, has the silkiness of Pinot Noir.

Red Rioja and Navarra are soft and smooth with a fragrant strawberryish quality

3   Intense, blackcurranty reds

Full-flavoured red wines with a distinctive blackcurrant flavour and those slightly bitter tannins from the grape skins that dry your mouth but make it water at the same time. They're made from Cabernet Sauvignon alone or blended with Merlot and other grapes to enrich the fruit flavours and soften the texture.

Cabernet Sauvignon is the grape to look for here. The Cabernet-based red wines of **Bordeaux** in France are the original blackcurranty wines with, at their best, a fragrance of cigar boxes and lead pencils. **New World Cabernets** have more blackcurrant, but also a vanilla-y flavour and sometimes mint. It's hard to know who's ahead on quality at the top. At the less expensive end it's perfectly obvious: the New World wins almost every time. The cheapest red Bordeaux is joyless stuff.

Nevertheless, Cabernet Sauvignon is one of the most reliable wines you can get. It retains its characteristic flavours wherever it's from, and at every price level – and that's rare in wine. Expensive ones should be ripe and rich with layers of intense flavour: cheaper ones have simpler flavours that are more earthy, more jammy, or more green-pepper lean.

For budget Cabernets, check out **Argentina**, **Chile**, **Australia**, **South Africa** and France's **Vins de Pays d'Oc**. If you want to pay a bit more, try **Penedès** in Spain, **South Africa**, **New Zealand** and **Chile** again, and, cautiously, Bordeaux or its better-value neighbour, **Bergerac**. **Australia** and **California** at the higher price level is outstanding. You'll also find these blackcurrant flavours in **Ribera del Duero** from Spain, although the grape here is Tempranillo, and a number of grapes give black fruit flavours in **Portugal**.

4 Spicy, warm-hearted reds

Dense, heartwarming, gloriously rich flavours of blackberry and loganberry, black pepper and chocolate, and mainly found in Syrah/Shiraz.

Australian Shiraz is the wine to try: dense, rich and chocolaty, sometimes with a twist of pepper, sometimes with a whiff of smoke, sometimes with a slap of leather. You can get good examples at all price levels. In France's **Rhône Valley** the same grape is called Syrah, and, of course, it was grown here long before the Aussies got their hands on it. Rhône Syrah tends to be a little more austere in style, and smoky-minerally to Australia's rich spice, but the best have lush blackberry fruit. Look for the label **Crozes-Hermitage** or **St-Joseph**.

For good value from France try **Vin de Pays d'Oc Syrah**, **Fitou**, **Minervois** or heavier styles of **Côtes du Rhône-Villages** (lighter ones are more in the silky, strawberryish style). **Portugal** offers good value with a whole host of indigenous grape varieties found nowhere else. In Spain, try the weighty plums and vanilla flavours of **Toro** and the more expensive **Montsant** and **Priorat**.

California Zinfandel made in its most powerful style is spicy and rich – and red. **Argentina**'s heart-warming **Malbecs** and **Chile**'s great big spicy-savoury mouthfuls of **Carmenère** are excellent value. Take a look at **South Africa**'s smoky **Pinotage**, too.

5 Mouthwatering, herby reds

Intriguing wines with sweet-sour cherry and plum fruit flavours and a rasping herby bite. These wines almost all hail from Italy and have a character that's distinctly different from the international mob.

Sicilian reds are rich and mouthfilling

It must be something to do with the Italian attitude to drinking wine. With food. Always. There's a rasp of sourness in these reds that's intended to cut through steak or pasta sauce, not be sipped as an apéritif. You'll find that same irresistible sour-cherries edge on wines made from all sorts of grapes – **Dolcetto**, **Sangiovese**, **Barbera** – in wines from **Chianti**, and in the rare but lip smacking **Teroldego**. Some have a delicious raisiny taste, too. Even light, low-tannin **Valpolicella** has this flavour at its best.

Up in Piedmont, tough, tannic wines from **Barolo**, made from the stern **Nebbiolo** grape, have a fascinating tar-and-roses flavour. Good Barolo is frighteningly expensive these days, but a decent **Langhe** will give you the flavour for less money. Down in the South, there's a whole raft of reds, made from grapes like **Negroamaro** and **Primitivo**, which add round, pruny flavours to the sour-cherry bite. **Sicilian** reds are rich and mouthfilling.

California and **Australia** are starting to get to grips with Sangiovese.

6 Earthy, savoury reds

These are the classic food wines of Europe, the kind where fruit flavours often take a back seat to compatibility with food and the ability to cleanse the palate and stimulate the appetite.

France, especially **Bordeaux**, is the leader in this style. I'm not necessarily talking about the glitzy, expensive Bordeaux wines, rare, difficult to obtain and costing increasingly silly amounts of money, but most Bordeaux reds do keep an earthy quality underpinning their richness. Even **St-Émilion** and **Pomerol** generally blend attractive savouriness with lush fruit. Below the top level are **Haut-Médoc**, **Médoc**, **Pessac-Léognan** and **Graves**, whose strong or earthy flavours are usually excellent. **Côtes de Bourg**, **Côtes de Blaye** and basic **Bordeaux** and **Bordeaux Supérieur** are usually marked by earthy, savoury qualities. You can find these flavours all over **South-West France**.

   Italy's main earthy, savoury type is **Chianti**, though the top levels move up into something altogether richer. Basic **Sangiovese** and **Montepulciano** wines throughout Italy often share this trait, as will whatever nameless carafe of red you pour with your pasta in a thousand villages nationwide. You'll find some of this style in the **Balkans**, **Greece** and **Hungary** and the more basic reds of northern **Portugal** and **Spain** follow this line, but generally it is cool climate wines that are most likely to taste like this.

   In the New World fruit is riper and held to be too important for many of these styles to thrive, but some Cabernets and Merlots from places like **Canada**, **New York State**, **New Zealand**, **South Africa** and even **China** may fit the bill.

Red wine wheel

Here's another way to get the flavour you want. I've arranged the world's red wines according to their intensity and the broad type of flavour. The wines at the outer edge have layer upon layer of flavour; those near the centre are light and simple.

Black fruits Blackcurrant, blackberry, dark plum, damson and black cherry flavours.

Red fruits The soft flavours of strawberries and raspberries and sharper hints of cranberries and red cherries.

Herbs/spices The wild flavours of herbs; peppery and aromatic spices; often mixed with tastes such as chocolate or liquorice.

Increasing intensity

KEY

The styles I have described in this chapter fit the zones of the wheel like this:

Juicy, fruity reds RED FRUITS or BLACK FRUITS, with light to medium intensity

Silky, strawberryish reds RED FRUITS, though the most intense have a shade of BLACK FRUITS, too.

Intense, blackcurrant reds BLACK FRUITS, maybe with a touch of RED FRUITS or HERBS/SPICES.

Spicy, warm-hearted reds HERBS/SPICES, but many combine this with RED FRUITS or BLACK FRUITS.

Mouthwatering, sweet-sour reds RED FRUITS and HERBS/SPICES.

Earthy, savoury reds BLACK FRUITS and HERBS/SPICES.

BLACK FRUITS

top Californian Cabernet Sauvignon

top Australian Cabernet Sauvignon

top Washington Cabernet and Merlot

top Bordeaux from the Médoc

top Pomerol-Léognan

top Chilean and South African Cabernet Sauvignon

Ribera del Duero

top Bordeaux from St-Emilion and Pomerol

top Chilean Merlot

BLACK AND RED FRUITS

mid-priced Australian Cabernet Sauvignon

top Argentine Malbec

Douro

mid-priced Californian Cabernet Sauvignon   New Zealand Merlot

New Zealand Cabernet Sauvignon

Navarra

mid-priced South African Cabernet Sauvignon

top Loire reds (Chinon, Bourgueil, Saumur-Champigny)

southern Portuguese reds

mid-priced Bordeaux (crus bourgeois)

Bulgarian Cabernet Sauvignon

Hungarian reds

cheap Chilean Cabernet and Merlot

Premier and Grand Cru Burgundy

North Italian Merlot

Loire reds (Chinon, Bourgueil, Saumur-Champigny)

Valdepeñas and La Mancha

LIGHT AND SIMPLE

Beaujolais crus

light Rioja

Australian Pinot Noir

Chilean and South African Pinot Noir

New York Pinot Noir

Oregon Pinot Noir

top Rioja Reserva and Gran Reserva

New Zealand and Californian Pinot Noir

good Burgundy

RED FRUITS

simple Burgundy and Beaujolais   basic vins de pays

cheap Argentine reds

Côtes du Rhône

Argentine Tempranillo and Bonarda   Provence reds (e.g. Bandol)

vin de pays Cabernet and Merlot

light Pinotage

Costières de Nîmes

southern Italian reds

Côtes du Rhône-Villages

Australian old vines

Gigondas and Vacqueyras

Grenache

Châteauneuf-du-Pape

RED FRUITS AND HERBS/SPICES

Barolo

Barbaresco

Chianti Classico Riserva

Brunello di Montalcino

Nobile di Montepulciano

Dolcetto

Barbera

Corbières

Valpolicella Classico

mid-priced Zinfandel

Dão and Barrada

Chianti Classico

Cahors

Coteaux du Languedoc and Côtes du Roussillon

Minervois

Fronton

Mexican Petite Sirah

Penedès

light Australian Shiraz

top-priced Argentine Malbec

BLACK FRUITS AND HERBS/SPICES

Austrian reds

cheap Bordeaux

cheap Burgundy and light German reds

simple and light German reds

cheap Italian reds

light Chianti

HERBS/SPICES

7 Delicate rosés

Good rosé should be fragrant and refreshing, and deliciously dry – not sickly and sweet.

France is a good hunting ground for this style of wine. Attractive, slightly leafy-tasting **Bordeaux Rosé** is usually based on Merlot. **Bordeaux Clairet** is a lightish red, virtually rosé but with more substance. **Cabernet d'Anjou** from the Loire Valley is a bit sweeter but tasty. Better still is **Rosé de Loire**, a lovely dry wine. Elegant Pinot Noir rosés come from **Sancerre** in the upper Loire and **Marsannay** in northern Burgundy. In the south of France and southern Rhône Valley (**Coteaux d'Aix-en-Provence**, **Lubéron** and **Ventoux**) produce plenty of dry but fruity rosés. **Costières de Nîmes** produces light, slightly scented styles. **Côtes de Provence** is usually dry but often expensive. **Bandol** and **Bellet** are pricier still from specific coastal regions of Provence.

Northern Italy produces light, fresh pale rosé called *chiaretto*, from **Bardolino** and **Riviera del Garda Bresciano** on the shores of Lake Garda and from the same grapes as neighbouring red Valpolicella, and **Lagrein** from high in the Dolomites. Finally, another wine to try is tasty Garnacha rosado from **Navarra** and **Rioja** in northern Spain.

8 Gutsy rosés

Dry, fruity rosé can be wonderful, with flavours of strawberries and maybe raspberries and rosehips, cherries, apples and herbs, too.

Most countries make a dry rosé, and any red grape will do. Look for wines made from sturdy grapes like Cabernet, Syrah or Merlot, or go for Grenache/Garnacha or Tempranillo from Spain's **La Mancha**, **Campo de Borja** and **Jumilla**. **Puglia** and **Sicily** in southern Italy make mouthfilling rosés, too. In the southern Rhône Valley big, strong, dry rosés from **Tavel** and **Lirac** go well with food. Drink them young at only a year or so old if you want a refreshing wine.

South America is a good bet for flavoursome, fruit-forward pink wine – try robust **Shiraz** and **Cabernet** from **Chile** or **Malbec** from **Argentina**. Other wines to try include dry, fairly full rosé from **California**, often from **Syrah** (not to be confused with the sweeter blush Zinfandel Californian rosés, labelled until 2008 as White Zinfandel), fruity Australian **Grenache** from the **Barossa Valley**, or **New Zealand** pinks.

9 Sweet rosés

The original examples are Rosé d'Anjou (from the Loire) and Mateus and Lancers rosé (from Portugal).

Blush Zinfandel, which is white with just a hint of pink from California, is fairly sweet, but OK as a chilled-down drink. Other sweetish rosés are **Rosé d'Anjou**, from the Loire Valley, usually sweetish without much flavour, and Portugal, famous for **Mateus** and **Lancers**.

10 Bone-dry, neutral whites

Crisp, refreshing whites whose flavours won't set the world alight – but chill them down and set them next to a plate of shellfish and you've got the perfect combination.

These wines may not sound very enticing, but there are plenty of occasions when you just don't want to be hit over the palate with oak and tropical fruit.

In France, **Muscadet** from the Loire Valley is the most neutral of the lot. Unoaked **Chablis** from Burgundy is the adaptable Chardonnay grape in a dry, minerally style.

Italy specializes in this sort of wine, because Italians don't really like their white wines to be aromatic. So **Frascati**, most **Soave**, **Orvieto**, **Verdicchio**, **Lugana**, **Pinot Grigio**, **Pinot Bianco** and **Chardonnay** from the **Alto Adige** all fit the bill. **Greek** whites are usually pretty neutral, perhaps just brushed with minerality.

You won't often find this style in the New World – winemakers there don't want neutrality in their wines. Even when they grow the same vines (and mostly they don't), they make fuller, more flavoursome wines from them. **Chenin Blanc** from **South Africa** at the lower price levels is about as close as you'll get.

11 Green, tangy whites

Sharp, zesty, love-them-or-hate-them wines, often with the smell and taste of gooseberries.

Sauvignon Blanc from **New Zealand** – especially from **Marlborough** – has tangy, mouthwatering flavours by the bucketful. **Chile** makes similar, slightly softer wines, **South African** versions can have real bite and Spain blends Sauvignon with Verdejo to give **Rueda** some extra zip.

Sancerre and **Pouilly-Fumé** from the Loire Valley in France are crisp and refreshing with lighter fruit flavours and a minerally or even a smoky edge. **Sauvignon de Touraine** offers similar flavours at lower prices.

The biggest bargain in Sauvignon Blanc is dry white **Bordeaux**. It's generally labelled as **Bordeaux Sauvignon Blanc** or maybe **Bordeaux Blanc**, and standards have risen out of sight in recent years. It's always softer than Loire or New Zealand versions.

The Loire also produces sharp-edged wines from **Chenin Blanc**, such as **Vouvray** and **white Anjou**. Loire Chenin has a minerally acid bite when young, but becomes rich and honeyed with age.

Riesling is the other grape to look out for here. Rieslings can be peachy, minerally or smoky when young, with a streak of green apple and some high-tensile acidity. With a few years' bottle age those flavours mingle and mellow to a wonderful honeyed, petrolly flavour – sounds disgusting, tastes heavenly. The leanest, often with a touch of sweetness to balance the acidity, come from Germany's **Mosel Valley**; slightly richer ones come from the **Rhine**; drier, weightier ones from **Austria** and **Alsace**. **Australian Rieslings**, particularly from the **Clare** and **Eden Valleys**, start bone dry and age to an irresistible limes-and-toast flavour.

12 Intense, nutty whites

Dry yet succulent whites with subtle nut and oatmeal flavours. These wines are generally oak-aged and have a soft edge with a backbone of absolute dryness.

If you like this style, you've got a taste for French classics, because the best expression of it is oak-aged Chardonnay in the form of white **Burgundy**. This is the wine that earned Chardonnay its renown in the first place and the style is sometimes matched in the best examples from **California**, **New York State**, **New Zealand**, **Australia** and **South Africa**. Not any old examples, mind you – just the best. Italian producers in **Tuscany** are having a go, too.

Top-quality oak-aged **Graves** and **Pessac-Léognan** from Bordeaux are Sémillon blended with Sauvignon Blanc, giving a creamy, nutty wine with a hint of nectarines. Unoaked **Australian Semillon** (note the 'unoaked' – it means it hasn't been aged in oak barrels) from the **Hunter** and **Barossa Valleys** matures to become waxy and rich. The best white **Rioja** from Spain, too, becomes nutty and lush with time.

None of these wines comes cheap and they all need time to show their best. Less costly alternatives which give an idea of the style are Spanish Chardonnays from **Navarra** and **Somontano**.

White wine wheel

This wheel of dry white wine styles works in the same way as the red wine wheel on pages 16–17. The wines at the outer edge have layers of intense flavour; those near the centre are light and simple.

Fruity Peachy, tropical fruit or honeyish flavours without the buttery overlay of oak.

Crisp Fresh, clean flavours with a bite, like lime, gooseberry or green apples.

Aromatic Wines with intense floral or exotic fragrances such as lychees and rose petals.

Oaky Wines with the toasty, buttery flavours that come from oak barrels.

KEY

The styles I have described in this chapter fit the zones of the wheel like this:

Bone dry, neutral whites The lightest wines in the CRISP zone.

Green, tangy whites CRISP wines, but shading into FRUITY and into AROMATIC styles.

Intense, nutty whites These are OAKY wines; the best are intense but subtle.

Ripe, toasty whites Wines full of OAKY and FRUITY flavours.

Aromatics They have the AROMATIC zone to themselves, but some are OAKY too.

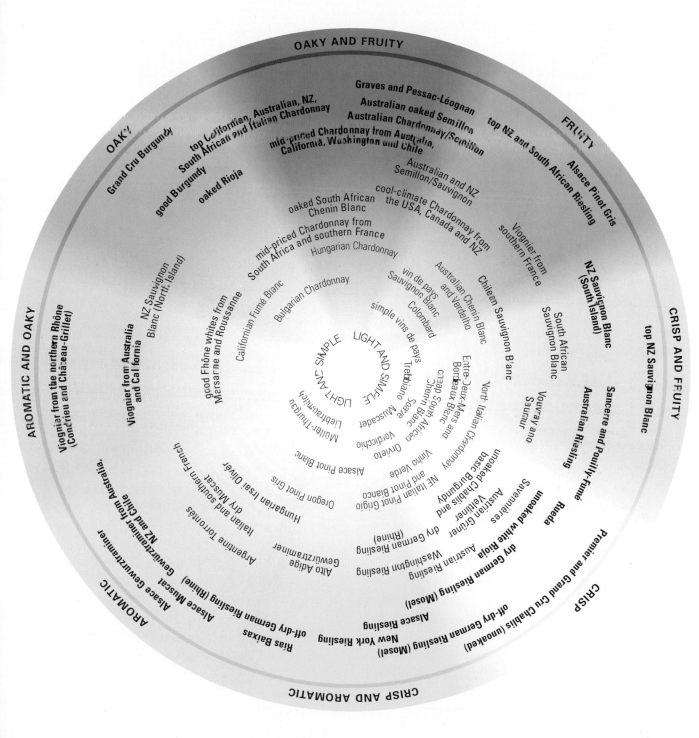

OAKY AND FRUITY

OAKY

Grand Cru Burgundy

top Californian, Australian, NZ,
South African and Italian Chardonnay

good Burgundy

oaked Rioja

Graves and Pessac-Léognan

Australian oaked Semillon

Australian Chardonnay/Semillon

mid-priced Chardonnay from Australia,
California, Washington and Chile

top NZ and South African Riesling

Alsace Pinot Gris

FRUITY

Australian and NZ
Semillon/Sauvignon

cool-climate Chardonnay from
the USA, Canada and NZ

oaked South African
Chenin Blanc

mid-priced Chardonnay from
South Africa and southern France

Hungarian Chardonnay

Viognier from
southern France

NZ Sauvignon
Blanc (North Island)

NZ Sauvignon
Blanc (South Island)

Californian Fumé Blanc

Bulgarian Chardonnay

good Fhône whites from
Marsanne and Roussanne

Australian Chenin Blanc
and Verdelho

Chilean Sauvignon Blanc

South African
Sauvignon Blanc

CRISP AND FRUITY

top NZ Sauvignon Blanc

vin de pays
Sauvignon Blanc

Colombard

simple vins de pays

SIMPLE

LIGHT AND SIMPLE

Trebbiana

Soave

Muscadet

Orvieto

Vinho Verde

Entre-Deux-Mers and
Bordeaux Blanc

crisp South African
Chenin Blanc

Vouvray and
Saumur

Sancerre and Pouilly-Fumé

Australian Riesling

AROMATIC AND OAKY

Viognier from the northern Rhône
(Condrieu and Château-Grillet)

Viognier from Australia
and California

LIGHT AND SIMPLE

Müller-Thurgau

Liebfraumilch

Alsace Pinot Blanc

Oregon Pinot Gris

Hungarian Irsai Oliver

Italian and southern French
dry Muscat

Argentine Torrontés

Alto Adige
Gewürztraminer

N Italian Chardonnay

unoaked Chablis and
basic Burgundy

NE Italian Pinot Grigio
and Pinot Bianco

Sauvennières

Austrian Grüner
Veltliner

dry German Riesling
(Rhine)

Washington Riesling

Austrian Riesling

unoaked white Rioja

dry German Riesling (Mosel)

Rueda

Premier and Grand Cru Chablis (unoaked)

CRISP

AROMATIC

Gewürztraminer from
NZ and Chile

Alsace Muscat

Alsace Gewürztraminer

Rias Baixas

off-dry German Riesling (Rhine)

off-dry German Riesling (Mosel)

New York Riesling

Alsace Riesling

CRISP AND AROMATIC

13 Ripe, toasty whites

Upfront flavours of peaches, apricots and tropical fruits, spiced up by the vanilla, toast and butterscotch richness of new oak barrels: delicious, instantly lovable and utterly moreish.

This is the flavour of the **Chardonnays** that shocked and thrilled the world when **California** and then **Australia** began making them 30 years ago. They changed our view of what was possible in white wine flavour and style. Since then we have begun to back off a little from such lush flavours and the producers have generally throttled back a bit. Many current Californian and Australian examples are relatively restrained. But the high-octane Chardies are still around if you hanker for the buzz.

The style was virtually invented in California and Australia, and it has been the hallmark of most Chardonnay in the **US** and **South America**, as well as being common in **South Africa**. Chardonnay from the north-east of **Spain** and many **Italian** versions – particularly those from the south – also fit in here.

Not that the style is confined to Chardonnay. If you ferment **Viognier** in new oak it also gives rich, exotic results. **Sémillon** in oak becomes mouthfilling and creamy, and barrel-fermented **South African Chenin** can be quite a mouthful. It's not so difficult to give lots of different whites that tropical flavour, and new oak barrels will supply the toast and butterscotch – but Chardonnay was the original and is still the best.

14 Aromatic whites

Perfumy white wines combining exotic fragrances with aromas of spring flowers.

It seems impossible that a wine could smell and taste the way **Gewurztraminer** from **Alsace** does. It's packed solid with roses and lychees, face cream and a whole kitchen spice cupboard. No, it's not subtle, but with spicy food, especially Chinese, it can be wonderful.

Viognier is at its apricots-and-spring flowers best in Condrieu

Nowhere else in the world has the nerve to produce such over-the-top Gewürztraminer. **German** versions are more floral, and the **Italians** prefer to make their Traminer rather more toned down. But **Slovenia, Slovakia** and the **Czech Republic** have a go, and **New Zealand** Gewürztraminer is a delight.

If you want this sort of full-blown aroma from other grapes, then it's back to Alsace. Dry **Muscat** here is floral with a heady, hothouse grape scent. **Southern France** and **Spain** make less scented styles, and you can get delicate floral Muscats in **northern Italy**, sometimes pink and sometimes as scented as tea-rose petals.

You still want more aromatic grapes? **Viognier**, at its apricots-and-spring flowers best in **Condrieu**, in the northern Rhône Valley, is planted in the **south of France, California** and **Australia** as well; and **Godello** from north-west Spain is also apricotty, but crisper. **Irsai Olivér** from **Hungary** and **Torrontés** from **Argentina** are both heady and perfumed. **Müller-Thurgau**, usually from **Germany**, sometimes from **Luxembourg** and **England**, can have a light, vaguely floral scent.

15 Sparkling wines

Fizz is there to make you feel brighter and happier – but good bubbly can have delicious flavours as well.

Champagne – the genuine article from the Champagne region of northern France – sets the standard. Good Champagne has a nutty, bready aroma, appley freshness and fine bubbles. Don't buy the cheapest, though: much of it is too acidic to be drinkable, let alone enjoyable.

Good Champagne has an appley freshness

Sparkling wine from **Australia**, **California** and **New Zealand** is made in the same way and it's often just as good and usually cheaper. Much of the best stuff in these countries is made by subsidiaries of French Champagne producers – Roederer, Veuve Clicquot and Moet & Chandon are the most active.

Other good French fizzes are the slightly honeyish **Crémant de Bourgogne** from Burgundy, the rather sharp sparkling **Saumur** from the Loire Valley and the appley **Blanquette de Limoux** from the south.

Italian sparklers made from **Chardonnay** and **Pinot Noir** are in the Champagne style, but light, creamy **Prosecco** and sweet, grapy **Asti** can be more fun. The best **Lambrusco** is red, snappy and refreshingly sharp, but the sweetened stuff is pretty dull. Spanish **Cava** can be a bit earthy, but is good value. German **Sekt** is often pretty poor, but when made from Riesling can be lean, sharp and refreshing.

Australian sparkling red wines are wild things, packed with pepper and blackberry jam. You'll love them or hate them, but you haven't lived until you've given them a try.

16 Rich, sweet whites

Rich, luscious mouthfuls for dessert time or when you're in a contemplative mood, often with intense flavours of peach, pineapple and honey.

In France the sweet wines of Bordeaux are at their gorgeous best in **Sauternes** and **Barsac**. These are rich and syrupy wines with intense flavours of peaches and pineapples, barley sugar, butterscotch and honey, all balanced by acidity, and they can age for 20 years or more. **Monbazillac**, **Cérons**, **Loupiac** and **Ste-Croix-du-Mont** are happy hunting grounds for cheaper, lighter versions. **California**, **New Zealand** and **Australia** have a few intensely rich wines in this style, too.

The Loire Valley produces rather unusual sweet wines that are less rich and often less expensive. They're quince-flavoured with a firm acid grip and a minerally streak. **Quarts de Chaume**, **Bonnezeaux**, **Coteaux du Layon** and **Vouvray** are the wines to look for. Only a few Vouvrays are sweet; they're labelled as *moelleux* or *liquoreux*.

Alsace sweeties are rich and unctuous. **Sélection de Grains Nobles** is sweeter than **Vendange Tardive**, and **Gewurztraminer** versions will be fatter than **Pinot Gris**, which will in turn be fatter than **Riesling**.

The sweet wines of **Germany** have a language all of their own. **Beerenauslese** and **Trockenbeerenauslese** are intensely sweet and extremely expensive; **Auslese** is less sweet and less expensive. All should be very high quality, and the best are made from Riesling: its piercing acidity keeps the sweetness from being overpowering. **Austria**'s sweet wines are similar in style to Germany's, but tend to be weightier.

There's also a rarity called **Eiswein** made from frozen grapes picked in the depths of winter, which manages a thrilling marriage of fierce acidity and unctuous sweetness. Apricotty **Canadian icewine** is made in the same way.

Hungary's **Tokaji** has a wonderful sweet-sour smoky flavour and quality is very high. Simple sweet **Muscat** from Spain, such as **Moscatel de Valencia**, is a simple-hearted splash of rich fruit but incredibly good value.

TWO TYPES OF SWEETNESS

Sweet wine is wine that is perceptibly sugary – you can detect the sweetness on your tongue tip. However, an ever-increasing number of modern dry wines emphasize ripe fruit flavours, which I often describe as **sweet fruits** to do them justice. Fruit is at its most delicious when it's ripe, and it's sheer joy to taste those flavours in a wine. But fruit loses much of its character when it overripens: the freshness disappears, the flesh becomes soggy and soft. There is a move towards making dry wines at high alcohol levels from overripe fruit. One expert calls these 'dead fruit wines'. A good term. They are heavy and lifeless and rarely have you angling for a second glass. If I like a wine, I always want a second glass.

17 Warming, fortified wines

Sweet wines tasting of raisins and brown sugar, plum and blackberry syrup, and able to take on board all kinds of other scents or flavours as they age.

Port, the rich red fortified wine of Portugal's Douro Valley, is the classic dark sweet wine and no imitator can match the power or the finesse of the best, though **Australia** and **South Africa** both make exciting port-style wines. The Portuguese island of **Madeira** produces some of the most fascinating warming fortifieds, with rich brown smoky flavours and a startling acid bite: **Bual** and **Malmsey** are the sweet ones to look out for.

Oloroso dulce is a rare and delicious sherry with stunning, concentrated flavours and black-brown **Pedro Ximenez** (or **PX**) is about as sweet a mouthful as the world possesses. Cheap sweetened 'brown' sherry is a weak parody of these styles.

Australian sweet **Muscat** from the **Rutherglen** region is astonishingly rich and dark, even treacly. From the islands off southern Italy, the fortified **Marsala** of Sicily and **Moscato di Pantelleria** are good brown-sugar drinks with a refreshing shiver of acidity.

18 Tangy, fortified wines

Bone-dry wines with startling stark, sour and nutty flavours. It's a taste that takes a bit of getting used to, but which is well worth acquiring.

These are the original sherries from Jerez in Andalucía, – check the label to make sure they're bottled where they were made – in southern Spain. **Fino** is pale in colour, very dry with a thrilling tang. **Manzanilla** can seem even drier, even leaner, and has a wonderful sourdough perfume and tingling acidity. **Amontillado** is chestnut-coloured and nutty. Traditionally amontillado is dry, not medium-sweet as we often see it. Dry **oloroso** adds deep, burnt flavours and at its intriguing best is one of the world's greatest wines.

Montilla-Moriles is the neighbouring region to Jerez and produces similar wines, but only the best of these reach the standard of good sherry. The driest style of Madeira, **Sercial**, is tangy, steely and savoury; **Verdelho** is a bit fuller and fatter.

Australia and **South Africa** make excellent sherry-style wines, though without the tang of top-class Spanish *fino* or *manzanilla*.

> Manzanilla can seem even drier, even leaner, and has a wonderful sourdough perfume and tingling acidity

discover grape varieties

The simplest way to become familiar with wine flavours is through grape variety. Each grape variety has its own hallmark flavours, so two wines with different names made in places thousands of miles apart will have a fair amount in common if they're made from the same variety.

Not all wines are made from a single grape variety. Red Bordeaux, for example, usually contains at least three, and one of Australia's classic wine styles is a blend of two famous varieties: Cabernet Sauvignon and Shiraz. But once you know the taste of different grapes you'll have a good idea of what to expect from a blend.

Red wine grapes

I'm going to start with the red grapes – some people call them black, but they're deep purple or bluish in reality, so I reckon it's easier to link them to the type of wine they generally make. There's more to red wine than sturdiness, power and 'good with red meats and cheese'. Delicacy, freshness and intriguing perfumes are all within the scope of the world's red grape varieties. It all depends on where you grow the grapes and what style of wine the winemaker wants to achieve. In general, red grapes grown in warm places will give richer, riper styles, and you'll get more delicacy, perfume and restraint from grapes grown in cool places.

WINE TERMS **Noble grapes**

Some grapes have achieved such a level of greatness in a particular region that they have been elevated to the peerage of the grape world and are often referred to as noble grapes. The major examples are: **Cabernet Sauvignon** in Bordeaux, France; **Chardonnay** and **Pinot Noir** in Burgundy, France; **Syrah** in France's Rhône Valley and in South Australia, where it's called **Shiraz**; **Chenin Blanc** in France's Loire Valley; **Sauvignon Blanc** in the Loire Valley and New Zealand; **Nebbiolo** in Piedmont, Italy; **Sangiovese** in Tuscany, Italy; **Riesling** in Germany; and **Zinfandel** in California. You can find out about them in the next few pages.

Cabernet Sauvignon

The epitome of the intense, blackcurranty style of red wine, Cabernet Sauvignon is never among the lightest of reds and it always has some degree of tannic backbone. The best mature slowly to balance sweet blackcurrant flavours with a scent of cedar, cigar boxes and lead pencil shavings. It is often blended with Merlot for a richer flavour.

Where it grows Almost every country where wine is made has a fair bit of Cabernet in its vineyards. Bordeaux is its homeland, but you'll find it in the south of France as well. Italy has some top-class versions; good Spanish ones come mostly from Navarra or Penedès; and it produces inexpensive wine over large tracts of Eastern Europe, notably in Bulgaria.

New World examples are vibrantly fruity, with rich texture, soft tannins and sometimes a touch of mint or eucalyptus. California and Australia have world-class examples; Chile's have piercing fruit and are excellent value; South Africa's are dry and blackcurranty; and New Zealand goes for a style closer to Bordeaux.

Keep it or drink it? Lots of people think of Cabernet Sauvignon as being a wine that needs to age in bottle after you buy it, but that's only because the best red Bordeaux and top California and Australian Cabernets need age. Most New World Cabernets, and most less expensive red Bordeaux, can be drunk straight away.

Splashing out Wine from Bordeaux villages like Margaux, St-Julien or Pauillac, from Coonawarra and Margaret River in Australia and Napa Valley in California.

Best value Chile and southern France are the places for tasty bargains. Bulgaria is, well, cheap.

Cabernet with food Modern Cabernet is an all-purpose red, but it's best with simply cooked red meats.

Not to be confused with Cabernet Franc, a related variety, or the white grape Sauvignon Blanc.

The Bordeaux region is renowned for its many stunning châteaux. This is Château Pichon-Longueville in Pauillac.

Merlot

Juicy, fruity wine that is lower in tannic bitterness and higher in alcohol than Cabernet Sauvignon, with which it is often blended. Blackcurrant, black cherry and mint are the hallmark flavours.

Where it grows Merlot started out as Cabernet Sauvignon's support act in Bordeaux, but has risen to worldwide popularity because of its softness. The great wines of Pomerol and St-Émilion in Bordeaux are based on Merlot, with Cabernet in the blend. These wines show Merlot at its sturdiest and most intense, but they're still fruitier and juicier than Bordeaux's top Cabernet-based wines.

Chile is Merlot heaven, at best producing gorgeous garnet-red wines of unbelievably crunchy fruit richness that just beg to be drunk. California and Washington State have more serious aspirations for the grape, but the soft, juicy quality still shines through. Australia and South Africa are only just catching on, but Merlot already makes some of New Zealand's best reds.

Merlot has become the wine drinker's darling because of its soft juicy fruit. These vines are in California, one of its success stories.

Italy uses Merlot to produce a light quaffing wine in the Veneto region, and offers more flavoursome examples from Friuli, Alto Adige and Tuscany. Hungary and Bulgaria are making rapid progress with the grape. In the hot South of France Merlot tends to lack distinctive character but produces a fair bit of gently juicy red.

Keep it or drink it? In general, drink it young, especially Chilean and Eastern European examples. Top Bordeaux Merlots, however, can last for up to 20 years.

Splashing out Château Pétrus and Château le Pin from the Pomerol region of Bordeaux are the two most expensive wines in the world. Other Pomerols and St-Émilions are less expensive lush mouthfuls.

Best value When it's good, you can't beat young Merlot from Chile.

Merlot with food Merlot is a great all-rounder – barbecue red, cassserole red, picnic red – but savoury foods with a hint of sweetness, such as honey-roast ham, particularly suit the soft fruitiness.

WINE TERMS **Varietals and blends**

A wine made solely or principally from a single grape variety is known as a **varietal**. These wines are often named after the relevant grape. This is the simple, modern way to label wine and I am all in favour, because it is the grape variety that contributes most strongly to the flavour. The law in the country or the region of production specifies the minimum percentage of the grape that the wine must contain to be given a varietal name. Very few stipulate 100%. A **blend** made from two or more varieties does not signify an inferior wine: on the contrary, many grapes need to have their weaknesses balanced by complementary varieties. The famous Châteauneuf-du-Pape red wine can have 13 different grape varieties, and rarely has less than four. Almost all the famous Bordeaux whites and reds are blends of two or more varieties.

Pinot Noir

At its best Pinot Noir is hauntingly beautiful with a seductive silky texture; at worst it is heavy and jammy or insipid and thin. Good young Pinot has a sweet summer-fruit fragrance and taste. The best mature to achieve unlikely and complex aromas of truffles, game and decaying leaves – and fruit, of course.

Where it grows Pretty widely these days, since winemakers tend to fall in love with it. Its home is in Burgundy, and the aim of all those acolytes worldwide is to make a wine that tastes like great red Burgundies such as Volnay or Vosne-Romanée. Outside Burgundy the most successful Pinots are from regions that have developed their own style – like Carneros and Sonoma Coast in California, and Wairarapa, Marlborough and Central Otago in New Zealand. Not very obliging, it obstinately refuses to taste as it should unless you treat it precisely as it likes. The best wines from California, Oregon and New Zealand show that winemakers there have cracked it and there are some good ones from Victoria and Tasmania in Australia and Overberg in South Africa. Chile's cooler vineyards can produce lovely delicate styles. Northern Italy produces an attractive, fragrant style and Germany more serious stuff. Other versions can be less convincing.

Keep it or drink it? Drink it, on the whole. Only the best ones repay keeping – and then not for as long as you'd keep the equivalent quality of Cabernet Sauvignon.

Splashing out Grand Cru Burgundies in the Côte d'Or are the pinnacle of Pinot Noir. Premier Cru Burgundy should still seduce you, but for a fraction of the price. (For more on Burgundy's Grands and Premiers Crus see page 114.)

The Romanée-Conti vineyard in the Côte d'Or is said to be the most valuable vineyard land in the world.

Best value Chile makes some reasonably priced examples, as does Marlborough in New Zealand. For a taste of true Burgundy, try a basic Bourgogne Rouge from a leading Burgundy grower.

Pinot with food This is food-friendly wine. It suits both plain and complex meat and poultry dishes. It also goes well with substantial fish, such as fresh salmon.

Also known as Spätburgunder in Germany, Pinot Nero in Italy and Blauburgunder in Austria.

Not to be confused with the white grapes Pinot Blanc and Pinot Gris, or the related red grape Pinot Meunier.

Fizz fact Pinot Noir is a major component in much white Champagne, even though it is a red grape.

Syrah/Shiraz

Intense is the word for Syrah/Shiraz wines. Intensely rich, intensely spicy, intensely ripe-fruited, or even all three at once. The most powerful begin life dark, dense and tannic but mature to combine sweet blackberry and raspberry flavours with a velvety texture. Others are gorgeous right from the word go.

Where it grows Most famously in France's Rhône Valley and Australia – and unusually, the two styles are running neck and neck in terms of quality. French Syrah is more smoky, herby and austere; Australian Shiraz is richer, softer, more chocolaty, sometimes with a leathery quality. But Australia is a big place, and styles vary across the country. Victoria Shiraz can be scented and peppery, Barossa Valley Shiraz leathery and chocolaty. Old vines Shiraz, wherever it's from, should be gratifyingly intense.

There's some Shiraz in South Africa, a bit in Italy and Switzerland. California, New Zealand and Chile are now making some good stuff in their cooler regions.

Keep it or drink it? All Syrah/Shiraz needs a year or two's aging to hit its stride. Top wines will last over ten years, and a great Hermitage might peak at 15.

Splashing out Hermitage or Côte-Rôtie from the northern Rhône; Grange from Australia (it's no coincidence that this wine was known for years as Grange Hermitage).

Best value Gluggers from southern France or Chile.

Syrah/Shiraz with food This is a wine that can stand up to powerful flavours. I love it with peppered salami and tangy cheese.

Why two names? It's Syrah in France; Shiraz in Australia. Other regions use either name.

Not to be confused with Petite Sirah, a grape grown in California and Mexico.

Baskets of luscious-looking Syrah grapes grown by top producer Guigal in the Côte-Rôtie vineyards, northern Rhône.

Other red wine grapes

There are literally hundreds, if not thousands, of different grape varieties grown around the world, but most of them have only a very local reputation at best. And many have no discernible character. But there's a second division of grape varieties with loads of character. Some of these grow in only a few specific places at the moment, but all have the potential to make good to excellent wine elsewhere in future.

Barbera is one of north-west Italy's best grapes and is excellent with food. Roberto Voerzio is one of leading new wave producers in the Alba region of Piedmont, making outstanding Barbera d'Alba and world famous Barolo wines.

Barbera

This is a high-quality, characterful grape, yet without a single world-famous wine style to its name. Its base is in north-west Italy, in Piedmont, where it makes wines so Italian-tasting that you find yourself instantly craving a plate of pasta. It's that herby, sour-cherries bite that does it: Barbera is the epitome of the mouthwatering, sweet-sour style I talked about earlier. But that rasping acidity is matched by plum and raisin fruit, and it's low in gum-puckering tannin.

It appears in umpteen guises all over Piedmont, but Barbera d'Alba and Barbera d'Asti are the best versions to go for. California uses Barbera for its simplest wines, but there's good stuff from Argentina.

Not to be confused with *Barbaresco, a tough, tannic wine from the same region of north-west Italy.*

Cabernet Franc

A relative of Cabernet Sauvignon which makes earthy, blackcurranty wines. Used in red Bordeaux blends and on its own in the Loire Valley and north-east Italy. Now starting to makes its mark in places like Chile, Australia, Virginia, New York State and Ontario.

Carignan

Widely grown red grape in southern France, used for rough everyday wines – but wine from old vines can be deliciously spicy or sturdy. There's lots in Spain, California and some in Chile.

Collecting crates of harvested Carmenère grapes in Lapostolle's Clos Apalta vineyard in Chile's Colchagua region. Carmenère has become a Chilean success story, producing some excellent wines with unmistakable flavours.

Carmenère ★

Red grape from Chile making delicious spicy wines. It was originally a Bordeaux grape thought to be extinct. It reappeared in Chile under the umbrella title of Merlot and is now proudly labelled under its own name. Makes marvellously rich, spicy, savoury reds. Some of the Cabernet in north-east Italy is now reckoned to be Carmenère.

Cinsaut

Red grape used in southern French blends, also grown in South Africa. Produces light, fresh wines.

Corvina

The major grape of Italy's Valpolicella, a cherryish and bitter-sweet red, with a gentle, easy-going texture.

Dolcetto

Vibrant, purplish-red wine from Italy, full of fruit flavour with a bitter-cherry twist. Drink it young.

Gamay

Gamay, to all intents and purposes, equals Beaujolais. It's one of those freaks of wine that this grape happens to flourish on an expanse of granite hills in the south of Burgundy, and effectively nowhere else. The Ardèche region of southern France has some, as does the Loire Valley in the west. But that's about it.

Gamay is never a grape to take too seriously. It makes refreshing light wines with sharp, candy-like cherry and raspberry flavours, perfect for drinking lightly chilled on hot summer days.

Grenache

The most widely planted red grape in the world. Most of its plantings are in Spain and the south of France where it makes wines high in alcohol with sweet and peppery flavours. It's most often used in blends – mainly with the more scented and powerful Syrah/Shiraz, the pallid Cinsaut or the rough and ready Mourvèdre. If you ever come across a heady, juicy rosé, there's a good chance that it's made from 100 per cent Grenache.

It's actually a Spanish grape, and its original name is Garnacha Tinta. It beefs up the blend of some red Riojas, makes juicy, herby reds in Campo de Borja and Calatayud, makes Rioja and Navarra *rosado* (the Spanish for rosé) in increasingly good light styles and produces extremely concentrated, usually expensive, rich, full-bodied reds in Priorat and Montant. Old vine Grenache makes some gorgeous sexy fruit bombs in South Australia, often from century-old vines. Morocco uses it for reds and pinks.

But Grenache is, as I said, at its best in good company, and it finds it in France, in the southern Rhône Valley. Grenache features among no fewer than 13 permitted grape varieties in this region's most famous wine, Châteauneuf-du-Pape – a complex, sweet-fruited super-rich red splashed with the scent of hillside herbs. The raspberry/strawberry character of this grape shines alongside a hint of hot, dusty earth in the softest Côtes du Rhône and Côtes du Rhône-Villages. Vin de pays Grenache from the neighbouring Ardèche region is light, fruity and good value. A lot of the juiciest, headiest rosés and rosados around the Mediterranean come from Grenache.

Also known as *Garnacha in Spain and Cannonau in Sardinia.*

WINE TERMS **Old vines**

This phrase is a great selling point on labels. **Old vines** (or **vieilles vignes** on French labels) mean more concentrated flavours and wine that is rare and desirable – that's the theory. And it's true. Old vines are something to boast of: they give more intensely flavoured wine, but in smaller quantities.

A lot of growers uproot vines that are over 25 years old, because that's the point at which their yields of grapes begin to drop. But that's exactly when the quality of the grapes starts to rise. So how old is old? Eighty or 100 years? Now that's old. Australia has some vines that old; so does California. Sixty? Yes, that's old. Forty? Merely middle-aged. Thirty? To call such vines old is a slight exaggeration. The trouble is that there is no agreed definition of what constitutes old. And we need one. Old vines is generally a reliable term, but it's appearing on more and more bottles. If the wine inside is rich and dense and mouthfilling, I'm not going to complain.

Grenache vines enjoying the heat in Châteauneuf-du-Pape, southern Rhône. The distinctive round pebbles, called galets, *soak up the fierce heat during the day and release it slowly at night-time.*

The high region of Luján de Cujo in Mendoza, Argentina, is making a name for its Malbec wines from magnificent old vines.

Malbec ★

The best red grape in Argentina, making smooth, rich reds at all price levels. It's also the major grape of Cahors in South-West France, which can be juicy and plummy at best. Chile, Australia, New Zealand, California and South Africa also have some Malbec. Expect to hear more of this variety as Argentina's reds become more famous.

Also known as Côt or Auxerrois.

Mourvèdre

Red grape that gives backbone to southern Rhône wines, also grown throughout southern France, Spain, Australia, California and South Africa. Can be hard and earthy, but develops smoky, leathery flavours as it ages.

Also known as Monastrell or Mataro.

Nebbiolo

If you taste it too young, Nebbiolo could well be the most fiercely aggressive red you will ever encounter. It takes a few years for the staggering levels of tannin and acid to relax their grip and release the remarkable flavours of tar and roses, backed up by chocolate, cherries, raisins and prunes, and an austere perfume of tobacco and herbs. It's the severest incarnation of the sweet-sour style of Italian reds, always at its best with sturdy food.

Nebbiolo is virtually exclusive to the Piedmont region of north-west Italy. The classic wines are the forbidding Nebbiolos from Barolo and Barbaresco. Modern styles mature in five years rather than the traditional 20, which is a relief for today's wine drinkers. Softer, plummier wines come from elsewhere in Piedmont – Nebbiolo d'Alba, Langhe, Gattinara, Ghemme and Carema.

A few committed Italophiles in California are pretty much the only other producers, though a few Australians are starting to look at it seriously and Argentina has some.

Also known as *Spanna.*

Pinotage

Conceived to meet the demands of the South African soil and climate, this grape produces both rough-textured damsony wines and smoother, fruity styles with flavours of plums, bananas, redcurrants and toasted marshmallows. Either way, it's a wine to love or hate. And it's not only drinkers who are divided: some producers adore it, others won't touch it. Spicy, warm-hearted reds are the best wines. Pinotage has not ventured far afield from South Africa, but that may be set to change. New Zealand has a few vines, and Chile and Australia are now experimenting with the grape.

Sangiovese

The name of the grape might not be familiar, but it's the principal variety behind Chianti, Italy's most famous red wine. It's responsible for Chianti's tea-like bitter twist and cherry-and-plum fruit. So it's one of those mouthwatering sweet-sour grapes, Italian down to its toes.

And it's not just grown for Chianti. You'll find wines made from Sangiovese in most of Italy, though not the very north, and some will be a bit dilute and thin and acidic, but a lot will be light, attractive everyday red with herby fruit and a rasping finish – just the thing with the lunchtime pasta.

In the best parts of Tuscany, however, it is taken very seriously indeed. Big, heavyweight wines like Brunello di Montalcino and Vino Nobile di Montepulciano are made entirely from Sangiovese. These are world-class wines that need aging, as do the best Chiantis, but most Sangiovese is best drunk young and fresh.

Sangiovese is the most planted red grape variety in Italy and reaches its greatest heights in central Tuscany. These vines are in the Chianti Rufina area east of Florence.

You'll find some Sangiovese in California, Australia and Argentina, as well, and they're starting to do interesting things with it; but for the moment there is nothing to equal the best Italian wines.
Also known as *Brunello and Prugnolo.*

Tannat

A sturdy, spicy red grape. It originates from Madiran in France, but also does well in Uruguay. First sightings in Argentina are promising.

Tempranillo ★

Spain's maid-of-all-work crops up all over the country, producing wines of all shapes and sizes. There are grand, prestigious wines in Ribera del Duero, mellow but ageworthy reds in Rioja and Catalunya, powerful beasts in Toro and young, juicy, unoaked styles in Valdepeñas, La Mancha, Somontano and many other regions. Its flavour is good but not always instantly recognisable the way that Cabernet Sauvignon or Pinot Noir is: Tempranillo's most distinctive feature is its good whack of strawberry fruit, but in the biggest, weightiest wines this tends to go plummy and blackberryish and spicy, overlaid with vanilla oak. Only the finest wines need aging – and the simplest really must be drunk young and fresh.

In northern Portugal Tempranillo is called Tinta Roriz and it is an important grape for port, the classic fortified wine, as well as appearing

The Ribera del Duero region in Castilla y León, Spain, produces mouthfilling reds from Tempranillo.

WHITE WINE FROM RED GRAPES

The juice inside a grape is clear, whatever the colour of the skin. So if you separate the juice from the skins before fermentation, hey presto, you'll end up with white wine.

The French call this style Blanc de Noirs and it works well with Pinot Noir in Champagne. A less edifying example of the white-from-red conjuring act is white or 'blush' Zinfandel. The problem is that you lose all the berry-fruit character that makes Zinfandel exciting.

However, making white wine from black grapes is not, apart from these two examples, all that common. In

Champagne the purpose of using Pinot Noir like this is to give weight and body to the blend, and in California the original purpose of white Zinfandel was to use up a grape that was temporarily out of fashion. Demand for red wine is just too high now for red grapes to be denuded of their colour without very good reason.

And another thing. Pretty much all the flavour and perfume of a red grape variety is also held in the skins. When you macerate the juice and skins together to extract colour, you also release all the grape's personality, too.

in reds from both Dão and Douro. Under the alias Aragonez it's responsible for some juicy numbers from Alentejo in the south.

Argentina grows it for its vivacious fruitiness and Australia, California, Oregon and the south of France are experimenting with it.

Also known as Ready for this? Cencibel, Tinto del País, Tinto del Toro, Tinto Fino, Tinto de Madrid or Ull de Liebre in Spain, Tinta Roriz or Aragonez in Portugal. And that's the abbreviated list.

Touriga Nacional ★

Red grape with plenty of colour, perfume and fruit used in port and modern Portuguese dry wines. Worldwide interest is increasing.

Zinfandel

California's speciality grape can be all things to all people. The best Zinfandel and the type I'm interested in is spicy, heart-warming dry red wine. Other styles range from off-white, sweetish and insipid 'blush' wines to high-intensity sweet port-style reds. All red California Zinfandel shares a ripe-berries fruitiness, but the intensity varies dramatically from light to blockbustingly powerful.

Cheap examples are usually lightweight juicy, fruity reds. The top-quality Zinfandels are at the sturdier end of the scale and they're expensive. Mendocino County produces strapping Zin full of blackberry fruit, spice and tannin. It's rich, ripe, dark and chunky in Napa, rounder and spicier in Sonoma and wild and wonderful from old vineyards in the Sierra Foothills. The full-throated, brawny flavours of these big Zins will wash down anything from barbecue ribs to the richest Pacific Rim cooking.

Zinfandel from regions outside the US, which place a lower value on the grape, are an economical alternative. It's grown in one or two outposts in Australia, South Africa, Brazil and Chile and not much money will buy you a sumptuous, rich, almost overripe mouthful.

Researchers have shown that Zinfandel is the same variety as the southern Italian grape Primitivo, and if you're looking for good value, Primitivo gives you the most bang for your bucks. Some Primitivo is even being labelled as Zinfandel to make it seem more fashionable.

Also known as Primitivo in Italy and it's probably the same as Croatia's Crljenak Kastelanski, too.

California Zin can be anything from strapping rich wines from old vines to light, sweetish wines often called White Zinfandel.

FETZER
VINEYARDS

CALIFORNIA
Valley Oaks

WHITE ZINFANDEL ROSÉ

Summer fruit aromas with wild strawberry and tropical fruit flavours.

White wine grapes

Green, yellow, pinkish or even brown on the vine, these are the grapes that promise refreshment. But that's not all: white wines range from the breathtakingly sharp to the most luscious and exotic flavours you will ever encounter.

CLASSIC BLENDS

The modern approach of labelling wines by the name of the grape variety has led to the great popularity of single-varietal wines. Cabernet Sauvignon, Merlot, Sauvignon Blanc and Chardonnay have all swept to fame on their own merits. But many of the classic flavours of France and other European wine nations are based on blends of two or more grape varieties.

Cabernet Sauvignon may be the most famous grape of red Bordeaux, but if the wines were made solely from Cabernet, most would be unbearably austere. Merlot and other grapes in the blend soften the wine and add exciting layers of flavour at the same time.

It's the same story with Bordeaux whites. Sémillon and Sauvignon Blanc are often better together than alone, and a grape called Muscadelle adds fatness to both dry and sweet wines. Champagne, Rioja, Chianti and port are all (for the most part) blended wines, and a bottle of Châteauneuf-du-Pape can include the juice of as many as 13 different grape varieties.

European blends are often emulated in the newer wine-producing nations, but new partnerships have become established too. Australia, in particular, has made modern classics of Chardonnay blended with Semillon and Cabernet Sauvignon with Shiraz.

Chardonnay

The world's most famous white grape variety can make anyone fall in love with wine, because it's so generous with its easy-to-relish buttery, lemony flavours. Chardonnay has an affinity for oak-aging and styles divide into unoaked which is lean, minerally and restrained, lightly oaked, when it can be nutty and oatmealy; and heavily oaked, which is where butteriness, tropical fruits and butterscotch come in.

Where it grows Chardonnay is everywhere. I'd be hard pushed to name a wine-producing country that doesn't grow it. It originates from the French region of Burgundy, where it produces stylish, succulent wines with a nutty richness from time spent in oak barrels yet still with bone-dry clarity. However, in the north of Burgundy is Chablis, where Chardonnay has a sharp, minerally acidity that may or may not be countered by the richness of oak – I prefer it all in its naked, unoaked glory.

The modern style has its origins in Australia and California: upfront, pineappley, oaky and sumptuous, but nowadays becoming a little more restrained.

New Zealand versions are either fruity or surprisingly nutty. Chilean versions are on the fruity side. South African ones are mixed in styles, but very good at their best. In Europe, modern styles come from southern France, Italy, Portugal, Greece and Spain.

Keep it or drink it? Most Chardonnay is ready the moment you buy it, but top wines from France, Australia and California will improve for five years or so.

Splashing out Of all Burgundy's mercilessly expensive Grands Crus, Le Montrachet is finest of the fine. Top Californian Chardonnays sell at almost the same price.

Best value Chilean, Australian or southern French.

Chardonnay with food The whole point of modern Chardonnay is that it will go pretty well with almost anything. It is wonderful with all fish, whether lightly grilled or drowned in a rich, buttery sauce. The richer the sauce, the oakier the wine can be.

Golden yellow Chardonnay grapes growing in California's sunshine.

Riesling

It's not a grape that everyone takes an instant liking to, Riesling, but it has undeniable finesse. Piercing acidity is the most startling and recognizable feature in styles ranging from thrillingly dry to richly sweet, with flavours that range from apple and lime zing to pebbles and slate to peaches and honey.

Dispel any confusion lurking in your mind between Riesling and Liebfraumilch, that simple, sweetish, first step in wine drinking invented in Germany which rarely contains any Riesling at all.

Where it grows Riesling is the grape of Germany's greatest wines. In the Mosel region it produces mostly light, floral wines with a slaty edge. Rheingau Rieslings are generally richer, fruitier and spicy. Both are surprisingly low in alcohol. They need a few years to mature before the flavours are at their best.

Across the border into France, Alsace makes a more alcoholic, dry, spicy Riesling. In Austria it's minerally and dry with a good, weighty slap of alcohol. Australian Riesling is different again – with an invigorating lime aroma that goes toasty with age. New Zealand, South Africa and the US have some decent wines, but Germany, Alsace and Australia have defined the key styles.

Keep it or drink it? Some German Rieslings can age almost indefinitely, but the simpler everyday ones can be drunk at 1–2 years old. As Riesling ages it often develops a petrolly aroma (nicer than it sounds). Top Australian wines will keep for 10 years or more.

Splashing out The great sweet German Rieslings. Alsace, Austria and Australia make superb dry versions.

Best value Mosel and Rhein Kabinetts from Germany and surprisingly good, big-brand Australians.

Riesling with food Good dry Rieslings, such as those from Austria and Australia, are excellent with spicy cuisine. Sweet Rieslings are best enjoyed for their own lusciousness but can also partner light, fruit desserts.

Also known as Johannisberger Riesling, Rhine Riesling or White Riesling – and Riesling Renano in Italy.

Not to be confused with Laski Rizling, Olasz Rizling, Riesling Italico or Welschriesling.

The steep slopes overlooking the Mosel river, here at Piesport, are home to some of Germany's top Riesling vineyards.

Sauvignon Blanc

This is the epitome of the green, tangy style: an unrestrained wine with aromas and flavours of green leaves, nettles, gooseberries and lime zest.

Where it grows New Zealand, particularly the Marlborough region, produces what has become the classic style, all pungent gooseberries and nettles. Australia seldom matches New Zealand for lean pungency. Chile delivers lean, fairly punchy flavours from cooler regions such as Casablanca and Leyda. South Africa is becoming increasingly exciting for Sauvignon Blanc, particularly from the cold west coast. California is a little warm for Sauvignon, but is now producing some good lean examples as well as fuller styles aged in oak barrels.

The grape's European home is in France's Loire Valley. The wines are milder and less pungent than New Zealand versions. Sancerre and Pouilly-Fumé are the Loire's famous wines; Menetou-Salon and Sauvignon de Touraine offer more green flavour for less money.

Sauvignon is also an important grape in Bordeaux, and elsewhere in Europe there are full-flavoured Sauvignons in Spain, especially in Rueda, neutral ones in the north of Italy and light ones in Austria. Eastern European versions vary, but tend to lack pungency, except from Hungary and Slovenia.

Keep it or drink it? Apart from a few top wines, Sauvignon Blanc is for drinking as soon as you can get the bottle home and the cork out.

Sauvignon Blanc from New Zealand's Marlborough region became an overnight bestseller in the 1970s.

Splashing out Cloudy Bay from New Zealand is a cult wine that sells out as soon as it hits the shops. Its Marlborough neighbours are just as good at around half the price.

Best value Entre-Deux-Mers in Bordeaux – and Bordeaux Blanc in general – is pumping out bargains with a good tangy flavour.

Sauvignon with food New World Sauvignon is a favourite match for the sweet-sour, hot-cool, spicy flavours of Chinese and South-East Asian foods; it goes well with some Indian cuisine and with tomato-based dishes in general. It's also a fine drink on its own.

Also known as Fumé Blanc in California and Australia.

Not to be confused with Cabernet Sauvignon, the famous red grape.

Albariño makes trendy white wines in the rolling hills of Galicia, Spain's rainy, green, north-west corner.

Other white wine grapes

Traditionally the world's leading white grapes have come from the cooler areas of France and Germany. But there's been an exhilarating re-invention of white winemaking in warm countries like Spain and Italy, and we'll see a lot more of their varieties in the future.

Albariño ★

Characterful, refreshing white from Spain tasting of lime zest and grapefruit, but with a soft, yeasty texture. It's trendy, so it's expensive. Also used in Vinho Verde in Portugal and starting to appear in places like California.

Aligoté

Grown in Burgundy and Eastern Europe to produce simple sharp wines. Burgundy's Aligoté de Bouzeron is best, stonily dry yet mouthfilling.

Chenin Blanc

What an extraordinary flavour – a striking contrast of rich honey, guava and quince with steely, minerally flavours and whiplash acidity. Chenin can produce gum-numbing dry wines, sparkling wines, medium-sweet styles or super-sweet wonders from noble rot-affected grapes. That's Chenin in France's Loire Valley. Chenin in South Africa might taste as pale as water. Let's deal with France first.

Chenin accounts for the white wines from the Loire's heartland – Vouvray, Savennières, Saumur and others. It can have a problem ripening here but global warming has recently provided a series of excellent vintages. Simple dry Chenin has a flavour of apple peel and honey but a good Vouvray has a streak of minerally flavour. The best sweet Loire Chenin comes from Bonnezeaux, Quarts de Chaume and Coteaux du Layon. These wines need to mature for years to attain their full quince and honey richness.

Chenin is South Africa's most widely planted grape. It generally makes rather hollow stuff but an increasing number of winemakers realize it could make South Africa's best whites if treated seriously. New Zealand and Australia produce small amounts of good fruity Chenin. California and Argentina use it for unmemorable gluggers.

Colombard

Reliable everyday white: fruity and crisp, occasionally with tropical fruits aromas. Widely grown in southern France, Australia, California and South Africa.

Falanghina ★

Once a fairly obscure white from Campania near Naples – If you've ever been to Capri and tried its white it was probably made from Falanghina. But the new wave of Italian winemakers has realized it can make really interesting, minty, apple-blossom-scented whites, and so it's spreading across southern Italy. Next stop, the New World.

Fiano ★

When I tasted a peachy, mint-scented Fiano from Adelaide Hills in South Australia, I realised this grape was no longer a south Italian secret. But most of it is grown from around Naples in Campania right down to Sicily and it's making some of Italy's most interesting new-wave whites.

Gewürztraminer

A fragrant blast of lychee and rose petals followed up by a luxurious, honeyed, oil-thick texture, a whiff of Nivea hand cream, a twist of fresh black pepper – dry or sweet, it's the most intensely aromatic wine in the world. 'Gewürz' translates as spice, although it's difficult to think of a single spice that exactly resembles Gewürztraminer. Still, if you're searching for a wine to match spicy Asian food, look no further. It's also wonderful to sip by itself.

Alsace is the place to go for Gewurztraminer (they take the accent off the 'u' here). Even the most basic wines have a swirl of aromatic spice, while great vintages can produce super-intense wines in styles from dry to richly sweet.

You have to keep your nerve to make Gewürz (its short nickname) work. If you don't like its perfume, why grow it? But the rise in popularity of Asian cuisine has seen producers become more confident. Germany, northern Italy (where the grape originates) and New Zealand all now produce a few deliciously indulgent examples.

Also known as Traminer.

These Gewurztraminer grapes come from Alsace, where the sunshine can continue well into November. If you leave the grapes on the vine this long the wines will be luscious and perfumed.

Malvasia

Widely grown in Italy and found in many guises, both white and red. It produces fragrant dry whites, rich, apricotty sweet whites and frothing light reds. Also grown in Spain and Portugal, it's the grape of the sweet fortified Madeira wine called Malmsey.

Marsanne

Originally from the Rhône Valley where it can make rich and honeysuckle-scented wines. It is also used in southern French blends. In Victoria, Australia it makes big, broad, honeyed wines.

Muscadet

The grape of Muscadet, the simple but refreshing white wine from the mouth of the Loire Valley around Nantes. It doesn't have much flavour itself, but the better wines are left in contact with their yeast lees in the vat, resulting in a very pleasant, prickly, creamy white which is perfect as a summer aperitif or accompanying the local seafood. Look for the words *sur lie* on the label.

Below left: Muscadet is just the perfect refreshing white wine to accompany a plate of local Breton seafood.
Below right: This is the leftover yeast at the bottom of the vat that helps make the most interesting Muscadet wines.

Muscat

The only grape to make delicious wine that actually smells of the grape itself comes in a multitude of styles. Rich, sweet and fortified, floral and dry or exuberantly frothy, Muscat wines all share a seductive grapy aroma. Intensely sweet Muscats often add an orange peel fragrance.

To start with the darkest and sweetest, Rutherglen in north-eastern Victoria, Australia, is a sticky heaven for those who crave its raisiny, perfumed fortified Muscats. Golden, sweet Muscats, again fortified, come from the south of France (from Beaumes-de-Venise, Frontignan, Rivesaltes and other villages) and Portugal, and have lighter, but sensuous, delicate orange-and-grape aromas with a touch of rose petals. Spain's Moscatel de Valencia is cheaper, more foursquare, but a good rich mouthful all the same.

Alsace is the place for dry Muscat – heavenly scented, thrillingly dry – though Italy, Spain, Portugal and Australia all have a go. And if you're in a bubbly sort of mood, Muscat makes delightful, grape and blossom-scented sparklers in Italy (Asti is the most famous) and Brazil.

Also known as Muscat Blanc à Petits Grains (its full name), Muscat de Frontignan or, in Australia, Brown Muscat. The Italians call it Moscato. The less thrilling Muscat of Alexandria (Spain's Moscatel) and Muscat Ottonel are related grapes. Orange Muscat does smell of oranges, and the rare pink Muscat (Moscato Rosa) does make divine wine smelling of tea roses. Black Muscat – well, I like it; we used to grow it in a greenhouse when I was little.

Not to be confused with Muscadet, the bone-dry white wine from the Loire Valley in France.

Palomino and Pedro Ximénez (PX)

The white grapes behind sherry and Montilla-Moriles: Palomino for dry styles, PX for sweet ones.

Pinot Blanc

A light quaffer. At best it makes creamy, floral, appley wine in Alsace; good in northern Italy too.

Muscat can be used for both delicious, dark sticky wines from Victoria, Australia and light, frothy Asti sparklers from Italy.

Pinot Gris

Intensity is a key issue with Pinot Gris. Whether you like your white wine bone dry and neutral or rich and spicy, or anything in between, the right Pinot Gris for you is out there somewhere. A hint of honey (sometimes admittedly very faint) is the linking theme that connects the grape's different incarnations.

Rich, smoky and honeyed dry whites from Alsace in France show Pinot Gris at its most pungent and impressive. The US has had success with lighter, crisper, spicy versions from Oregon, while New Zealand is producing a fair number of soft, pear-scented examples. Eastern Europe produces outstanding dry or off-dry and spicy wines.

Germany takes the grape into sweet-wine territory and sometimes calls it Ruländer. Dry German Grauburgunders aged in oak are fat and smokily honeyed. Fairly neutral wines, and plenty of them, labelled as Pinot Grigio, come from Italy. But really good Italian Pinot Grigio is floral and honeyed.

Also known as Pinot Grigio in Italy, Ruländer (usually sweet) or Grauburgunder (usually dry) in Germany, Malvoisie in Switzerland.

Not to be confused with the other Pinots: Pinot Noir, Pinot Blanc and Pinot Meunier(one of the official Champagne grapes).

Roussanne

A white Rhône grape – a more aromatic and elegant cousin of Marsanne, with which it is frequently and successfully blended.

Semillon

Semillon comes into its own in two key areas, France's Bordeaux and Australia, and it comes in two totally different styles: dry and sweet. By the way, the French put an accent on the 'é'. Either way, it can produce wonderful quality.

It pops up in various parts of Australia for dry wine, but Hunter Valley Semillon is the most famous. The traditional style here is unoaked. When young, unoaked Hunter Semillon tastes neutral, even raw, with just a bit of lemony fruit. But unoaked Hunter Semillon should not be drunk young. It needs up to a decade in bottle – and then it will amaze you with its waxy, lanoliny, custardy fruit. Oaked Australian Semillon, often from the Barossa or Clare

Oregon's Willamette Valley is becoming renowned for crisp styles of Pinot Gris.

Valleys, is different. Dry, toasty, waxy and lemony, it's good young but the best can age for a few years, too. Riverina makes light, waxy Semillon, much of which is blended with Chardonnay.

In Bordeaux Sémillon is usually blended with Sauvignon Blanc, which adds a refreshing streak of sharp acidity. The best dry versions come from Graves and Pessac-Léognan: oaked with flavours of cream and nectarines, they improve for several years in bottle.

Sweet wines are another story. Here Sauternes is the star: this Bordeaux appellation produces extraordinarily concentrated wines from grapes affected by noble rot, with flavours of barley sugar and peaches. This golden, sweet style is imitated, in small amounts, in California, Australia and New Zealand. Hand-picking the noble rotted grapes, sometimes berry by berry, means these wines can never be cheap; but the flavour is so special it's worth the money.

Torrontés ★

The star white grape of Argentina, producing highly aromatic wines, especially from high-altitude vineyards in the north.

Verdejo

Increasingly popular grape variety from Rueda in northern Spain, where its sharp acidity and greengage fruit is prized.

Verdelho

Originally a grape grown for the fortified wine of Madeira, but it also produces full-bodied, leather- and lime-scented dry whites in Australia.

The Bodega Colomé estate, high in the Calchaquí Valley in north-west Argentina, has some very old plantings of Torrontes, Argentina's number one white grape variety. This is some of the highest vineyard land in the world and the high altitudes and very dry climate mean the grapes produce intense flavours.
PS There is also a gorgeous hotel here – the drive here is so tough, you'll need some pampering and a stopover.

Verdicchio

One of Italy's non-aromatic white grapes, now gaining some respect for its ability to impart a richness like baked cream and a haughty, dried herb scent to its wine. Best known for the wine of the same name from eastern Italy – Verdicchio.

Vermentino

Light, perfumed dry white from Sardinia, or green-apple fresh from the Tuscan coast. As Rolle it is Provence's best white grape.

Vernaccia

White grape that makes an Italian equivalent to sherry in Sardinia and a tasty golden dry white in Tuscany.

Viognier

Heady, hedonistic, with a rich scent of apricots and breeze-blown spring flowers, Viognier is an aromatic dry wine so luxurious that it seems almost sweet.

It used to be confined to a few small areas of the northern Rhône Valley in France, but fashion is a powerful force. Suddenly Viognier is appearing all over the south of France – never in large quantities, to be sure, but at prices that give a taste of the grape to those of us who can't fork out the premium-plus rates for classic top-quality Condrieu and Château-Grillet from the northern Rhône.

California, Australia and South America are trying their hands at it, too. Results vary, but are distinctly promising to very good. Viognier should be drunk young and fresh – the ravishing scent fades rapidly after a year or two.

Viura

The main white grape of Spain's Rioja, light and apple-fresh in its simplest form, but full, custardy and orange-scented when fermented in oak barrels. It is most commonly used in blends.

Also known as *Macabeo in Spain and as Macabeu in Languedoc-Roussillon.*

The Condrieu vineyards high above the river Rhône are the original home of the Viognier grape.

INSTANT RECALL: RED GRAPES

Barbera A snappy, refreshing Italian red

Cabernet Sauvignon The blackcurranty red par excellence

Carmenère Dark, blackcurrant- and pepper-flavoured Chilean red

Gamay The juicy red grape of Beaujolais

Grenache Ripe strawberry and spice, often in a blend

Malbec Full, lush, plummy red, especially from Argentina

Merlot Juicy and plummy; part of the classic red Bordeaux blend

Nebbiolo The stern and tannic dark grape from north-west Italy

Pinot Noir A capricious grape, at best making elegant, silky reds with a haunting fragrance

Pinotage A love-it-or-hate-it sturdy, smoky red from South Africa

Sangiovese The main grape of Chianti; mouthwatering, sweet-sour red fruit flavours from Italy

Syrah/Shiraz Spicy and warm-hearted; at home in France's Rhône Valley, Australia, California, Chile...

Tempranillo Spanish strawberries and plums

Zinfandel California's all-purpose grape variety, often seen as a sweetish pink, but best as a spicy red

INSTANT RECALL: WHITE GRAPES

Chardonnay From ripe peaches and toast to steely, stony and austere: the classic international white grape in numerous styles

Chenin Blanc The quirky, fruity-minerally white grape from the Loire Valley

Gewürztraminer The uniquely spicy and exotic white, at its best in Alsace

Muscat Dry and sweet wines that actually taste of grapes

Pinot Gris Neutral in Italy (as Pinot Grigio), rich in Alsace, always with a hint of honey

Riesling The steely, citrussy aristocrat of white grapes, best in Germany, Austria, France's Alsace and Australia

Sauvignon Blanc Gooseberry and nettle tang, originally from France's Loire Valley but now better known in New Zealand, Chile and South Africa

Semillon Lemony, waxy dry whites and golden sweeties from Bordeaux and Australia

Viognier The sumptuous, apricotty white of the northern Rhône Valley

what makes each wine unique

It doesn't take much to make wine. In fact, a grape is quite capable of doing it by itself.
The moment the skin of a ripe grape splits, the sugary juice on the inside comes into contact
with yeasts that live naturally in the air and on the surface of the grape skin. Yeasts have a
voracious appetite for sugar and as they eat their way through it they convert it into alcohol.
The process is called fermentation.

But leaving nature to make wine for you like this is a bit like leaving your car out in the rain to get washed: the results will not be entirely what you were hoping for. Some 500 chemical compounds have been identified in wine, and most are produced naturally during fermentation. The winemaker's job is to ensure that the right compounds – the ones that taste good – are formed, and that the wrong ones – the ones that taste of rancid butter, or vinegar – are not.

Given 500 different components, it's not surprising that no two wines taste quite alike. But the winemaking process is only part of the story. The grape variety, the yield from the vine, the climate and the location of the vineyard all contribute to the flavour of the wine.

Climate and location

First off, grapes need sun, otherwise they can't ripen. And without sugar in the grapes there will be nothing to ferment into alcohol. The riper the grapes, the higher the sugar content and the more alcoholic the wine will be. If you're after a great big beast with a hefty wallop of ultra-ripe fruit, well – get that sunshine switched on to full.

But traditional wisdom asserts that great wines are produced only at the 'margin'. What does it mean? Well, we're talking about climate. It means that the most complex wines, the ones with perfume, appetizing balance, depth, and the ability to evolve with age, are produced In places where it is a marginal bet whether there will be enough sun to ripen the grapes at all. The grapes creep and stagger to ripeness through a long, unpredictable, not-too-hot summer and autumn. When it comes to traditional wines, like France's Champagne, Chablis, Bordeaux and Burgundy, I have to agree with the traditional view. But there are also many modern classics from California, Australia, Chile, Argentina and South Africa, where grapes ripen fully every year without much effort at all.

Perhaps the best of both worlds is to have cool climate vineyards in areas with warm, reliable sunshine. How is that possible? Well, how about a coastal vineyard in northern California? Grapes soak up that famous Californian sun while simultaneously being cooled by the breeze and chilly mists that roll in from the Pacific. Or how about a high-altitude vineyard in the Andes? Plenty of clear skies and sun, but the higher you go, the cooler it gets, which slows down the ripening period and creates the balance we're talking about.

Every grape variety requires different conditions to ripen. Riesling can ripen perfectly in the cool valleys of Germany, Syrah can't. But Riesling would bake in the Rhône Valley, where Syrah gaily broils to perfect ripeness under the sun's bright glare.

And don't forget the soil, and the site. Waterlogged soil is cold and hinders ripening; well-drained soils promote it. Hillsides drain well and, if they're facing in the right direction, catch more sun; valley floors drain less well and often cop a snap of frost too. And these conditions can lie right next to each other, in the same village. They'll produce totally different wines.

Grapes and yields

The majority of the world's wines are produced from one or more of the 15 or 20 most popular grape varieties. The grapes have certain characteristics that are inevitably inherited by their offspring, the wines. Pinot Noir grapes give wines with red-fruit flavour. No black fruit, no citrus. You're a red-head, son, just like your old man. But the thrusting young Californian Pinot is a different chap from the cynical old Burgundian. Sauvignon Blanc gives green and tangy wines. That is the colour of Sauvignon's eyes. But Sauvignon Blanc arrives at the party in different styles: bold and boisterous from New Zealand, charming and subtle from France, alternative from northern California – it all depends on where she grew up and who shaped her growth.

Facing page: The Marlborough region in New Zealand's South Island enjoys long dry autumns (most years, that is).

This French term doesn't really have an English translation but it is at the root of the French attitude to wine. The **terroir** of each vineyard is what makes it unique: it can be defined as a combination of soil, climate and exposure to the sun. It thus sums up every possible factor: the type of topsoil and subsoil, the direction of the wind, the degree of shelter from frost, whether the ground slopes and how much, and whether it faces north, south, east or west. New World winemakers are more inclined to focus on **climate** as being the main determinant of wine style, with the soil sometimes being dismissed as merely the stuff that holds the irrigation water to keep the grapes growing. But the more good, different wines these guys taste, the more they realize flavour and personality need more than simply sunshine and a reliable water supply. That's when they thoughtfully kick the earth in their vineyards and think – perhaps there's something in this 'terroir' business after all.

After about 20 years vines become less vigorous and produce smaller, more concentrated crops. Australia has plenty of vines much older than that. These ones are in the Clare Valley, South Australia.

The number of grapes each vine produces affects both the flavour of the wine and the price. Higher yields should mean lower prices. But do low yields mean higher quality? To a large extent, yes. A Pinot Noir vineyard in Burgundy where the vines are pruned hard every winter to prevent the vine producing too many bunches will make better wine, other things being equal, than one where the vines are allowed to crop too heavily. More grapes, in this instance, mean more dilute juice and less flavour.

But the equation is not always a straightforward one. Each vineyard, and each grape variety, has its own optimum yield. To allow the vines to produce more than that level means a drop in quality. It's a question of knowing your vines.

I'll give you an example. The warmer parts of Australia have heavily irrigated vineyards churning out wine like milch cows, and it's amazingly cheap. Clever winemaking and vine-growing techniques mean that it tastes pretty good, too. On the other side of the coin are the lovingly tended, 100-year-old vines boasted by the early-settled parts of Australia: these gnarled centenarians give tiny quantities of intense, concentrated, high-quality wines that cost a bomb. Their yield is perhaps one-twentieth of that of the irrigated vineyards. But if you treated those factory-farmed vineyards the same way as the centenarian ones, you still wouldn't get the quality of the latter. And yet the wine would cost nearly as much to produce.

And all this means...

Ideally, it all means perfect grapes. Or as good as the grower can get them: picked at optimum ripeness, with an optimum balance of sugar and acidity. Grapes like this, delivered in perfect health (no rot, no mildew) are at the absolute peak of their potential. Whether the wine lives up to that potential depends entirely on the skill and attentiveness of the winemaker.

Making wine

So much for the background; what about the sticky business of transforming fresh-picked grapes into the world's most delicious and intriguing drink? You won't see many jolly peasants treading the grapes these days; think, rather, of stainless steel, computers and laboratory-style hygiene. Constant experimentation with equipment and techniques is part and parcel of the modern wine industry, but for all that, winemaking remains a magical, messy process.

Grape juice

The first thing you need to do is get at the juice. A little controlled violence has to be applied in the form of a machine called a crusher, which breaks the skins of the grapes. If you are making white wine, the next job after crushing is to get the fermenting juice (known as the must) well away from all the skins and stems. They add tannin and colour to the wine – exactly what you don't want for a white wine. So you transfer the crushed mass to a press without delay and squeeze out all the liquid, then pump it into a container called a vat to ferment. Some winemakers put uncrushed bunches of grapes straight into the press to get even fresher juice.

Fermentation

Fermentation is the process in which yeasts – either natural ('wild') or specifically chosen – convert the sugar in the grape juice to alcohol, carbon dioxide and heat. The latter two bubble out and the alcohol remains in the juice.

The single greatest advance in winemaking in the 20th century was the advent of temperature-controlled fermentation – for which

Winemaking is hard work. Well, most of it is.

WINE TERMS **Winemakers**

The winemaking process, or **vinification**, is the point at which the natural events of fermentation are shaped and controlled with a view to creating a particular end product. The person who makes the decisions is the **winemaker**. The concept of the winemaker as an interventionist who determines the character of the wine is a modern one, developed in California and Australia in the 1970s. Previously it was an unsung role. An attentive winemaker can make decent wine even from unexceptional grapes, and a talented one can produce stunning wine from top-quality raw materials. A poor winemaker, on the other hand, can turn out dreadful wine even as neighbouring producers are creating classics. For this reason the name of the **producer**, the company or person that produces the wine, is a better guide to a wine's quality than the grape or the region.

read cool fermentation. Cool fermentation is one of the reasons why the least expensive Australian or Chilean wine, grown in conditions that are too hot for comfort, still tastes fresh and fruity. Most modern easy-drinking whites are made in great big refrigerated steel vats, but some top dry whites will be fermented in small oak barrels, which add buttery, vanilla richness to the wine.

You make red wine by fermenting the juice and the skins together, since the skins contain the colour as well as flavours, perfumes and the preservative tannin. This is generally done in a vat made of stainless steel, concrete or sometimes wood. Let the temperature go much higher than for whites to extract as much colour and flavour from the skins as possible. You'll have to stir the vat or pump the juice from the bottom over the skins floating on top, but otherwise just sit back and watch the deep purple colour ooze out of the skins. When the fermentation is over and you have all the colour and tannin you want, drain the free-running juice into a fresh container and put the remaining pulp into a press to squeeze out the rest.

For rosé wine, start as if you were about to make red wine, but separate the juice from the skins much earlier, so that the wine has just a tinge of colour. Then proceed as if you were making white wine. You can cheat by mixing a bit of red wine into a white wine, but that's not real rosé and it won't taste as good.

Fining and filtration

Fermentation is complete when all the sugar in the wine has turned to alcohol, or the alcohol level becomes high enough to kill the yeasts. Before bottling, most wine will go through fining and filtration so that it is nice and clear when it reaches the consumer. This could be done straight off with an ultra-fine filter but that would strip out a lot of quality and flavour from the wine too. Instead, winemakers get all the tiny particles that are making the wine cloudy to stick together and drop to the bottom (this process is called fining), and then use a gentler filter that will leave the wine clear but with quality intact. Traditional fining agents include egg whites, isinglass (a product of the sturgeon fish) and gelatine; they are not present in the finished wine, but if a wine is labelled 'suitable for vegetarians or vegans' it refers to what has been used in the fining process.

If wine is fermented or matured in oak barrels, it will acquire characteristic oak flavours from the wooden staves, particularly if the winemaker chooses brand new, fairly small barrels called **barriques**. Wine tasters describe these **new oak** flavours as toastiness, spiciness, butteriness, butterscotch and vanilla. Many of the world's best reds and whites are fermented or matured in oak; but large oak barrels that are reused from year to year add little to the flavour.

Barrels are expensive: an economical alternative is to submerge oak planks in a vat of wine, or to add oak chips in a kind of oversize tea bag while the wine is fermenting.

Stainless steel or concrete tanks, which don't affect the flavour, are preferable for fresh-tasting and ultra-fruity styles.

Blending

The winemaker has the opportunity to transform the wine by blending the contents of two or more vats together. That could mean putting together different grape varieties to add a whole new dimension of flavour.

Maturing the wine

The wine is still not ready to bottle: you need to mature it for anything from a few days to several years, depending on the flavour you are aiming at. Storing the wine in small oak barrels called barriques adds rich, toasty flavours. The newer the barrels, the greater their influence on the flavour. Oak-aging doesn't automatically make a wine better – it suits gutsy wines like Cabernet Sauvignon, but would overpower a delicate Riesling.

Stainless steel and concrete tanks are inert, so they add no flavour and preserve the wine's fruit; they are ideal for fresh-tasting wines such as tangy Sauvignon Blanc.

While they are maturing, wines, especially reds, benefit from a naturally occurring process called malolactic fermentation. A strain of bacteria converts the acid in the wine from harsh malic acid (the acid of unripe apples) to softer lactic acid, which is the main acid of milk. This isn't appropriate for some white wines, in which case the bacteria are filtered out or killed off with sulphur.

Producing grape juice and then fermenting it into wine is a messy old business.

Making sparkling wine

All the very best sparkling wine is made by the method developed in Champagne in France. Any sparkling wine that is labelled 'traditional method', 'classical method' or something similar is made in this way.

The traditional or Champagne method

First you need to make some still wine, called the base wine, which is often unbearably acidic but has the potential to make good fizz, because carbon dioxide has the effect of softening wine and fully ripe base wine would produce flabby fizz. The next step is to create the bubbles. Put the still wine into strong bottles with a little yeast and sugar to start a second fermentation. Seal them with strong stoppers, because fermentation produces vast amounts of carbon dioxide gas, which builds up a lot of pressure in a sealed container. Since it cannot escape, the carbon dioxide dissolves into the wine, impatiently waiting for the day it will be released as jubilant foam and elegant trails of tiny bubbles.

Unfortunately the dead yeast leaves a decidedly un-celebratory deposit of gunge in the bottle. To get this out you first have to tip this muck towards the bottle's opening. Traditionally the bottles are stored in angled racks where they are turned and gently tapped by hand every day for a couple of months to achieve this. Mechanized racks now do the job in a few days.

Right: This is the dead yeast gunge that has to be removed from the bottle before you can enjoy a glass of fizz.

Once all this sediment is in the neck of the bottle, you freeze the neck and whip out the stopper: the sediment will shoot out like a pellet but the bubbles stay dissolved in the wine. Add a little sweetening if you want to take the harsh edge off the acidity and push in the famous super-strong Champagne cork – and you've got Champagne-method bubbly.

Making sweet wine

For wine to be sweet, there must be a noticeable amount of sugar left in it after fermentation. This is known as residual sugar. The simplest method, for the simplest wines, is to stop the fermentation before all the sugar has been turned into alcohol – you just kill the yeasts with sulphur or remove them with a filter or a centrifuge.

Good sweet wines need grapes that are so ripe that the yeasts cannot ferment all the sugar before the alcohol level kills them off and the remaining sugar constitutes the sweetness in the wine. Intense sweet wines – notably Sauternes from Bordeaux – come from grapes affected by a fungus called botrytis or noble rot. It's 'noble' because rather than ruining the grapes like any other disease would, it reduces their water content and concentrates the sugar and acidity. If you have a warm autumn, you can also make sweet wines by letting the grapes shrivel on the vine. An Italian technique is to leave the grapes to shrivel on mats or racks for several months after picking before making the wine. The wines are called *passito* or *recioto*.

I love a glass of good fino sherry with its sharp, pungent tang.

Facing page: Opportunities to taste 19th-century Burgundies are as rare as hens' teeth nowadays. I once tasted an 1865 Romanée – a magnificent vintage. Mmmm...

Making fortified wine

Sweet or dry wines with 15 per cent alcohol or more are usually made by adding brandy or pure spirit to the wine. The practice of fortifying certain wines with extra alcohol was first developed in order to help them travel well.

Port

Red wines from the Douro were notoriously rough. By mistake someone added the fortifying brandy to the wine before the fermentation had finished. As I've already explained, yeasts die if the alcohol level rises too high (anything much above 16 per cent or so), so they were left with a sweet red wine which wouldn't go on fermenting. Genius. Port was born.

Sherry

Sherry is different from port: the brandy is added after the fermentation has finished, so the wine is dry. In barrel, fino sherry grows a layer of yeast called flor, which gives it its typical pungent, almost sour flavour. Sweet sherry is sweetened before bottling.

ORGANIC WINES

There is a strong move in grape growing, as in many other crops, towards organic methods of cultivation. All over the world there are growers who are eschewing chemical pesticides, herbicides and fertilizers, and returning to natural methods. There are no international standards for what constitutes organic viticulture, but there are local organizations in many regions.

However, vines face tough problems in most parts of the world. Fungal diseases like downy mildew and powdery mildew can wipe out a crop, and insect pests can spread deadly viruses or themselves weaken vines. The risk of abandoning chemicals altogether can be just too great. So a popular alternative to full organic viticulture is to reduce the use of chemicals to the bare essentials.

Biodynamics takes the concept of working with rather than against nature a stage further than full organic viticulture. Vineyard practices are timed to gain maximum benefit from natural biorhythms, even taking account of the phases of the moon and the movement of the planets.

VINTAGE WINE

It's a phrase you often hear bandied about to suggest high living: drinking vintage wine, it is implied, is far, far smarter than drinking mere wine. Well, I've got news for you. Most wine is vintage wine.

Vintage wine is simply wine from a single year: the vintage is the name for the annual grape harvest. It does not carry any connotations of greater age or distinction, like vintage cars. If a bottle has a year on it that tells you when it was made, then it's vintage wine.

Not all wine is vintage wine, and not all is the worse for it. For example, most Champagne and other good sparkling wines are non-vintage, meaning that they're a blend of wines from two or more years. Blending different years here ensures consistency of flavour and style.

MEASURING CARBON FOOTPRINT

Gauging the carbon footprint of a wine means considering not just transport, but also the energy expended during production. A gleaming, well-staffed, modern winery is likely to have used far more energy per bottle than an artisan winemaker. Other factors include:

Transporting the wine

Let's have a quick look at logistics. The cost of transporting wine from New Zealand to Europe or the US is a relatively reasonable 13p (21 cents) per bottle. It is good value to ship wine in containers and shipping itself represents an efficient mode of transport. Transporting wine from, say, southern Italy to the UK is considerably more expensive, as the bottles will be trucked overland. Trucking wine is an expensive business.

Bottling at destination

Sometimes wine is shipped in sealed tanks from the source country and bottled at the destination. It makes sense. More wine can be shipped for less money and it's an efficient use of fuel. The carbon footprint per bottle is greatly reduced, and the price saving can be passed on to customers. But so far no seriously high- quality wine has been shipped in this way. However, as standards of bottling and techniques of transporting the wine improve, quality is rising and this is likely to become more common.

Heavy bottles and alternative packaging

Some producers like to put their wine in thick, chunky, distinctive bottles. Unfortunately, they couldn't be more environmentally unfriendly if they tried, and anyone with an interest in being green should steer well clear of them. Anyway, the wine inside is more than likely to be thick and chunky as well. Heavy bottle producers like that kind of wine. I don't.

Glass is wonderfully inert and innately beautiful but also heavy and fragile. Could plastic be an alternative? Or even juice-style cardboard containers? So far I'm not convinced. But with the climate change crisis we *will* see greater acceptance.

From grape to glass – a tale of two wines

What I want to do here is tie everything together, to trace two different wines from grape to glass and bring the whole process to life. The point is not to compare the wines but to contrast the stories. It is a real and personal business.

On the one hand, I'll look at a **big-selling Sauvignon Blanc from New Zealand**: high-volume, popular wine to retail in the UK at £5–£10 and in the US at between $10 and $20. And on the other, I'll look at a **small producer in Burgundy**, making a fraction of the quantity at over four times the price. For the sake of argument I'll make him a decent producer of mid-priced wine.

Below left: Marlborough, a modern wine region created as recently as the 1970s. Below right: Vineyards have been cultivated in the heart of Burgundy, here in the village of Pommard, since the early Middle Ages.

Background

Our Kiwi Sauvignon, let's call it **OZZIE'S HILLS**, is based at a large, purpose-built, state-of-the-art winery in Marlborough, which houses industrial-scale crushers and pressers, long rows of enormous fermentation vats and layered cellaring facilities. It is the workplace of wine professionals, from winemakers to accountants, scientists to cellar door managers. It is a slickly run operation.

The company owns a substantial portion of land in Marlborough but not enough to satisfy demand, so they also buy grapes from specialist contract growers. **Ozzie's Hills** themselves started out as contract growers in the 1980s, and have managed to successfully turn their hand to winemaking.

Over in Burgundy, **MONSIEUR LE CLARKE** runs the family business from home. He employs three people: his wife, his son and a reliable chap called Jacques from the village. The effortlessly charming Madame le Clarke

Above: Traditional Burgundian basket press. Facing page: Stainless steel vats are used at most New World wineries.

runs the 'office' in a constant battle with their temperamental home computer, while his son is learning the ropes of the business. He makes the odd balls-up but has a useful degree in enology – which is winemaking to you and me. **Monsieur le Clarke** himself is only happy in the vineyards or the cellar, and that's where you'll always find him. His wife tried to make him use a mobile phone, but he said he can't have any interruptions when he's looking after his vines.

All the winemaking equipment is kept in the garage, next to the tractor. The beautiful house has been in the le Clarke family for 250 years, which is about as long as the family has been making wine.

Vineyards, climate and grapes

The Marlborough vineyards sweep across rolling hills and valleys for as far as the eye can see. The growing season starts in September/October and summer consists of long warm days of bright sunshine that ripen the grapes fully, while cool breezy nights maintain the essential balance. This is the backbone of a wine that will be bursting with flavour but also crisp and dry.

Much top-spec technology is utilized to help grow the best-quality grapes in large quantities. Great gleaming tractors make short work of zipping up and down the rows. Helicopters may be used for spraying.

M. le Clarke, meanwhile, has no outright vineyards to manage but owns many parcels of vines spread across 18 different vineyards in three adjacent villages. This is the norm. Napoleonic laws of inheritance have resulted in fractured ownership of land. While M. le Clarke tends his rows of grapes very carefully, the rows on either side of his are not so well loved. Quality varies enormously within every vineyard. Each parcel of vines is made into separate wine.

The climate in Burgundy is much more marginal than in New Zealand, which makes growing grapes more precarious. The growing season begins in April/May and all fingers are crossed for a warm, long summer. Delicate Pinot Noir, **M. le Clarke**'s main interest, seems to give its best in exactly this kind of climate. He has one small tractor to help with spraying but it's old and cumbersome. Some of his neighbours are talking of returning to using horses. He thinks they may have a point. Free manure, for a start.

Making the wine

In New Zealand the grapes are picked in late February and March by machine harvesters that gently shake the grapes from the vine. The **Ozzie's Hills** winemakers wait to direct the process in the winery, having spent the last six months abroad, honing their skills in the northern hemisphere.

Fermentation at cool, controlled temperatures in stainless-steel vats is the next key to this style. Their adoption in New Zealand from the dairy industry revolutionized winemaking in the 1980s. The stainless steel vats are inert and allow the winemaker to maximize the flavour of fruit and freshness in the grape. Nothing is

lost and everything enhanced. Coupled with fully ripe yet crisp Sauvignon Blanc grapes, the final result simply explodes out of the glass.

Back in Burgundy, harvest is in September and **M. le Clarke** organizes a team of experienced pickers to help him hand-pick the grapes. Some of the pickers come from families who've been helping with the harvest for a hundred years. They know the vines almost as well as M. le Clarke does. If anything's not right, they'll tell him.

Once the harvest is in, he sets about making the wine in his garage on his annually primed and cleaned equipment. He has bought one new piece of equipment: a basket press for gentler separation of the juice from the skins – very important for Pinot Noir. Funnily enough, the design of the basket press, with its slatted wooden sides, is almost exactly the same as that of the one his grandfather used. In Burgundy, progress is often a case of going back to see what worked best in the old days. He's overseen 28 vintages in his time and saw many more as a boy. There is little he hasn't seen.

Some new French oak barrels have been purchased from a local cooper for maturing the wine, and are stored in cool, underground cellars. The main cellar is beneath the house, but as he's gradually bought more parcels of vineyard he's needed to expand and so also rents a cellar underneath the priest's house. Any difficult wines are stored there, and they do seem to calm down and develop a delightfully tranquil nature under the divine influence of the prelate. Actually, M. le Clarke stores only his top wine in 'new' oak, because he doesn't want too much vanilla and toasty spice in his Burgundy; it will swamp the subtleties of all his different vineyard sites. He uses barrels for several vintages before selling them off to a merchant in the nearby town. He knows the exact state of each barrel, in each cellar. Maturation may go on for many months and he will often be making winemaking decisions well into the following growing season, further complicating the balancing act of what to do and when. He waits and waits until the wine feels right, and then it is ready.

Bottling

Ozzie's Hills will be bottled under screwcap, thus essentially eliminating any chance of cork taint. The embracing of screwcap technology is fully indicative of New Zealand's forward-looking mentality, and has helped push reluctant consumers toward modernity.

M. le Clarke has not yet learnt the French word for screwcap, and has never tasted a screwcapped bottle of wine. For him, it is cork or nothing.

PART TWO
ENJOYING WINE

Wine is part of everyday life and treating it with reverential awe won't make it taste any better. The rituals of opening, serving, tasting, buying and storing wine are mostly built on sound reasoning, but they are meaningless if they don't help you to enjoy yourself and get the best out of your wine. If you don't get pleasure out of a glass of wine, there's no point to it. But for some of you, these rituals of serving and the responsibility of owning and storing wines will add to the pleasure. And you may take pleasure in arguing the toss in wine shops and restaurants with sales assistants and wine waiters. Fantastic. But if you don't get a buzz out of such things – don't worry. Just have confidence in the fact that the most important thing is that you are happy and having fun yourself. In this book I try to make life easier for everyone who enjoys wine, at whatever level.

buying and storing wine

I have a chaotic jumble of bottles under the stairs in my house, and stray bottles tucked into odd corners in the kitchen, the box room and behind the TV. But however much wine I accumulate, it's never going to stop me dropping into my local wine shop to browse, have a chat and pick up a bottle for the evening. This is the way we buy most of our wine these days, not by the case, not for laying down, just as part of our daily shopping.

OZ'S TIPS FOR FINDING OUT MORE ABOUT WINE

A selection of useful internet sites
- www.wine-searcher.com
- www.decanter.com
- www.winespectator.com
- www.winemag.com
- www.bluewine.com

A few good wine blogs
- www.wineanorak.com
- www.jancisrobinson.com
- www.wineloverspage.com
- www.wine-pages.com
- www.natdecants.com
- www.quaff.com.au
- www.matchingfood andwine.com

Where to buy wine

Shopping for wine can be so much more, though, than a dash to your local store: it can be a pleasure and a leisure pursuit in itself. Here are some of the options, starting with the easiest, buying from your home.

Using the internet and mail-order shopping

For sheer range of choice, the best thing to do is stay at home. Seriously. The internet has revolutionized wine buying. Plenty of established merchants and internet-only wine 'e-tailers' have websites which you can browse at leisure, comparing prices and digging out far more information on individual wines than you'll be likely to find on a shop shelf.

Of course, it's just an advanced version of traditional mail-order shopping, which has been a mainstay of wine retailing for years. Both methods have the advantage that you don't need to worry about carting the wine home and, more importantly, give you access to a vast number of wines not available in your local area.

And if you want to experience the warm sense of being part of a like-minded fellowship, well, there are a significant number of wine clubs out there that will not only sell you wine but will also keep you involved, with newsletters, tastings and events.

A good wine shop

What the internet lacks is the quiet meditative atmosphere of a really good wine shop – the cool, even slightly musty air, the calming lighting, the stillness. It slows the pulse rate and gives you the space and time to browse, choose with care and touch and dream about bottles you may never be able to afford. These are all signs of a shop that stores the wine in appropriate conditions and has knowledgeable staff. You may pay a bit more for your wine here, but this is where to come when you need inspiration.

Most shops offer a discount on a 12 bottle case, and this is the minimum quantity you can buy from many internet and mail order merchants. You don't have to buy a whole case of the same wine: you can usually order a selection of bottles (called a mixed case).

This is the kind of wine shop I enjoy – it's well stocked and laid out and the lighting is not too strong.

A good supermarket display with clear signs and a wide range of wines on offer.

A good wine shop doesn't have to have been established for hundreds of years. Many corner shops have some good wines, and the best of the franchise operations try to encourage the operators to stock decent stuff. Many of the best independent merchants have actually been established for less than a generation and many operate out of an industrial estate. Wine warehouses may not look very sophisticated – they're not trying to – but they usually offer very good ranges of wines, as do the larger branches of the supermarkets. And if you're getting the wine bug, wine brokers offer keen, up-to-the-minute prices, but usually only on top-end stuff and for orders of at least a case or to a minimum value. They advertise in wine magazines and online wine sites.

Getting good service

If you want to know about any of the wines in a shop, ask. Enthusiastic and knowledgeable staff are usually bursting to tell you about their wines. If none of the staff knows anything about the wines, or you get the impression that they are blustering, it's probable that they don't handle the wines too carefully either. Shop elsewhere.

WINE TERMS **En primeur**

En primeur is a French term for wine that is sold before it is bottled, sometimes referred to as a 'future'. If you're interested in *en primeur* offers – that is, investing in wine that is still at the winery or château and not yet bottled – make sure you go to a merchant with a good track record in handling such transactions and with a solid trading base in other wines. In tough times, some always go bust.

However well a merchant does handle the wines, it's impossible to guarantee that every bottle is faultfree. Most shops will happily exchange the wine for a replacement bottle if you suspect a fault after opening the wine.

It's worth buying regularly from one merchant. Let them know which wines you liked and which you weren't so keen on. The more a merchant knows about your preferences, the better he or she will be able to guide you.

Getting information

Wines are reviewed on TV, on the radio, in newspapers and magazines and on dedicated wine websites, but sharing your experiences with friends is one of the best ways of gathering recommendations. Some shops have informative cards on the shelves and many wines have detailed descriptions on the back label.

All wine merchants publish lists of the wines they stock. The simplest name the wines and their prices, and give details of the merchant's terms of business. More ambitious lists review all the wines (sometimes with the whiff of marketing hype) and may include details about the merchant's pet wine regions and winemakers.

Most merchants hold regular wine-tastings. Some are formal occasions, others simply a matter of opening a few bottles for customers to sample during shop hours. Surprisingly few merchants will pressure you to buy any of the wines being tasted.

Auction houses

A wine sale catalogue from a top auction house will have wine enthusiasts drooling over wine names they certainly don't see in their local wine shop every day. Better still, the lots are often of mature vintages that are difficult to buy elsewhere. Top auction houses today make a considerable effort to check the provenance of their wines. If you've never bought wine at an auction before, a good place to start is at a local auctioneer rather than at the famous international houses of Sotheby's, Christie's or Acker Merrall & Condit who hold regular auctions in London, New York and Hong Kong. Online wine auctions are also popular, too, and have similar pros and cons to live auctions.

OZ'S TIPS

Buying direct from the producer

Some châteaux and wineries are only too happy to sell wine from the cellar door or by mail order. For some, it's the only way they sell it. If you're visiting, call first to check opening times and if necessary to make an appointment. But beware: even in this age of online shopping you can still run up against archaic trade barriers. Wherever you live you'll generally have to pay a customs duty on wine shipped to you from abroad. And in some US states it is actually illegal for consumers to buy wine direct from outside the state.

IDEAS FOR WINE TOURING

Two general websites to get you started

- www.winetravelguides.com
- www.travelenvoy.com/wine.htm

Country by country websites

Most of the sites below have links to regional organizations with more ideas for wine routes, wineries to visit, seasonal events and so on.

Europe
- www.englishwineproducers.com
- www.vins-bordeaux.fr
- www.bourgogne-wines.com
- www.champagne.fr
- www.italianwinetours.com
- www.winesfromspain.com
- www.viniportugal.pt
- www.germanwine.de/english.html

North and South America
- www.appellationamerica.com
- www.wineinstitute.org
- www.newyorkwines.org
- www.washingtonwine.org
- www.oregonwine.org
- www.winesofchile.org
- www.winesofargentina.com.ar
- www.winesfrombrazil.com.br

Rest of the world
- www.wineaustralia.com
- www.visitvineyards.com
- www.newzealand.com/travel and www.nzwine.com
- www.wosa.co.za
- www.platterwineguide.com

Wine touring

Many of the world's most stunning vineyard areas make great holiday destinations, too, and I can think of few greater pleasures for wine lovers than tasting wine in the place it's made. Specialist wine tours are a fantastic way to learn about wine in a way you'll never forget, and it's all done for you – visits planned, experts to show you around, translators on hand – but independent travellers can have just as much fun, too.

In France, Alsace, Burgundy and the Loire Valley are perhaps the most delightful regions for the wine lover, but wherever vines are grown in France you're likely to see signs by the road saying *dégustation et vente* (tasting and sales) or *vente directe* (direct sales). In Bordeaux, by all means visit the famous châteaux – you'll need to make an appointment and the top ones won't let you in, anyway. They don't always let *me* in – who could blame them? But the less famous ones will welcome you. In Champagne most of the big houses in Epernay and Reims offer guided tours.

Cantinas (wine cellars) can be found all over Italy, but Piedmont, Tuscany and the Veneto are the regions that have been at it the longest, and are most geared up for tourists. In Spain you'll find *bodegas* set up to welcome tourists in three main regions: Rioja, Penedès, inland from Barcelona and famous for Cava fizz, and the town of Jerez in Andalucía with its sherry bodegas.

Wine tourists in South Africa, Australia, New Zealand and many US states, in particular California, are well catered for by friendly people, and many wineries offer fine dining experiences, too.

Storing wine

Very few of us have a big, dark, cool cellar under our house where we can lay down wines to mature for years on end. Just as well then, that plenty of modern wines aren't designed to benefit from extended aging anyway. It's still worth keeping a few bottles in a rack to save running down to the shop all the time. Store the wine you buy out of direct sunlight and away from major heat sources and it will be happy for a few months.

However, a fiercely tannic red will only reveal its sweeter nature after several years, and many high-quality white wines develop with time. If you just keep them standing about the house for years on end, the light, warmth and dry air will conspire to ruin the wine.

You need somewhere fairly cool and humid that isn't subject to fluctuations in temperature, darkness (draping a blanket over the bottles will also help keep their temperature fairly even) and lack of vibration. And lie the wine on its side to keep the cork damp and swollen, which preserves the airtight seal. An understairs cupboard is a good storage place. For perfect storage conditions you could buy a temperature- and humidity-controlled cabinet or even have a cellar installed under your house, but both options are expensive.

For more expensive purchases, you can pay your wine merchant to store the wines. Make sure that you receive a stock certificate and that your cases are clearly identified and stored separately from the merchant's own stock.

Simple racking systems like this one are not expensive and are easy to install. I spend far too much time drooling over the bottles on my racks.

Finding out about vintages

Some of the world's most sought-after wines come from places where the grapes are poised on a knife-edge of ripening or failing every year. These are the regions where vintages really matter, because the wines can be so different from one year to the next. In regions with a more reliable climate, the vintage year on the bottle is really no more than an indication of the wine's age.

You'll find vintage charts, giving a mark out of ten to each vintage in the world's main wine regions, in many places – you may even have one in your diary. How closely should you follow them?

The answer is that such general information can only ever be a rough guide. Weather conditions are not necessarily the same for a whole region, and in any case a good producer will make better wine in a poor year than a lazy one will make in a good year. So consult vintage charts for general advice – but don't treat them as gospel.

Age and maturity

As wine lies in its bottle, it evolves. Tannins soften, acid mellows, red wines grow paler and develop sediment, whites darken to a rich, nutty amber. Wines with plenty of acid and tannin will become more approachable and less fierce-tasting with time, and if they have the vital extra ingredient – loads of intense fruit flavour – the true quality of the wine will be revealed only after a few years' aging in the bottle.

But older wine is not always better wine. For most wine the best vintage is the most recent one. Everyday wines simply taste more and more stale, faded and dull as the aging process goes on.

understanding wine labels

A wine label is not just the attractive final touch to the bottle or an advertisement for the producer's sense of style, it is a guide to the contents of the bottle and should give you a pretty good idea of the style and flavour of the wine inside. However, there are certain legal requirements that vary from country to country, which I will cover briefly in the following pages.

You can see for yourself whether the wine is white, red or rosé. Next I would want to know which grapes the wine is made from, where they were grown, who made the wine and when. With this information, you'll be in a position to know what you're getting.

It seems simple enough to offer this passport-style information, and many wine labels lay it all out with commendable clarity. Others can seem seriously obscure, though really it's only a question of understanding a little more about how the world of wine works.

What will it taste like?

The simplest labels to understand are those that state the grape variety. Most labels of New World wines do this, although there's also a fashion for naming top-class wines after a bin number or a vat number or the vineyard or the proprietor's daughter. But in such cases the back label often gives the game away and tells you the grapes used. The grape variety is the biggest clue the label gives to the taste of the wine. The next biggest is the place. If you've read as far as this you'll know that Sauvignon Blanc from New Zealand has a particular style and flavour; when you see a bottle you know more or less what to expect.

In the case of European wines, the grape varieties are not often stated. However, they tend to be defined by the rules that apply in the region that the wine is named after. That's why I've put together the Appellation Decoder on pages 186–188 to link classic wines with their grape varieties. Because what you need to be able to do, when looking at a wine label, is put it in context.

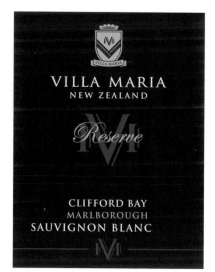

This is a typical New World label where the name of the producer, here Villa Maria, and the grape variety, here Sauvignon Blanc, are more important than that of the region (Marlborough) and wine name (Clifford Bay).

I mentioned the term terroir on page 52. Terroir is the basis of the French appellation system. In the French view, terroir is what makes each vineyard different from its neighbour. So it makes sense to take an area that shares more or less the same terroir and give it one name (or appellation), then take another area with basically a slightly different terroir, and give it another name. Even if the grapes are the same, the style of the wine should be different. Five appellations in the northern Rhône Valley, and not very far removed from each other, produce red wines based on the Syrah grape but each (in theory) has its own unique character.

Which producer?

The producer is the company or person that makes the wine. They have control over the choice of grapes and who makes the wine and how, and so are responsible for the quality of the wine. High quality doesn't necessarily mean a high price: one thing that marks out a good producer is how much better the wines are than poorly made or unexciting ones of a similar price. A poor producer can follow all the rules and come up with poor wine; a good producer will make creditable wine in almost any circumstances.

There are thousands and thousands of wine producers in the world and you can't hope to know all of them, or even all the good ones, even in one country. If you know nothing about the producer of the wine then buying it is a risk. It's a matter of taking advice and experimenting to find producers whose wines you like. You'll find some of my recommendations in the The World of Wine section on pages 106–185.

Easily recognized brand-name wines offer a safe route out of the producer maze. The quality of these wines is generally good these days, although they can be overpriced. But if I buy a brand name, I'm buying a non-specific wine, blended to a happy-medium sort of a taste. It will probably be perfectly nice, and reliably so, but it's unlikely to be exciting.

European appellation systems make it difficult for the less knowledgable wine lover to tell from the label what grape varieties have been used in the wine. Red Rioja is made principally from a blend of Tempranillo and Garnacha (Grenache) grapes, but this classy example, Castillo Ygay, is mainly Tempranillo with a little Mazuelo to bring a hint of acidity and colour to the blend.

For wines from all countries except Germany, you can generally assume that the wine is dry unless otherwise stated. However, the wines from Alsace in France are currently involved in a bit of a rumpus because a lot of them are quite sweet yet don't say so on the label. With global warming, and a general trend towards very ripe flavours – especially in the US – you might think that quite a lot of the wines you taste, for instance, Sauvignon Blanc and Chardonnay, are not quite dry. And you'd be right.

FRANCE

Sec is dry; **demi-sec** off-dry; **doux** or **moelleux** sweet; and **liquoreux** very sweet. Be aware that wines from appellations that apply specifically to sweet wines, such as Sauternes, make no mention on the label of the fact that the wine is sweet.

ITALY

Dry is **secco**, medium-dry is **semisecco**. Medium-sweet is **abboccato** or **amabile**. Sweet wines are **dolce**.

SPAIN

The terms are **seco** (dry), **semi-seco** (medium) and **dulce** (sweet).

GERMANY

Wines here tend to be at least slightly sweet unless otherwise stated. The terms **Kabinett**, **Spätlese**, **Auslese**, **Beerenauslese**, **Trockenbeerenauslese** and **Eiswein** refer to ascending levels of sweetness. **Trocken** is dry while **Halbtrocken** off-dry.

AUSTRIA

Dry wines are more common here than in Germany, but with a warmer climate, they are also a little fuller and riper. Austrian sweet styles are, in ascending order of sweetness: **Spätlese**, **Auslese**, **Beerenauslese**, **Ausbruch**, **Trockenbeerenauslese** and **Eiswein**.

Classifications on the label

The most pressing question, the one that none of the information on the label will answer directly, is whether the wine is good, bad or indifferent. And, try as they might, official classification systems don't help much with indicating the quality of the wine.

The most basic way of classifying wine is by the place of origin. Outside Europe most countries are settling for something like the US AVA (American Viticultural Area) system. Each area is supposed to be homogeneous in some way – climate, for example – but in practice many AVAs have boundaries that simply follow county lines. This sort of system guarantees the geographical origin of the wine, but carries no quality connotations.

All the European systems are based to some extent on the concept of terroir (see page 52). To ensure that the intrinsic character of each region's wine is maintained, it is deemed necessary to regulate most aspects of wine production.

The most strictly regulated wines in France (and each European country has an equivalent classification – see the box on page 76) are Appellation Contrôlée wines. The words Appellation Contrôlée on a label are not, however, a guarantee of quality – instead they guarantee that the wine is from the region, hopefully possesses the character of the region (using the correct grape varieties and vineyard and winemaking practices), and has been made in accordance with the rules of that region. This is why you can't grow any old grape varieties in Bordeaux and then claim the Bordeaux appellation. Rules for vins de pays wines are far more relaxed; and vins de table can be pretty much anything that won't kill you.

Interestingly, it is at the top end that fraud is of the most concern. As the price of top wines has spiralled upwards, and as they are sold more and more to new markets like China and Russia that don't have a long experience of how the labels, corks and capsules should look and how the wines should taste, fraudulent bottles have become surprisingly common. Top producers are now employing various techniques in labelling, capsuling and corking their top bottles that guarantee authenticity and help to trace any fraudsters.

see page 52 ... see the box on page 76

OZ'S TIPS
Imposters!

Rules about how wines may be described on labels are tighter than ever. It's true that sparkling wines from America, North and South, can call themselves 'Champagne' as long as they're not shipped to Europe, but there has been progress. Australia has virtually phased out the misleading use of classic European wine names – Chablis, Sauternes and so on – for its own wines.

What we have to look out for now is wines from unfashionable areas being repackaged to look like wines from fashionable ones. It's quite simple and quite legal: you take your Eastern European white and red, give them a brand name like Kangaroo Creek and leave the details of where they were made for the small print.

No, it's not a capital offence. And as long as the wine tastes as modern as the packaging, I can't entirely condemn it. But it's a shame that they think we'll only buy their wine if it looks like something else. Especially when experience shows we'll buy anything, if it's good enough.

WINE CLASSIFICATIONS: EUROPE

The French appellation system is the most widely known system of quality control. Other European countries have roughly equivalent gradings, though some have more categories. Quality within any of the bands is not consistent and a good example of a simple wine will be better than a poorly made wine that has complied with the rules to achieve a higher status.

	FRANCE	ITALY	PORTUGAL	SPAIN	GERMANY	AUSTRIA
Special-quality wine	No category	Denominazione di Origine Controllata e Garantita (**DOCG**)	No category	Denominación de Origen Calificada (**DOCa**)	Qualitätswein mit Prädikat (**QmP**), but since 2007 called Prädikatswein – divided into 6 styles	Qualitätswein – divided into 6 styles
Quality wine	Appellation d'Origine Contrôlée (**AC/ AOC**) or the lower Vin Délimité de Qualité Supérieure (**VDQS**) – but the latter is being phased out after 2010.	Denominazione di Origine Controllata (**DOC**)	Denominação de Origem Controlada (**DOC**) or the lower Indicação de Proviniência Regulamentada (**IPR**)	Denominación de Origen (**DO**) Vino de Pago is a new category for single-estate wine	Qualitätswein bestimmter Anbaugebiete (**QbA**)	DAC is a new regional appellation for wines of a particular style from a particular region
Regional wine	Vin de pays	Indicazione Geografica Tipica (**IGT**)	Vinho regional	Vino de la tierra or vino comarcal	Landwein	Landwein
Basic wine	Vin de table	Vino da tavola *System currently being overhauled to reduce the 500-plus DOCGs, DOCs and IGTs to 180 or so DOPs (Denominazione de Origine Protetta) and IGPs (Indicazione Geografica Protetta)*	Vinho de mesa	Vino de mesa	Deutscher Tafelwein	Tafelwein

What the label tells you

The majority of modern wines will tell you what grape was used to make the wine, and what country the grapes were grown in. These are the two most important indicators as to the style of the wine. The producer's name is also crucially important as in any walk of life, some are better than others. You should also find the year the grapes were harvested – the vintage. After that, here is a list of things you may find: the region and the country the wine comes from; the wine's classification, if it has one; the alcohol level, increasingly important in our health-conscious age; and where the wine was bottled – ideally by the producer, next best is in the region of production, and least good is in a country thousands of miles away from where the grapes were grown. However, with worries about carbon footprint, the quality of wines shipped in bulk is sure to improve.

A good label should give you lots of clues about the wine, but beware of florid marketing hype on the back label.

OZ'S TIPS

Five things to look for on the label

1 **Estate bottled** This should mean that the grapes have been grown, made into wine and bottled in one place, which should in turn mean that the wine has been made with pride and has individuality – in an ideal world, that is. On French labels the equivalent terms are *mis en bouteille au château/domaine/à la propriété*. Australia has a tradition of making high-quality blends of wines from different estates and regions, so the term is less significant there.

2 **Cru** A French wine term used to indicate a village or vineyard of high quality, particularly in the regions of Bordeaux, Burgundy, Champagne and Alsace.

3 **Traditional method** Sparkling wine made the same way as Champagne. *Méthode traditionelle* in French.

4 **Old vines** The grapes that grow on old vines tend to have more concentrated juice and so make more densely flavoured wines than those from youngsters. The French phrase is *vieilles vignes*.

5 **The vintage** No, I'm not suggesting that you become a vintage bore. But at the very least, knowing how old the wine is will give you an idea of whether it will taste young or mature.

Five things to be wary of on a label

1 Reserve In some countries (notably Spain and Italy) reserve wines are matured in oak for longer than the standard wines and a full set of rules is in force. Elsewhere the term might be used to indicate this style of wine, but then again it might just mean nothing at all.

2 Supérieur Surely a superior wine is better? Sorry, wrong. This French term and its Italian equivalent **superiore** indicate only that the wine has a slightly higher alcohol content than the ordinary wine of the same name.

3 Grand Vin In Bordeaux, Grand Vin indicates that it is the main wine of the property, as opposed to a second wine. It does not mean 'great wine'.

4 South-Eastern Australia No, there's nothing wrong with this – just bear in mind that South-Eastern Australia includes the vast majority of Australia's wine-producing areas – just about everything except Western Australia. So while the name of the wine might imply a particular place and the label might imply a specific appellation, it's not as specific as all that. Far from it. It's like saying 'this wine could come from anywhere in France except Champagne and Alsace'.

5 Anything that claims to be special – exceptional, classic, a limited release, from the founder's bin... Just ignore these terms and stick to the basics of who, what, when and where in deducing the likely quality of the wine.

European wine labels

The front label varies with the type of wine and from country to country but it should tell you all the necessary information about the wine. The two European wine labels here show two very different approaches.

PLANETA a modern, dynamic producer from Sicily

1 Name of the producer this modern label from a go-getting company is more reminiscent of labels from outside Europe, especially from California and Australia. The producer name is the most important element on the label.

2 Name of the wine 'Burdese' gives the consumer no clue as to the style of wine inside. I would hope the back label explains more!

CHÂTEAU LAFON-ROCHET a traditional Bordeaux producer

1 Classification This tells you that the wine was included in the famous 1855 Classification of the red wines of Bordeaux.

2 Traditional imagery The vast majority of Bordeaux labels still feature a straightforward illustration of the château building. Any that do not are probably making a statement about their modern approach.

3 Château name Any wine estate in France, especially in Bordeaux, can take a château name, regardless of whether it has a grand building. Castello is the equivalent word in Italy, Castillo in Spain and Schloss in Germany.

4 Appellation European wine regulations expect the appellation name to tell you all you need to know about the taste of the wine, its quality classification and place of origin. St-Estèphe in Bordeaux is best known for its slow-maturing, tannic red wines based on Cabernet Sauvignon.

5 Vintage The year the grapes were harvested. In most parts of the world the year's weather influences the style of wine, its ripeness, alcohol level and longevity. It's also important to check the vintage to see whether the wine is ready to drink.

6 Château bottling Once rare, this is now the norm in Bordeaux, and means that the wine was bottled on the estate. Anything not bottled at the château or 'à la propriété' is most likely an undistinguished offering from a large merchant or co-operative.

7 Meaningless statements 'Grand vin de Bordeaux' sounds good but in fact says nothing about the quality of the wine. 'Grand Vin' on its own on a Bordeaux label indicates that the wine is the château's main wine, rather than one of its lesser ones, but again says nothing about its quality.

8 Alcohol level the regulations for each appellation specify the required minimum alcohol level.

9 The quantity of wine in the bottle 75cl is the standard bottle size for wine.

German wine labels

For some time now German producers have been moving away from traditional Gothic script on their wine labels to a design that is more user friendly, especially to consumers outside Germany. Optional information is moved to the back label.

LOOSEN

1 Name of the producer Dr Loosen is a top German producer making exciting wines.

2 Vintage This style of wine is best drunk young so the year of vintage is clear to read.

3 Grape variety The grape variety is the most prominent name on the label. Riesling is Germany's best white grape.

LANGWERTH VON SIMMERN

This beautiful label is an example of the more traditional style of German label. But all this information still gives the less knowledgable consumer little indication of the style of wine inside the bottle.

1 Name of the producer Freiherr Langwerth von Simmern based in the village of Eltville.

2 Gutsabfüllung means 'bottled by'.

3 Village and vineyard site The vineyard name usually follows the name of the village. Marcobrunn is a famous Riesling vineyard in the village of Erbach in the Rheingau.

4 Auslese indicates the level of sweetness. Auslese wines are usually fairly sweet.

5 Grape variety The name Riesling is in small letters and is not seen to be a selling point.

GERMAN WINE STYLES

Prädikat (the top overall classification) comes in six styles or grades, defined by the ripeness of the grapes used.

Kabinett The lightest Prädikat wine. It will be slightly sweet unless labelled as **Halbtrocken** (off-dry) or **Trocken** (dry).

Spätlese ('late-picked') Many are sweetish, though Halbtrocken and Trocken versions are also common.

Auslese ('selected') Wine made from selected bunches of very ripe grapes. Most are fairly sweet but some are dry.

Beerenauslese ('selected berries') Luscious sweet wine made from selected single grapes, almost always affected by the noble rot fungus.

Trockenbeerenauslese ('shrivelled selected berries') Intensely sweet wines made from individually picked grapes shrivelled by noble rot.

Eiswein ('ice wine') Made from frozen grapes picked in winter.

Other wine labels

Labels from wine regions outside Europe are usually clearly laid out and easy to understand.

HOWARD PARK

1 Name of the producer Wines produced outside the traditional appellation areas of Europe often promote the producer name over that of any region.

2 A simple graphic image is commonly used for wine labels in the same way as a European coat of arms.

3 Wine name The name doesn't give the consumer a clue as to the style of wine inside the bottle, but I know that Abercrombie is Howard Park's flagship wine.

4 Grape variety Cabernet Sauvignon is a key selling point on this label, and is one of Western Australia's success stories.

5 Region Western Australia is a key wine state in Australia.

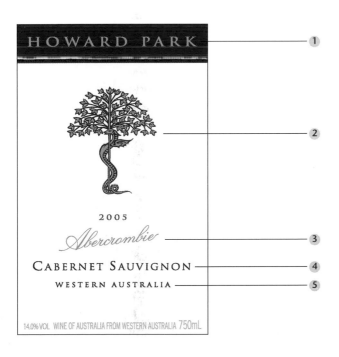

Back labels

Buying wine would be far easier if the label told you how the wine tasted; some back labels do. Many retailers also have helpful systems for grading each of the wines they sell on a scale from bone dry to very sweet for whites, and from light to full-bodied for reds. Back labels can tell you how oaky the wine is and which grape varieties were used to make it. Or they can tell you whether the wine is suitable for aging and what foods will go well with it. But they can also be complete waffle and marketing gobbledegook.

It's up to you to make the distinction between useful information and the interventions of an enthusiastic marketing department. Treat back-label information as a general guide to the wine and don't let yourself be drawn in by florid accounts of the winemaking.

REGULATIONS OUTSIDE EUROPE

In the US, South America, Australia, New Zealand and South Africa, regulations govern statements about the place of origin of the wine and the grape varieties used. They help to ensure that the labelling is honest, but don't generally tell you anything about quality.

The US uses the AVA (American Viticultural Area) system which merely requires that at least 85% of grapes in a wine come from the specified AVA. Canada has a quality-based system; look for the letters VQA on the label. In Australia the Label Integrity Program (LIP) guarantees all claims made on the label and the GI (Geographical Indication) system is being rolled out across the country. In New Zealand labels guarantee geographic origin and in South Africa the Wine of Origin (WO) system specifies regions, districts and further subdivisions.

opening the bottle

The gentle creak, squeak and pop of a cork being pulled – that's a sound I like a lot. It's the overture to a celebration, the moment when work stops and the evening begins. Even the most hopeless corkscrew will work most of the time, but a well-made one is less likely to wreck the cork or leave cork crumbs floating in your wine.

BOXES, CARTONS AND CANS

Wine boxes with a tap on the side are a perfectly sound idea, especially if you just want a glass or two per day. The technology is fine; the problem is that the choice is limited and the wine in the box is rarely exciting.

Cartons like the ones used to store milk are effective, but they're awkward to open and, again, the wine put into them is nothing to write home about. As for **ring-pull cans**, don't even think about it – yet. But for a party or a picnic drink, the idea is fine – it just needs more serious technology applied.

Don't be a cork snob – bottles come with all sorts of seals nowadays. But I do still love a good, old-fashioned real cork.

Choosing a corkscrew

Look for a corkscrew with a comfortable handle, an open spiral and a lever system that you like using. Corkscrews with a solid core that looks like a giant screw tend to mash up delicate corks or get stuck in tough ones. With a simple T-shaped corkscrew the effort of pulling the cork can turn into a circus-strongman act, but it does bring a certain sigh of satisfaction when – if – you remove the cork without giving yourself a hernia.

Using a corkscrew

First tear off or cut away the metal foil or plastic seal around the top of the bottle, known as the capsule. You can buy a device called a foil cutter for this job; some corkscrews include one in the handle. Wipe the lip of the bottle if there is dirt or mould around the top of the cork.

Press the point of the corkscrew gently into the centre of the cork. Turn the corkscrew slowly and steadily and try to drive it in dead straight. If it veers wildly off-course at the first attempt, it is better to unwind it and start again than to press on and risk breaking the cork. Some corkscrews remove the cork by driving straight through it, but for others, stop turning as the point emerges at the bottom of the cork and then ease the cork out gently.

The standard restaurant corkscrew is called a **waiter's friend**. It has a lever at the top to help ease out the cork and folds away neatly. I find it the simplest, most compact opener – I never go anywhere without one.

The **Screwpull** brand is a very simple design, which has never been bettered. It relies on the high quality open spiral for its effectiveness. This long-handled version gives you extra leverage and makes light work of even the stiffest corks, although the foil-cutting knife is a bit tricky to use.

The most irritating design is the ubiquitous **'butterfly'** – not only does it feature the sort of thick, solid-cored screw that mashes up corks, but I always find it impossible to remove the cork in one sweep of the lever arms.

OZ'S TIPS

Don't be a cork snob

The only requirements for the seal on a bottle of wine are that it should be hygienic, airtight, long-lasting and removable. Cork has been successsfully employed since Roman times at least, and I do love the ritual of extracting a cork from a good bottle, but cork is simply the bark from the cork oak tree and as such is prone to inconsistency, infection and shrinkage. Modern alternatives lack cork's cachet and mystique, but they will give you fresher wine on a regular basis.

Screwtops are seriously challenging cork for supremacy. They are consistent and inert, so the wine is reliable every time. They don't let oxygen in so the wine stays fresher longer and, in fact, wines age more slowly under screwcap. Their only major drawback is that the wine can develop a sulphide-y off-odour, but this is due to lack of oxygen and can easily be addressed by the winemaker.

Plastic corks are OK for early-drinking wines, but noone is convinced of their ability to age.

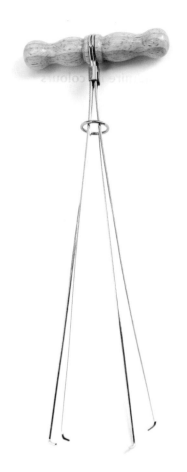

Opening sparkling wine

The pressure in the bottle does the work, so all you have to do is control it. If you don't, you'll get a loud pop, a rush of foam and a half-empty bottle of rapidly flattening fizz. You might injure somebody, too.

Tear off the foil to reveal the wire cage that restrains the cork. Place one thumb over the top of the cork and undo the cage. From the moment the cage is released there is an ever-present danger of the cork shooting off, so point the bottle away from people, windows and other breakables.

Some people say you have to turn the bottle, not the cork. Well, I say grasp the cork with one hand and hold the bottle firmly with the other. Then either turn the cork, or the bottle, whichever grabs you, but the most important thing is, keep a thumb or a hand over that cork to stop it flying out and removing someone's eye. If you keep a lot of downward pressure on the cork you should be able to ease it out gently – and you may even experience that ol' timers' delight, the cork slipping out with a sigh like a contented woman. Hold the bottle at an angle of 45° for a few moments to calm the initial rush of foam, then pour the first glass.

Always make sure the bottle is thoroughly chilled before you attempt to open it. A warm bottle is quite likely to explode its cork in dramatic fashion, however hard you try to restrain it.

If you've very lucky, you might own this device called a butler's friend which is brilliant at fishing out pieces of broken cork.

Broken corks

To remove a broken cork that is still wedged into the bottle neck, drive the corkscrew in at the sharpest available angle and press the cork fragment against the side of the neck as you work it gently upwards. If you're having no luck, push the cork down into the wine. You might get bits of cork in your glass, but the wine will taste none the worse for it – just fish them out.

If a sparkling wine cork breaks in the bottle, then your only option is to resort to a corkscrew. But take the cork out very cautiously – remember, there's still all that pressurized gas in the bottle.

serving wine

If you want to taste wine at its best, to enjoy all its flavours and aromas, to admire its colours and texture, choose glasses designed for the purpose and show the wine a bit of respect.

Glasses

The ideal wine glass is a fairly large tulip shape, made of fine, clear glass, with a slender stem. Anything that approximates to this description will do. When you pour the wine, fill the glass no more than halfway so that you can swirl the wine around and allow the aromas to develop. For sparkling wines choose a tall, slender glass, as it helps the bubbles to last longer.

Coloured glass obscures the colour of the wine, flared glasses dissipate the aromas rather than concentrating them, and heavy, thick glasses are, well, heavy and thick.

Detergent residues or grease in the glass can affect the flavour of any wine and reduce the bubbliness of sparkling wine. Always rinse glasses thoroughly after washing them and allow them to air-dry or keep a lint-free cloth for drying glasses only – Ulster and Chinese linen are traditional choices. Ideally wash the glasses in really hot water and use no detergent at all. Store your wine glasses upright to avoid trapping stale odours.

Decanting

There are three reasons for putting wine in a decanter: one, to separate it from sediment that has formed in the bottle; two, to let the wine breathe; three, to make it look nice. You don't need a special decanter, a jug is just as good. Equally, there's no reason why you shouldn't decant the wine to aerate it and then pour it back into the bottle again for serving.

A bottle of mature red wine that contains sediment needs careful handling. Stand it upright for a day or two before you want to serve it, to let the sediment settle to the bottom. You can serve the wine

Careful decanting is only necessary when the wine contains sediment. Stop pouring when the dark grains or sludge reach the neck of the bottle.

straight from the bottle if you pour it carefully, but it's safer to decant it. Place a torch or a candle beside the decanter and, as you pour the wine, place yourself so that you can see the light shining through the neck of the bottle. Keep pouring in one steady motion and stop when you see the sediment rushing into the neck.

Breathing

Most wines do not need to be opened early in order to let the wine breathe. A few fine red wines – top-class red Bordeaux, top Italian reds, top Syrah/Shiraz and a few others – can benefit from it, but almost all inexpensive ones, and all white wines, can simply be opened and drunk. There are no set rules, however, and only experience will tell you if a wine will improve with breathing.

The reason for letting a wine breathe is that contact with oxygen in the air makes the flavours more open. But if you leave the wine for too long before you drink it you may find the flavours going flat and dull from excessive oxidation. If you're the sort of person who plans ahead, open your reds an hour or so before you intend to drink them. That way they won't suffer from oxidation, and they may even improve. And always beware of opening even top wines too early. Very old examples can lose all their flavour if they are exposed to the air for too long.

SERVING TEMPERATURES

Wine should be warm enough to be flavoursome and cool enough to be refreshing. High-quality whites taste good at higher temperatures than lesser whites of the same style. It is better to serve a wine too cool and warm it in your hands than to serve it too hot, when the flavours fall apart.

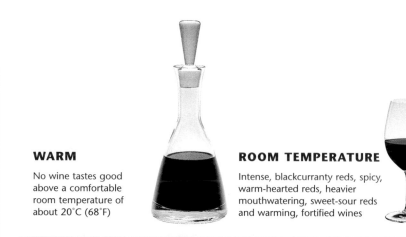

WARM

No wine tastes good above a comfortable room temperature of about 20°C (68°F)

ROOM TEMPERATURE

Intense, blackcurranty reds, spicy, warm-hearted reds, heavier mouthwatering, sweet-sour reds and warming, fortified wines

| over 20°C | 15° to 20°C |

Simply uncorking the bottle and leaving it to stand will have little or no effect, as only a small surface area is exposed. Pouring off a small amount will help, but decanting will expose the wine to far more air. For instant results with a wine that has been uncorked just this minute, a quick swirl of your glass will work wonders. Interestingly, many screwcap wines taste better on the second glass because they've been bottled with virtually no oxygen, and they need a few minutes to wake up. If a wine has a rather sweaty, meaty smell – the expert term is 'reduced' – put a copper coin in the glass and swirl it round. The wine will taste as fresh as a daisy in a minute or two.

Leftovers

You can keep leftover wine for several days without it losing much of its flavour. All you need to do is hold off the effects of oxidation. The simplest way is to push the cork back in and stick the bottle in the fridge. Alternatively, you can buy reasonably effective devices which suck out the air or which inject a dense inert gas.

Special stoppers are available for recorking sparkling wine, but a conventional cork does the job well enough. Either way, keep the wine well chilled.

If you have two leftover bottles of the same wine, pour the contents of both into one. The fuller the bottle the longer the wine will last. White wines last better than reds.

COOL ROOM TEMPERATURE	COOL	COLD	CHILLED	WELL CHILLED
Silky, strawberryish reds	Juicy, fruity reds, light mouthwatering, sweet-sour reds, tangy fortified wines and golden sweet wines	Intense, nutty whites, ripe, toasty whites and aromatic whites	Green, tangy whites, sparkling wines, delicate rosés and the lightest tangy fortifieds	Bone-dry neutral whites and cheap sparkling wines
13° to 15°C	11° to 13°C	8° to 11°C	6° to 8°C	4° to 6°C

how to taste wine

At last. You must have thought we were never going to reach the business end of things – opening your mouth and taking a deep draught of delicious wine. That's if it is delicious. You're the only one who can say – it's your palate. But as you try more and more wines, your awareness of flavour and your personal preferences will develop. And the good thing is that you'll be able to apply this knowledge when choosing wine in a wine shop or restaurant.

But what's so special about wine that you have to go through a whole ritual just to say what it tastes like? Well, wine doesn't just taste of wine. Any number of aromas and flavours mingle together in the glass – we're talking dozens, sometimes hundreds – and if you just knock it back the same way you do a cold beer or a soft drink, you could be missing most of whatever flavour the wine has to offer.

Giving wine a bit of thought while you're drinking it is by far the best method for finding your way around the grapes, regions and styles of the wine world. THINK WHILE YOU DRINK. It's more fun than studying and one delicious sip will stay in your memory far longer than any book. In fact, you'll enjoy this book much more if you've got a glass by your elbow – and my words will probably make more sense, too. If you get really interested in wine, you can join wine-tasting groups but let's start with you, and ideally a friend or two getting used to thinking while you drink, but above all, enjoying it. You'll soon work out what you like and knowing what you like should give you the confidence to try more and more styles.

Look at the wine

Pour the wine into a wine glass so that it is about a third full. A big tulip-shaped glass that is broad near the base and narrower at the top will help to concentrate the aromas of the wine. Tilt the glass against a white background so you can enjoy the range of colours in the wine from the centre to the rim. But don't spend too long on this: you're wasting good drinking time.

Smell the wine

Give the wine a vigorous swirl in the glass to release the locked-in aromas. Stick your nose right into the glass and inhale steadily and gently, as if you were smelling a flower.

These initial split seconds of inhalation will reveal all kinds of familiar and unfamiliar smells. Always interpret them in terms that mean something to you. If the smell reminds you of honey, or chocolate, or apples, or raspberries, then those descriptions are sure to be right for you. Remember, it's your nose that counts here. It doesn't matter if someone else interprets the smells differently – that's their nose – and anyway, it's all part of the pleasure of wine. It's only by reacting honestly to the taste and smell of a wine that you can build up a memory bank of flavours against which to judge future wines and to help you recognize wines you have already encountered.

At first you may find that you can't put a name to smells you do recognise or that there are too many smells to untangle in your mind, or even that the wine smells of nothing much at all. Your nose tires quickly, so give it a break after a few seconds, then go back to the wine. It's worth jotting down a note of your thoughts before you forget them – a glance at the notes can bring the aromas flooding back weeks later. And if you're with friends, say what you think and listen to what the others say. Everyone's view is valid and useful.

Take a sip

At last! It's time to drink the wine. So take a decent-sized sip – enough to fill your mouth about a third full. Draw a little air through your lips and suck it through the wine to help separate the aromas from the liquid, then start to enjoy all the personality and flavour that the fumes impart.

The tongue can detect only very basic flavour elements: sweetness at the tip, acidity at the sides (saltiness too, but you won't find that in many wines) and bitterness at the back. The real business of tasting anything, not just wine, goes on in your nasal cavity. So hold the wine in your mouth, and consciously breathe out through your nose. The nasal cavity has millions of receptors searching for every scent and flavour known to man and ready to transmit the aroma straight to your brain. If you're not sure about this nasal business – hold your nose and take a mouthful of wine. Can you taste anything? No. Then release your nose, breathe out through it – and your mouth will fill with flavour. All the flavours that give us so much pleasure in our daily eating and drinking are carried from our mouth to our brain by aromas we breathe up into our nasal cavity.

Evaluate the wine

Ideally make a few notes: jot down first impressions, then record the taste that develops after the wine has been in your mouth for a few moments. First note any sweetness, acidity and tannic bitterness that your tongue detects. Some flavours are upfront and unmistakable, others shift subtly, just out of reach. A few words jotted down and the flavour can come flooding back. And if you really want to become a good wine taster, your memory is as important as your palate. And stay relaxed. This is supposed to be fun. The more tense you are, the less likely you are to enjoy the wine – or remember what it tastes like.

Swallow or spit it out

Why do wine tasters spit wine out after they have tasted it? Quite simply, it's the only way to taste a lot of wines and remain sober. I often have to taste and make notes on 100 wines at a time and the spittoon can easily hold the equivalent of two to three bottles of wine – all spat out by me. Winetasters like a drink as much as the next person – but not when we are 'tasting'. We're trying to stay sober and make accurate, useful judgements on all the wines that we can refer to later. If you're visiting a producer's cellar or attending a professional wine-tasting, believe me, spit.

At home, if you've organized a tasting session – well, if noone's driving – you could all just sit around the kitchen table and get happy. But if you want to do it the proper way, you don't need a special spittoon, just use a bucket, preferably placed on some newspaper; if you and your friends aren't practised spitters you could make a right old mess otherwise. And when you've spat – OK, or swallowed – make one final mental or actual note on any lingering aftertaste. And decide whether you liked the wine or not – and why.

THE BUILDING BLOCKS OF WINE

All wines have some basic elements in common:

Acid and sugar are present in the juice of the grape. The sugar is turned into alcohol during fermentation, but some can remain. A lot of leftover sugar makes for a sweet wine. Acid sounds unpleasant and aggressive, but when present in the right proportion it makes the wine intense and refreshing. All wines contain acid, as do all fruits.

Tannin is the stuff in red wines that stains your teeth and dries your mouth, but in the right amounts can do marvellous things to the flavour and texture of the wine. White wines don't have noticeable levels of tannin. Tannin and acid both have the added benefit of acting as preservatives, and wines with high levels of either (or both) have the potential to last for many years in the bottle.

Alcohol isn't just there for the sake of getting you lit up. It balances other flavours, for example softening the attack of the acid, and makes the wine feel richer in your mouth. And without it, you'd just be downing a glass of grape juice.

TASTING BASICS

Nose is the name for the smell of the wine. Alternative terms are **aroma**, usually used of young wines, and **bouquet**, usually used for mature wines. But hey, **smell** will do.

Palate is the taste of the wine in your mouth. Call it **taste** if you prefer.

Sweetness or the lack of it is the first sensation as the wine hits the tip of your tongue. Sweetness always needs to be balanced by acidity or it will be cloying. All but the very driest of wines will have some sensation of sweetness.

Acidity makes wine taste crisp and refreshing. You notice its effect on the sides of your tongue. It must be balanced by sweetness, alcohol or body: if a wine has too little of these, too much acidity will taste unpleasantly tart. A wine with too much sweetness, alcohol or body and too little acidity will taste flabby and flat.

Tannin is the mouth-drying substance found in red wines. It mostly comes from the skin and pips of the grapes. When it is balanced by good fruit flavours it adds enormously to the mouthwatering, savoury character of good red wine. Too much and the wine will taste hard and bitter. Not enough and it can taste as soft and innocuous as fruit juice.

Alcohol is found in all wines, but levels vary from as little as 8% for a light German Riesling to maybe 15% for a rich, ripe Aussie Shiraz – and higher for fortified wines. High alcohol levels make wine feel rounder in your mouth. It is possible by scientific methods to reduce the level of alcohol in wines by a degree or two without ruining the flavour, but too much de-alcoholization leaves a drink that is devoid of alcohol's round, warming texture and usually tastes like a less interesting version of grape juice.

Fruit flavour in wine comes from the grapes, yet wine seldom tastes of grapes. Indeed, most wine grapes don't taste of much until fermentation transforms them. Then the resulting wine can develop hundreds of flavours, but we have to borrow language from elsewhere to describe them. Often we use fruit flavours – plums, strawberries, blackberries, limes and many others. But we also find flavours like nuts, coffee beans, chocolate and fudge, biscuits and bread, herbs and leaves, coal dust and smoke – honestly, the number of flavours in wine goes into hundreds – and they're borrowed from every walk of life.

Weight or **body** describes the different impressions of weight and size wines give in the mouth. This is what is referred to by the terms full-, medium- and light-bodied. Different wine styles will be at their best with different body and weight. And more is *not* always better.

Length is the flavour that persists in your mouth after you've swallowed the wine. A flavour that continues or even improves for some time after the wine is gone is a mark of quality.

Balance is the relationship between all these elements of the wine: sweetness, acidity, tannin, alcohol, fruit and body. An unbalanced wine will taste as though it is lacking something – and it is.

There's more to describing wine than saying it's good or bad. Tasting terms are a way of sharing our perceptions of a wine's qualities; they should never be a secret code for experts. Fruit flavours are direct comparisons, so if I know the fruit, I will recognize the flavour you are talking about. The same goes for honey or nuts. These less obvious terms are useful too.

Aggressive A wine with acid that makes your gums sting or that dries up the back of your throat due to an excess of tannin.

Aromatic All wines have an aroma, but an aromatic wine is particularly pungent or *spicy*, and is usually from an aromatic grape variety like Gewürztraminer.

Astringent A wine in which the mouth-drying effect of tannin is very marked.

Big A full-bodied wine with lots of everything: fruit flavour, acidity, tannin and alcohol.

Bold A wine with distinct, easily understood flavours.

Buttery Oak barrels and malolactic fermentation (see page 55) can both give a buttery taste.

Chewy Wine with a lot of tannin and strong flavour, but which is not *aggressive*.

Clean Wine free of bacterial and chemical faults. Also describes simple, refreshing wines.

Complex A wine that has layer upon layer of flavours.

Crisp A refreshing white wine with good acidity.

Deep Subtle, *rich*; allied to *complex*.

Dry Not at all *sweet*.

Dull A wine with no well-defined, pleasing flavours. Often a sign of too much exposure to oxygen.

Dusty A dry, slightly *earthy* taste sometimes found in reds. Can be very attractive if combined with good fruit.

Earthy A smell and taste of damp earth – appealing in some French reds from the Loire Valley and Bordeaux.

Fat Full-bodied, unctuous.

Firm Well-balanced, well-defined wine; the opposite of *flabby*.

Flabby Lacking in acidity, feeble.

Focused A wine in which all the flavours are well defined.

Fresh Young wine, with lively fruit flavours and good acidity.

Full A wine with a weighty feel in the mouth.

Grassy Commonly used though not strictly accurate term for the green leaf, lime zest or capsicum flavours typical of Sauvignon Blanc.

Green Can mean unripe, in which case it's pejorative. But green leaf flavours are common in cool-climate reds, and greenness in association with flavours such as gooseberries or apples implies the fresh, tangy flavours found in many white wines.

Hard A red with a lot of tannin or a white with too much acid. Uncompromising rather than *aggressive*, but rarely enjoyable.

Jammy Red wine in which the fruit has the boiled, cooked flavours of jam.

Light Low alcohol or little body. Not necessarily a bad thing.

Meaty A heavy red wine with solid, chunky flavours. A few wines actually do taste of grilled meat or bloody beef.

Minerally How you might imagine a lick of flint or chalk to taste. Common in wines from Germany and Austria, and from Chablis and the Loire Valley in France.

Neutral Little distinctive flavour.

Oaky The slightly sweet vanilla flavour in red and white wines that have been fermented and/or aged in new oak barrels. Oak also adds tannin.

Petrolly A surprisingly attractive petrol- or kerosene-like smell that develops in mature wines made from Riesling.

Piercing Usually refers to high acidity. But particularly vibrant fruit flavours can also be piercing.

Powerful A wine with plenty of everything, particularly alcohol.

Prickly Slight fizziness caused by residual carbon dioxide gas, meaning that fermentation is not quite finished. Very refreshing in simple whites but a fault in red wines.

Rich Full, well-flavoured, with plenty of alcohol.

Ripe Wine made from well-ripened grapes has good fruit flavour. Unripe wines can taste *green* and stalky.

Rounded Any wine in which the flavour seems satisfyingly complete, with no unpleasant sharpness.

Soft A wine without harsh tannins or too much acidity, making it an easy-going drink. Often a good thing, but a wine can be too soft.

Spicy Exotic fragrances and flavours common in Gewürztraminer; also the tastes of pepper, cinnamon or clove in reds such as Australian Shiraz. Spiciness can be an effect of oak aging.

Steely Good acidity and a wine that is firm and lean, may be *minerally* but not *thin*.

Stony A dry, chalky-white taste, like *minerally* but without quite the excitement.

Structured 'Plenty of structure' refers to a wine with a well-developed backbone of acidity and tannin, but enough fruit to stand up to it.

Supple Both vigorous and smooth. A description of texture rather than flavour.

Sweet Not only a wine with high levels of sugar, but also the *rich* and *ripe* quality of some of the fruit flavours in many modern dry wines.

Tart A very sharp, acid taste like an unripe apple.

Thin, lean, stringy Terms for high-acid wine lacking in flavour.

Toasty A flavour like buttered toast that results from maturing a wine in oak barrels.

Upfront A wine that wears its heart on its sleeve: expect obvious flavours, not subtle ones, but sometimes that's just what you want.

how to spot a faulty wine

There are fewer poor wines nowadays because winemaking is better understood today than ever before. This is a result of a new generation of winemakers, in particular from Australia and California, who have studied the science of winemaking and then set off to work in vineyards around the globe sharing their knowledge. Even so faulty bottles do crop up. You can spot faults in the same way as you can any wine flavour, by using your senses of sight, smell and taste.

Use your eyes

Whatever its colour, wine should be clear and bright. Cloudy wine usually indicates bacterial spoilage, but it's extremely uncommon these days. Don't confuse cloudiness with shaken-up deposit: an aged red wine that has developed a dark, powdery or gritty deposit just needs to stand upright until the deposit settles again.

The colours of wines vary according to their grape variety and the climate in which they were made. But if a white wine you expect to be pale has a brownish-yellow tinge, or if a young red has a brownish tinge, then beware: it's probably oxidized. Oxidized wine tastes dull and flat.

If wine has seeped past the cork, making the neck of the bottle sticky, then it probably hasn't been very well kept and air might have got in. This, too, can mean oxidized wine.

Use your nose

These smells are all tell-tale signs of trouble:

Sherry-like smells Only sherry should smell of sherry. Such smells on unfortified wines can indicate oxidation.

Vinegary smells If it smells like vinegar, then that is what it is turning into.

Rotten eggs This horrible, horrible smell of hydrogen sulphide can form during fermentation and is a sign of poor winemaking.

Mouldy, musty smells This is 'corked' wine, caused by a contaminated cork. A slight cork taint may just dull the wine but not make it undrinkable

Reduced smells You get this slightly meaty, cheesy smell sometimes, especially on screwcap wines. It's a sort of sulphide usually created by the wine not having enough oxygen, rather than too much. I always carry an old copper coin with me. If the wine is 'reduced', pour yourself a glass, slip in the coin, swirl the wine about and in a minute or two all the sulphidy smells will have disappeared. It's something to do with smelly sulphide reacting with copper to create odourless copper sulphite. I think. And do remember to remove the coin from the glass before drinking the contents.

Use your taste buds

Your palate should normally confirm what your nose has already told you – but sometimes a fault will show more on the nose than on the palate, or vice versa. Use nose and palate in conjunction when judging a wine.

UNSIGHTLY BUT NOT FAULTY

Pieces of cork floating in your wine glass are nothing to do with cork-tainted wine. They are unsightly but have no effect on the flavour.

White crystals often form on the cork and at the bottom of bottles of white wine. These natural deposits, called tartrates, are harmless and do not alter the taste of the wine.

Sediment often develops in red wines after a few years in the bottle. This is best dealt with by decanting.

drinking wine in a restaurant

The key here is: if in doubt, ask. This applies regardless of the sort of restaurant you're in. If there's a well-informed wine waiter or sommelier (that's the person who is in charge of the wine) and the wine list seems to have been put together with care, then he or she will be only too pleased to tell you anything you want to know – and will probably have some suggestions about which wines will go particularly well with the food you have chosen.

A lot of restaurants, of course, have neither a particularly good wine list nor a decent wine waiter. If the list doesn't tell you the producer, or the vintage, or some other vital piece of information about a wine, ask to see the bottle. At least you can then make your own mind up. The quality of a wine list is not measured by its length. A short, well-chosen list is often better, as is one that specializes in the wines of one region.

Ordering your wine

So, you've decided what you're going to eat, and you've had a look at the wine list and decided what price you want to pay. This is very important. Being pressured into paying more than you can afford can ruin your evening. And a good wine waiter wants to know your price limits so that he can work within them. What you don't know is what any of it tastes like. The wine waiter approaches. How do you begin? Try something like this: 'Oh, hi. Look, we're both having fish, but we want to drink red. We were thinking about this Chilean Merlot, but perhaps it would be too heavy. What would you recommend?'

That's a very broad outline, and you don't have to blurt it all out at once, but the point is that you've given the waiter all the clues he or she needs – food, style and price range – to make an appropriate suggestion. And now you've broken the ice you can come to a final decision calmly rather than in a state of blind panic. The worst thing, if you don't know what to choose, is to sit staring in terror at the wine list, and refuse to ask because you think you'll lose face. You won't.

However, it is a good idea to make a preliminary choice before you seek advice: if you don't like the advice you get, it will leave you with something to fall back on.

When the bottle comes and is shown to you, check it. Sometimes the wrong wine arrives because somebody misheard. Sometimes the vintage has changed, and nobody's told you. If it's not the vintage you ordered, query it. If you don't want the replacement, choose something else.

When the waiter pours the wine, sniff it and taste it. You're checking to see if it's faulty, not if you like it. Take your time. If you suspect it might be faulty, express your doubts, take another taste

and perhaps ask the waiter to try it. If it is faulty they should immediately replace it.

This is where most of the problems with wine waiters arise. Bad wine waiters refuse to accept that a faulty wine is faulty. Bad customers insist that a wine is faulty when there's nothing wrong with it – it may just be unfamiliar.

If you have a disastrous experience (and everyone who eats in restaurants has a bad wine waiter story) don't pick a row: it will spoil the evening. A quiet, reasoned complaint to the manager at the end of the meal will do more good. And if you've had bad service, don't leave a tip.

OZ'S TIPS

Top 10 restaurant tactics

1 Try a glass of house wine first – it allows you to take your time when choosing the wine and if it's good you could stick with it.

2 Order water to quench your thirst so you can savour the wine.

3 Discuss your choice of wine with the wine waiter if there is one. Don't treat him or her as an enemy – or a hired slave.

4 If you're going to have two bottles, don't blow your budget on the first.

5 Don't worry too much about matching the wine to your food: New World Cabernet Sauvignons, Shirazes and Merlots are good all-round reds; New World Chardonnays, Sauvignons and Semillons are useful whites; and Alsace whites go well with a great variety of dishes. This is particularly important in Asian restaurants where the flavours of the national cuisines have evolved without any wine culture. You could say the same for Cajun, Mexican and Caribbean food. With these foods you don't want hard edges on your reds, or vanilla oakiness on your whites. Fruit and balancing acidity are the most important factors here, and if I had to choose two, I'd say New Zealand whites and Chilean reds do this best.

6 On an uninspiring list, opt for wines from Australia, New Zealand or South America – they are the most likely to be reliable and good value.

7 Take a chance on up-and-coming regions of Italy, Spain or Portugal – Sicily or Puglia in Italy, wines from the Garnacha grape in Spain and wines from Alentejo, Beiras or Dão in Portugal – they could well be the best value on the list.

8 Feel the temperature of the bottle when it arrives. If the wine is too warm, whether it's red or white, ask for an ice bucket; and if it gets too cold, don't feel you have to keep it in the bucket just because the waiter has put it there.

9 Don't be bullied by over-assiduous waiters – make sure the bottle is within your reach and top up your glasses when *you* want to.

10 Enjoy yourself: you're the one who's paying.

matching food and wine

Good wine is tasty on its own, but to get the best out of wine you need a group of friends around, and a bite to eat. So, how do you go about choosing the wine for the meal? The pleasures of eating and drinking operate on so many levels that there's far more to perfect wine and food partnerships than clinical flavour matching. If you're in the mood for Champagne then don't let anyone stop you drinking it, whatever you're eating; and if the spirit of place, or the weather, or the company you're in begs for a particular wine, go for it.

Wine affects the flavour of food; food affects the flavour of wine – pretty obvious, I suppose. When the fundamental characteristics of the wine and the food are in harmony, the flavours of both should sing out. Sometimes a well-judged contrast does the trick just as well as a perfect match. Frankly, most combinations are perfectly enjoyable and a few are sensationally good, but a real mismatch can take the fun out of both the food and the wine.

Fortunately, it's easy to avoid disastrous pairings. Don't drink dry wine with sweet food – the wine will taste unpleasantly thin and acidic – and stick to red meat if the wine is a high-tannin red, such as Barolo from Italy, Dão or Bairrada from Portugal, or red Bordeaux. Fish is fine with low-tannin reds such as young Pinot Noir, but too much tannin with your fish will give a metallic taste. And that's about it. Now you can get on with looking for combinations that bring out the best in both the wine and the food.

Sense of place

My best memories of sublime wine and food partnerships come from picnics while travelling in France and Italy. I'll stop in the villages of Tuscany or southern France to pick up bread, sausage, cheese and tomatoes, buy wine straight from the local winemaker's barrel and gulp it all down ten minutes later at the side of a country lane. Wine and food will never taste better than this.

Weight As well as matching the taste of the wine to the flavour of the food, it's a good idea to match the weight (or body) of the wine to the intensity of that flavour. A heavy, alcoholic wine suits hefty food; choose a light wine for delicate dishes.

Acidity The acidity of the food should balance that of the wine. High-acid flavours, such as tomato or lemon, need matching acidity in the wine. You can also use an acidic wine to cut through a creamy or oily dish, but make sure the wine has plenty of flavour, like New Zealand Sauvignon.

Sweetness With desserts and puddings, find a wine that is as sweet as or sweeter than the food. Some savoury foods, such as carrots, onions and parsnips, taste slightly sweet, and if they are prominent in the dish a really ripe-fruited wine like Viognier will work well.

Age/maturity A mature wine will have developed a complex taste and aroma over the years. To get the most enjoyment out of it, keep the food simple – plain grilled or roast meat is ideal.

Sauces and seasonings Always bear these in mind. It may be more important to match the wine to a rich sauce or spicy seasonings than to the main ingredient. As a general rule tannic reds and oaky whites don't like spicy sauces of any kind.

Oak A heavily oaked wine can ride roughshod over food that isn't richly flavoured, and really isn't the thing with spicy Asian food.

The magic resides in the simplicity of the meal and the joy of basking in the same sunlight that is ripening the vines. There's a lesson to be learnt from this for wine and food matching at home. Regional wines and foods aren't necessarily ideal matches from a scientific point of view, but a technical approach takes the fun out of the wine and the food. It's much better to make a bit of a holiday of your meal and think along the lines of southern French wine with Provençal food or a light Italian red with pizza.

International cuisines

Wine and food are both international travellers these days and they pick up new friends wherever they go. Many of the food styles popular around the world today grew up in cultures that don't have wine in their repertoire. Rich and spicy Asian, Indian, African and Mexican dishes and the mixed cuisines of fusion food and Pacific Rim cooking demand wines with a character that the traditional wine cultures of Europe never had to provide. But fruit-driven modern styles can deliver the perfect match.

Nevertheless, some European classics *do* deliver the fruit: Alsace wines, particularly Gewurztraminer and Pinot Gris, and German Riesling. Riesling from any country is a good choice, as are the intense Sauvignon Blancs from New Zealand and South Africa. Juicy fruity reds like Garnacha from Spain, Merlots from Chile and the lighter Malbecs from Argentina can do the trick, and the less powerful California Zinfandels are a good choice.

Wine and cheese

I'm really not sure why cheese is always seen as a natural partner for wine. Only occasionally do I come across an exciting combination. The enduring cliché, perpetuated by a host of back labels, that red is the wine for cheese, is even more perplexing, as white is frequently a better partner. Red wines are OK for hard cheeses like mild Cheddar or Gouda and bland ones such as mozzarella. For mature Cheddar and other strong hard cheeses you need a powerful red like Rhône Syrah or Australian Shiraz, or even port. Goat's cheese is better off with white Sancerre or other wines made from Sauvignon Blanc. Ripe cheeses like Brie or Camembert are hostile to most wine flavours, but sparkling wines can tame them. Otherwise, I'd drink Normandy cider. Strong blue cheeses call for sweet wines: the classic combinations are port with Stilton and Bordeaux's sweet white Sauternes with Roquefort.

Vegetarian dishes

The clean, bright, appley flavours of Pinot Blanc from Alsace and the simple fruitiness and low tannins of reds like Grenache and Tempranillo make them good all-rounders for modern vegetarian cooking. Dry rosé is a good idea, too. Anything spicy calls for fruity and acidic reds and whites. So do tomato-based sauces. Cream and cheese sauces need softer wines: Semillon or ripe, toasty Chardonnay would be good. Salads with vinegary dressings can be murder on wine. Go for tangy whites, such as dry Riesling or Sauvignon Blanc.

WINE'S WORST ENEMIES

Artichokes, chillies, oysters, kippers and **mackerel, salsas** and **vinegars, salted peanuts** and **chocolate** can all flatten the flavours of wines. If you want to drink wine with these foods, the general rule for reds is to avoid very tannic wines and go for juicy young ones instead; or choose whites with plenty of fruit and fresh acidity.

With mackerel and kippers try a dry fino sherry, and with chocolate go for fortified Muscats, the Italian sparkling wine Asti or perhaps some port. Vinegary dressings, chillies and salsas need a match for their acidity, so team them with Sauvignon Blanc or dry Riesling. Oysters need bone-dry whites.

Eggs can be tricky to match with wine. Choose light, unoaked Chardonnays or neutral whites – oaky and very fruity ones don't work so well. Only the very lightest reds, such as Beaujolais, go well with eggs.

Red wine and food: some suggestions for the wine styles described on pages 12–16.

	Juicy, fruity reds	Silky, strawberryish reds	Intense, blackcurranty reds	Spicy, warm-hearted reds	Low-tannin, mouthwatering, herby reds	Earthy, savoury reds
EXCELLENT MATCH ✓ ✓ ✓	Roast or grilled red meats Barbecues Roast or fried chicken Ham Roast pork Spicy food Indian and Tex-Mex food Cold meats and pâtés Pizza Grilled fish Creamy or cheesy sauces	Red meat in rich sauce, e.g. boeuf bourguignon Roast game birds Roast or grilled red meats Chicken in red wine sauce or cooked with garlic Substantial fish, such as grilled salmon or tuna	Roast or grilled red meats – especially lamb Venison Duck and goose Roast chicken and turkey Cold roast beef	Peppered steak Sausages Warming, herby stews Duck and goose Roast or grilled red meats Venison stew Barbecues Hard cheeses Indian food Tex-Mex food Chilli con carne Spaghetti Bolognese Salami	Pizza Lasagne Tomato-based dishes Spaghetti Bolognese Cold meats and salamis Roast pork Garlicky and herby dishes	Rich game dishes Warming, herby stews Roast or grilled red meats Mushroom or meat risottos Roast chicken or turkey with stuffing
OK MATCH ✓	Spaghetti Bolognese and lasagne Soft cheeses Tomato-based dishes	Roast pork Rich, lightly spiced Oriental dishes	Red meat in rich sauce	Roast chicken or turkey with stuffing	Roast or grilled red meats Grilled fish	
DISASTER WARNING ✗	Only the standard warning that goes for all dry reds – avoid sweet foods.	These wines lose their charm with fiery spicy food.	They overwhelm fish, taste bitter with tomatoes and spicy foods, and don't suit cold pork or chicken.	These are food-loving wines, but they will swamp delicate food.	No problems – these wines are real all-rounders.	These wines only come into their own with robust, meaty meals. They clash with cold pork or chicken.

102 ENJOYING WINE

White wine and food: some suggestions for the wine styles described on pages 19–22.

	Bone-dry, neutral whites	Green, tangy whites	Intense, nutty whites	Ripe, toasty whites	Aromatic whites	OTHER WINE STYLES
EXCELLENT MATCH ✓ ✓ ✓	Plainly cooked fish and shellfish Grilled chicken Spaghetti carbonara Quiche Salads Cajun and Tex-Mex food Salami Pork Thai and Chinese food Cold meats Tomato-based dishes Pizza	Anything in tomato sauce, including shellfish Tomatoes Pizza Indian food Salads with sharp dressing Sushi Goat's cheese South-East Asian food Tex-Mex food Chinese Szechuan food Grilled or baked salmon and tuna	Creamy and buttery sauces Plain grilled white fish Grilled or roast chicken and turkey Smoked salmon Spaghetti carbonara Grilled or baked salmon and tuna Seafood in a white wine and cream sauce Pork Rabbit Pheasant or partridge	Grilled or baked salmon and tuna Creamy and buttery sauces Grilled or roast chicken and turkey Barbecues Pheasant or rabbit Spaghetti carbonara Seafood in a white wine and cream sauce	Pizza Lasagne Tomato-based dishes Spaghetti Bolognese Cold meats and salamis Roast pork Garlicky and herby dishes	**Rosés** that are dry and fruity make excellent partners for a whole range of dishes from delicate fish to rich spicy food, but, as they're light, steer away from heavy meaty dishes. **Dry sparkling wines** are good all-rounders too, and particularly good with shellfish and smoked fish. Champagne with oysters is a classic luxury match, although non-vintage Champagne is more suitable than richer, more expensive vintage.
OK MATCH ✓	Creamy and buttery sauces	Asparagus		Smoked fish Mildly spiced food	Roast or grilled red meats Grilled fish	**Tangy fortified wines** are good with nibbles such as olives and salted almonds, go well with soups and smoked fish and are the classic partner to tapas.
DISASTER WARNING ✗	Avoid pairing any dry white with sweet food, but otherwise you can't go wrong with these wines.	These wines work with all sorts of hard-to-match foods, but they don't suit simply cooked red meats.	For all their intensity, these are subtly flavoured wines, and spices will destroy all that subtlety.	Heavily oaked wines overwhelm delicate fish – but they won't stand up to too much spice or acidity.	Aromatics are great food wines, but they're better suited to complex dishes than simple ones.	**Warming fortified wines** suit cheese and chocolate. **Rich sweet wines** go with both sweet food and blue cheese.

wine and health

The image of wine as a healthy drink is both an ancient and a very modern one. Wine was once highly prized for its medicinal qualities, largely because it was more reliably hygienic than water. It made a reasonable antiseptic and a good base for medicines. Some doctors went further, and recommended particular wines for particular ailments. Scientists are constantly researching the links between wine and health, but remember it's not just wine – anything you eat and drink can have benefits or cause problems.

The damaging effects of alcohol have been known for a long time and the anti-alcohol lobby has tried for years to persuade us that all alcohol is bad for us. However, there's now a wealth of medical evidence to suggest that moderate consumption of alcohol, particularly wine, is actually better for most people's health than total abstinence.

A poster from 1937 advertising the joys of French wine, bringing its imbiber health, laughter and hope. If only it were so simple today.

Health benefits

The main research finding is that drinking wine in moderation reduces the likelihood of dying from a heart attack, stroke or other form of vascular disease. It does this by helping to prevent clogged arteries and blood clots. Some of the benefits are due to the alcohol in the wine. Alcohol acts as an anticoagulant, which eases blood flow and prevents clots forming. It boosts HDL – or 'good' cholesterol – which actually cleans fatty deposits out of our arteries, and reduces LDL, the 'bad' cholesterol that puts them there in the first place.

Wine has an extra trick up its sleeve in the form of powerful anti-oxidants, which reduce the amount of fatty LDL deposits that can stick to the walls of our arteries. This benefit was originally attributed only to red wines, but subsequent research has shown that white wines are also effective. It also appears that wine may reduce the risk of some cancers and aid mental alertness into old age. And of course, we don't need researchers to tell us about the relaxing effects of a glass or two at the end of the day.

Social drinking can sometimes get a bit out of hand. I drink a large glass of milk before a big evening and try to drink a glass of water between each glass of wine. None of us wants to spoil the party but most of us have to work the following day.

Moderate consumption

All advocates of wine as a healthy beverage stress that the benefits of wine come only with moderate, regular consumption. Excessive amounts of alcohol increase the likelihood of many health problems, including all those that moderate consumption can guard against. In addition, alcohol is not recommended for people suffering from certain diseases, and pregnant women in particular should take medical advice regarding alcohol.

Individuals should talk to their doctors and make up their own minds, but my feelings on the matter are simple. Drink water for your thirst and enjoy good wine for its flavour. If you're not drinking enough to harm yourself, then the pleasure and sense of wellbeing that wine adds to your life are benefits enough.

PART THREE
THE WORLD OF WINE

Once the only important places on the wine map of the world were

European nations with long traditions of winemaking.

Then, in the late 1970s, came the challenge from

the so-called New World countries with their

innovative ideas and bright, fresh, modern interpretations of the

classic wines of Europe. California and Australia led the way and

were joined by New Zealand and, more recently, Chile, Argentina and

South Africa. And now, there are more 'new' countries, eager to impress.

India, China, Uruguay and Brazil, Canada and the northern European

countries like England, Holland, Belgium and Denmark. But New World

and Old World are attitudes of mind as well as places, and tradition and

innovation now go hand in hand throughout the world of wine.

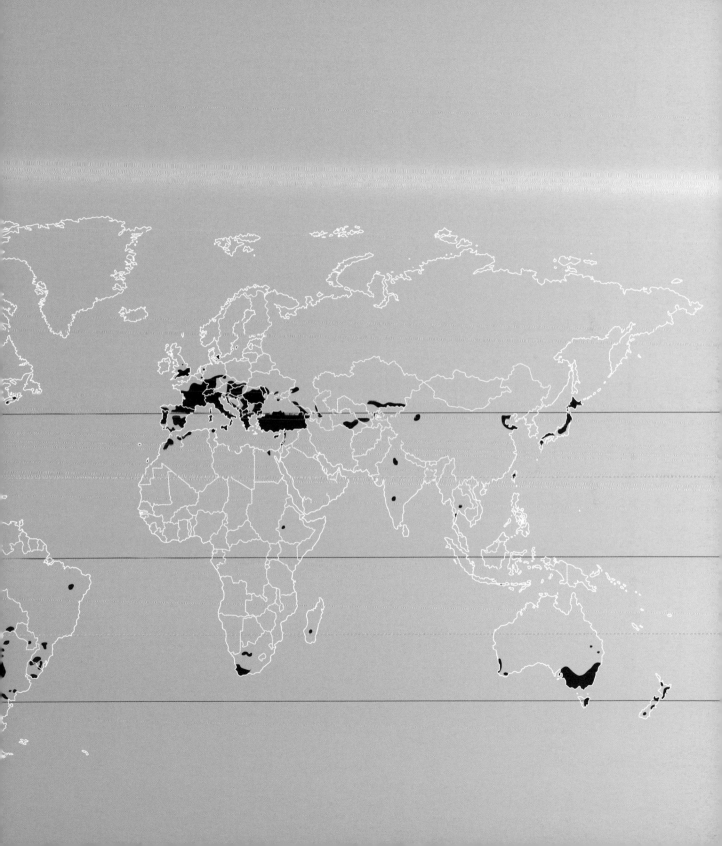

france

Ah, France. Say the words 'French wine' and everybody's got a response: it's the best, the worst, too expensive, cheap plonk... whatever you think about France, the opposite is probably just as true. But nobody can deny that France is at the very heart of the world of wine.

Facing page: The Jurançon vineyards in the deep south-west of France make some ravishing, peachy, dry and sweet white wines.

Right: The turreted Château Palmer in the Margaux appellation of Bordeaux makes magical red wine that can last for decades.

What thrills me is the range of flavours I can find here. For a start, so many international wine styles have their origin in France. The worldwide vogue for Cabernet Sauvignon sprang from the cedary, blackcurrany flavours of red Bordeaux. Burgundy inspired the worldwide love of Chardonnay and Pinot Noir. Champagne has spawned a thousand sparkling imitators across the globe.

But the influence of the New World is being felt here as much as anywhere, and flavours have become softer and richer than they used to be. All the same, you should still expect French wines to be less obviously fruity than their New World counterparts. More subtle, in some cases; more austere in others.

Bear in mind, too, that France's reputation as a producer of great wines is based on the very top layer of quality. Below that things have always been more mixed. And if you go for the very cheapest French wines – well, frankly, you could be getting better value and better flavours in a dozen other countries.

FRENCH CLASSIFICATIONS

France, like all European Union countries, has a tiered classification system. The higher the grade, the stricter the rules covering place of origin, grape variety, method of growing and method of making. But don't ever mistake the Appellation Contrôlée classification for a guarantee of quality: it's not. Instead it's a guarantee that the wine comes from the region stated on the label, and was made in accordance with the law – just that and no more.

Appellation d'Origine Contrôlée (AC or AOC) The top grade of French wine applies stringent rules. Producers may only grow certain grape varieties in each area, and yields per hectare are regulated.

Vin Délimité de Qualité Supérieure (VDQS) A sort of junior AC. It accounts for just one per cent of French wine and is being discontinued after the 2010 vintage.

Vin de pays Relatively loosely regulated regions producing 'country wines' that are supposed to have the character of their region. Innovative winemakers love this category, because it allows them to do pretty well what they like. Most of the wines will have the grape variety on the label. You'd think that was just about the most helpful piece of information they could give, but, amazingly, most AOC wines aren't allowed to mention the grape variety.

Vin de table The most basic wine. The label won't state the region, and much is blended from all over France. It's seldom a good buy: stick to vin de pays instead.

Bordeaux

If there is one single wine that for generations has carried the reputation of France, it is red Bordeaux. It is a benchmark wine throughout the world, and the origin of the intense, blackcurranty style of red, but there's one thing I want to make clear. Don't assume that because Château Margaux makes spectacularly wonderful wine, then the word Bordeaux on the label automatically equals prestige and quality. It doesn't. The wines of this region reach the heights, but they also plumb the depths of quality. The worst red Bordeaux is just dire, and it's not even cheap.

When I talk about the flavours of red Bordeaux I mean good to very good wines. Those flavours are, at their best, a complex blend of blackcurrants and plums, cedarwood and cigar boxes, with perhaps a touch of violets, perhaps a touch of roast coffee beans. They come especially from the Cabernet Sauvignon grape, which is always blended here, usually with both Merlot and Cabernet Franc. Wines with a lot of Merlot in the blend taste softer and more generously fruity.

The finest estates produce sublime wine, of immense complexity and fascination. If you can afford these treasures, good for you. Top red Bordeaux is out of reach for most of us, except for the most special of special occasions. Thankfully, more and more good wines – still expensive, but not prohibitively so – become available every year.

Bordeaux also makes a fair bit of white wine, which can be sweet or dry. The most famous golden, sweet whites are those of Sauternes and its neighbour, Barsac, and there are various lesser regions that produce lighter versions of this style. Oddly (considering my strictures on the lesser red wines) these wines can be rather good buys.

Dry whites also come up with the goods at the cheaper end. Basic white Bordeaux is a good bet these days. At the very least it will be fresh and clean and have some attractive grassy fruit. These wines are simple, less pungent versions of the green, tangy style typified by New Zealand Sauvignon Blanc. The same grape variety grows here, too, and is sometimes blended with Sémillon, sometimes not. At the top end, creamy, nectariny dry whites from Pessac-Léognan can be some of the best in France.

Bordeaux Clairet is, depending on your point of view, a dark rosé or a very light red wine. Either way, it's a good-value dry wine with a refreshing taste of summer fruits.

Do regions matter?

The simple answer is yes. The basic distinction is between those regions that grow a lot of Cabernet Sauvignon (the Médoc, Haut-Médoc, Pessac-Léognan and Graves) and those that specialise in Merlot (St-Émilion and Pomerol). Cabernet Sauvignon-based wines have more tannin and a more austere flavour than the Merlot-based wines, especially when young.

On the map you'll see some less illustrious regions marked, like Côtes de Castillon, Côtes de Bourg, Côtes de Blaye and Fronsac. All these places make red wine, and they're often good spots to look if you want simpler flavours and lower prices. Flavours are at best juicier and fruitier than those of top wines, but at worst leaner and more austere, and which you get depends as much on the producer as the region. If somebody points you towards a good one, try it. Lalande-de-Pomerol produces some goodies in the Pomerol mould of rich, plummy fruit, and since Pomerol is rare and expensive these wines make a useful substitute. St-Georges-St-Émilion and Puisseguin-St-Émilion make simpler, earthier versions of St-Émilion and if they're a bit cheaper, especially if they come from a single property, then give them a go.

The very best dry white Bordeaux comes from Pessac-Léognan and Graves. Simpler wines come from Entre Deux Mers or may just be labelled Bordeaux Blanc.

Sauternes and Barsac are the top sweet wine areas, but others, including Loupiac, Cérons and Ste-Croix-du-Mont, have some pretty good wines. Curiously, Monbazillac, the region that comes closest to Sauternes in style, is actually just outside the borders of Bordeaux.

Do vintages matter?

Vintages matter more in Bordeaux than in most places. The weather here can be blissfully warm and sunny one year, and cool and wet the next, so the wines can vary from intense and deep-fruited to lean and underripe. See the Quick Guide on page 112. All good red Bordeaux needs to age for a few years, but some vintages mature faster than others.

The simplest whites are less susceptible to vintage variation, and in any case should be drunk young. With top whites, take care with the vintage, and give them some age. Vintages matter terrifically with Sauternes because the noble rot fungus, which gives the wines their sweetness and character, can't be relied upon to show up every year.

When do I drink them?

If you're going to open a really good bottle of red Bordeaux, then it's an event. There's an air of formality about good Bordeaux that demands respect. Keep it for when you've got time to appreciate it and cook something that will flatter the wine (roast lamb, just cooked pink, is ideal).

Sauternes is just as special. Do what the Bordelais do, and drink it with Roquefort cheese. Believe me, the

---

BORDEAUX HIERARCHIES

Bordeaux has three tiers of AC wines. The basic AC Bordeaux covers the whole region, which is subdivided into districts with their own appellations. Within these are a few small appellations based around communes with exceptionally good land, e.g. Pauillac.

But the château is the crucial indicator of the quality of the wine, and top districts have lists of top performers, known as **crus classés** or classed growths. The most famous classification (made in 1855) rates the top 61 red wine châteaux on the Left Bank of the Gironde from First Growth (Premier Cru) to Fifth (Cinquième Cru). Sauternes gives the top award of First Great Growth (Premier Grand Cru) followed by First and Second Growths. Graves simply picks out Crus Classés; St-Émilion has Premiers Grands Crus followed by Grands Crus.

Even the most flexible of these systems doesn't keep pace with changes in quality year by year, so it's rather refreshing that Pomerol doesn't bother with *crus* at all.

---

combination is sublime. The simple whites, however, have no social pretensions at all: take them on a picnic if you want, or drink them out of a tumbler. They won't mind.

Can I afford them?

Look, you've got to live a little. Once in your life fork out for a top bottle of red, or share the cost with friends. Treat it properly and it shouldn't disappoint. Good whites, dry and sweet, are expensive too, but the everyday whites are excellent value. I think you will have gathered by now what I think about most of the everyday reds – but Côtes de Blaye and Côtes de Castillon can give you some delightful – and affordable – surprises.

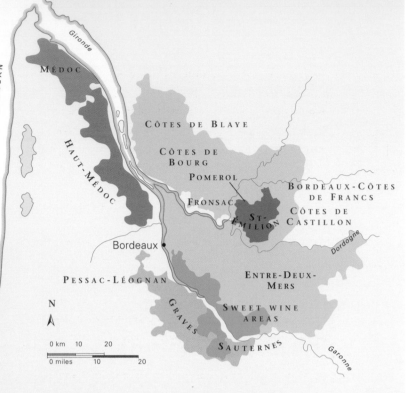

WINE TERMS **Claret**

For 300 years, from 1152 to 1453, Bordeaux owed allegiance to the English crown. No wonder that England, and later on, the English-speaking world, developed such a taste for the wine. Some of it was known as **clairet** because of its light style compared to the gutsier wines of Spain or Portugal; and the name became Anglicized to **claret**. The name claret is still widely used in Britain, and applies to all red Bordeaux, while *clairet* is now the name for rosé-style wines from this region.

QUICK GUIDE ▷ *Bordeaux*

Location Bordeaux is situated on the Atlantic coast in South-West France.

Grapes Intense, blackcurranty reds are made from blends of varying proportions of Cabernet Sauvignon, Merlot and Cabernet Franc, with smaller amounts of Petit Verdot and Malbec. Sémillon and Sauvignon Blanc are the main white grapes for both dry and sweet wines.

Cabernet-dominated communes Listrac, Margaux, Moulis, Pauillac, St-Estèphe, St-Julien (all in the Haut-Médoc); Graves, Pessac-Léognan.

Merlot-dominated communes Pomerol, St-Émilion, Côtes de Castillon.

Local jargon *Left Bank, Right Bank* – reds from the Médoc, Haut-Médoc, Graves and Pessac-Léognan, the appellations on the left bank of the Gironde, are colloquially known as Left Bank wines; those from St-Émilion, Pomerol and other regions on the river's right bank are called Right Bank wines. Left Bank wines are Cabernet-dominated; Right Bank wines major on Merlot. *Grand Vin* – this means that the bottle contains the main wine of a château; it doesn't refer to the quality of the wine. *Second wine* – some châteaux produce a second wine from younger vines, or lesser parts of the vineyard than the Grand Vin. They can be a good buy. *Petit château* – a general term for the mass of unclassified châteaux in Bordeaux. Some are good, but many produce dross.

Vintages to look for 2009, 2008, 2006, 2005, 2004, 2001, 2000; 2009, 2007, 2005, 2003 and 2001 for Sauternes.

Vintages to avoid 1997; 2006, 2004 and 2000 for Sauternes.

Ten to try
RED
• **Château d'Angludet** Margaux ❹

• **Château des Annereaux** Lalande-de-Pomerol ❸
• **Château Balestard-la-Tonnelle** St-Émilion ❺
• **Château Léoville-Barton** St-Julien ❺
• **Château la Tour-de-By** Médoc ❷

DRY WHITE
• **Château Haut Bertinerie** Premières Côtes de Blaye ❸
• **Château Reynon** Sauvignon Blanc ❷
• **Château Smith-Haut-Lafitte** Péssac-Leognan ❺

SWEET WHITE
• **Château Lafaurie-Peyraguey** Sauternes ❺
• **Château Loubens** Ste-Croix-du-Mont ❹

Burgundy

Burgundy, like Bordeaux, is a classic region of France. The French name for the region, and the one you'll see on the label, is Bourgogne. It's home to three famous grape varieties, which make three benchmark styles of wine: silky, strawberryish Pinot Noir; intense, nutty Chardonnay; and juicy, fruity Gamay, the grape of Beaujolais.

Top Chardonnays and Pinot Noirs fetch millionaire prices, and are available in tiny quantities. Beaujolais is far less serious, and even at its best has no such aspirations. The first two have been imitated with great success elsewhere in the world, using the same grape varieties. Beaujolais has acted more as an inspiration – for juicy, fruity reds from a whole host of different grapes.

Pinot Noir is the most fascinating grape of all, the hardest to grow and the trickiest to vinify. Whereas Cabernet Sauvignon is robust and easy-going and seems to taste reliably Cabernet-like almost no matter what you do to it, Pinot Noir is light and subtle and will, at the least provocation, lose its freshness or its perfume or its ineffable silky quality. It takes a very good grower along with a very good winemaker to make good Pinot Noir.

To get a picture of red Burgundy you have to add to the truculent nature of the grape the complexities of vineyard ownership in Burgundy. While Bordeaux is composed of large estates with clear boundaries, a Burgundian estate may consist of tiny parcels of vines in perhaps 20 different vineyards. Likewise, each vineyard in Burgundy is divided between many different owners. It's due to the way the French inheritance laws work. Each estate will make a different wine from each block of vines. Each wine will have a different name, and (in theory) a

The colourful glazed roof tiles of the Hospices de Beaune are typical of the region and give a clue to the wealth of medieval Burgundy.

Generic appellations As well as basic Bourgogne Rouge and Bourgogne Blanc, which can come from anywhere in the region, there are two undistinguished red styles that are seen relatively little these days, Bourgogne Grand Ordinaire and Bourgogne Passe-Tout-Grains. .

Regional appellations For example, Côte de Nuits-Villages, or Côte Chalonnaise. The Côte d'Or region is divided into the Côte de Nuits and the Côte de Beaune appellations.

Village appellations Most villages in the Côte d'Or have their own appellation, such as Gevrey-Chambertin, and so do some in the other regions, notably in Beaujolais.

Premier Cru This term means First Growth but applies to the second-best vineyards in each village. The vineyard name will appear prominently on the label – though Burgundy also has some vineyards which are not Premier Cru that may also appear by name on the label, in smaller type. Either way, a vineyard name is a good sign.

Grand Cru These are the very best vineyards. They are appellations contrôlées in their own right, so may dispense with the name of their village on the label. Le Chambertin, for example, is a Grand Cru wine from the vineyard of Le Chambertin in the village of Gevrey-Chambertin.

different character. These facts alone make Burgundy far harder to grasp than Bordeaux. In Bordeaux the name of the vineyard and the name of the producer are identical and interchangeable; in Burgundy, you need to know the name of both the vineyard and the producer – more than anywhere else, it pays to seek knowledgeable advice. Buy from a bad producer and you'll wonder what all the fuss is about.

Chardonnay in Burgundy is easier to grow, easier to make and easier to buy than Pinot Noir. It's far more reliable, but it's in just as great demand, so prices are high. It comes in a number of styles. Chablis is as lean and minerally as Chardonnay gets, but ages to a nutty complexity after several years. In the Côte d'Or, the world-famous heart of the region, flavours range from the apple and nuts of the simpler wines to the long-lived buttered-toast, oatmeal and cream of the very best. The style is leaner again in the Côte Chalonnaise, but fatter and fruitier down in the Mâconnais. Chardonnay is also the grape of most sparkling Crémant de Bourgogne, a lean but honeyish fizz. There's also a little crisp, lemony wine made from Aligoté, a white grape grown in small quantities but to good effect. It rarely attains the weight of a really good Chardonnay, and is usually best drunk young.

And Beaujolais? It's a region devoted to one red grape, Gamay, and offers several variations on a basic light and bright, juicy, fruity taste. Beaujolais-Villages has the juiciest flavours. Simple Beaujolais and Beaujolais Nouveau can be as good but often lack fruit. Drink them all young. A Beaujolais from one of the ten top villages, known as the Beaujolais *crus*, should have more character and depth. The most notable *crus* are light Chiroubles, fragrant Fleurie and heavier wines from Morgon and Moulin-à-Vent.

Do regions matter?

Absolutely. If you want Chardonnay, it is lean and minerally in Chablis, fuller and more complex on the Côte d'Or, more austere and chalky in the Côte Chalonnaise, fatter and softer in the Mâconnais. If you want Pinot Noir, the finest wines come from the Côte d'Or; wines from the Côte Chalonnaise are earthier. Within the Côte d'Or each village has its own style, and within each village there is a hierarchy of vineyards. If you want Gamay you have the choice between juicy, simple Beaujolais, the *cru* wines, which are more serious and will often age for a few years, or the mostly unexciting reds of the Mâconnais.

Do vintages matter?

Yes, but the name of the producer matters more. See the Quick Guide (right).

When do I drink them?

The best Burgundies are indulgent, hedonistic wines and I drink them with indulgent, hedonistic friends. I wouldn't waste them on people who take themselves too seriously. When I'm drinking good Bordeaux I feel I ought to be wearing a tie and sitting up straight. Give me a glass of good Burgundy and I'll take off my jacket and relax. Give me a good Beaujolais and I'll kick off my shoes as well.

Can I afford them?

Good Burgundy is expensive, but if you're clever (and get clever advice) you can find some wines that are reasonably good value. The trick for reds is to go for a good producer based in the Côte d'Or, but buy the simpler wines, like Bourgogne Rouge, Auxey-Duresses, Monthelie or Chorey-lès-Beaune. The price will be far less than that of grander appellations. You won't get the full weight and complexity, but you'll get the elegance and silkiness. The same goes for Chardonnay. The very top villages like Meursault and Puligny-Montrachet get more expensive every year. However, Chardonnay grows well in a leaner style in the Côte Chalonnaise and the number of good producers is increasing. The Mâconnais region is also seeing a resurgence of quality for fatter, fruitier styles.

As for Beaujolais: yes, you can afford it. It's probably overpriced for what is an everyday country wine, but it's uplifting and delicious when it's good.

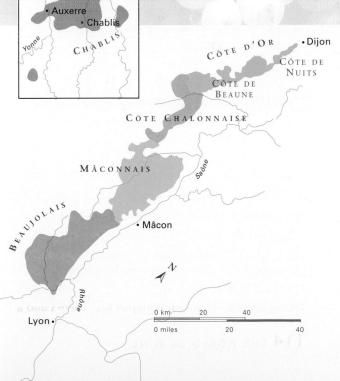

Champagne

Champagne is the world's benchmark sparkling wine. Even when Australian or Californian producers set out to make a slightly different style, Champagne is the point they start from, and they often use the same grapes – Chardonnay, Pinot Noir and Pinot Meunier. It's one of the most famous wines in the world, and because most is sold under big brand names it's one of the simplest to buy.

The key to the flavour of good Champagne is that it doesn't taste obviously fruity. Instead it mingles fruit with biscuits or fresh bread or nuts or even chocolate, and it softens and mellows with age to a glorious nutty complexity. At least, that's the ideal. The method of production, which I've outlined on page 56, is what gives Champagne this flavour – as well as the bubbles.

Not all Champagne measures up; some can be lean and green and mean. Partly it depends on the weather – cold wet summers produce unripe-tasting Champagne – but mostly it depends on the producer. Happily most big names are reliable these days, though a bit more homogenized than before.

Champagne can benefit from bottle age, even after you've bought it. If you tuck a non-vintage Champagne away in a cupboard for six to twelve months it will gain extra roundness; and vintage Champagne isn't at its best until at least a decade after the vintage.

Do regions matter?

Only if you're visiting and have to find your way around. But with global warming, more single producers are starting to sell wine under their own label, and local variations in style will become more important.

The finest Pinot Noir destined for Bollinger Champagne.

Do vintages matter?

Most Champagne is non-vintage, which means that it is
a blend of several vintages. All houses keep stocks of
older vintages so that they can blend to a consistent
style year by year. Vintage Champagne, in which the
vintage obviously does matter, is (in theory) only
produced in the best years. You'll pay extra for vintage
wines, and what you get for your money should be
extra depth, extra character, extra weight – extra
everything. Yet vintage Champagnes are not just bigger
versions of non-vintage. There should be extra
complexity, too, and the character of the year should
show through. See the Quick Guide, page 118.

When do I drink it?

Any time, any place, anywhere. It's great to drink on the
beach, in the bath, for breakfast, at smart parties –
anywhere. Vintage Champagne is a more serious sort of
wine than non-vintage and you probably ought to pay
proper attention to it. Vintage Champagne goes well
with food and non-vintage is the better choice for
parties, if that's any help.

Can I afford it?

When you really want it, of course you can. Just give
up something else. The cheapest Champagne can be
pretty grim, but lots of good merchants have an
excellent own-label Champagne at well below the big-
brand prices.

QUICK GUIDE ▷ *Champagne*

Location The most northerly major wine region in France, situated east of Paris.

Grapes Chardonnay gives elegance to Champagne; Pinot Noir gives weight; and Pinot Meunier gives softness. Most Champagnes are a blend of all three grape varieties.

Local jargon *nv* – a commonly used abbreviation for non-vintage (see box, page 116). *Grand Cru* – wine made entirely from grapes from the region's very best vineyards. *Premier Cru* – wine made entirely from grapes from vineyards just one notch down from Grand Cru. *Blanc de Blancs* – white wine made entirely from white grapes: Chardonnay, in other words. Blanc de Blancs Champagne should be fresh, creamy and bright. *Blanc de Noirs* – white wine made entirely from the region's black grapes, Pinot Noir and Pinot Meunier. Blanc de Noirs Champagne should be weightier than other styles.

Vintages to look for 2009, 2008, 2002, 1999, 1996, 1995, 1990, 1989.

Vintages to avoid 2003 is overripe and 2001 underripe.

Ten to try
All these producers make good vintage Champagne as well as non-vintage (nv), but Billecart-Salmon's is particularly reliable.
- **Billecart-Salmon** Cuveé N F Billecart vintage ⑤
- **Bollinger** nv ⑤
- **Alfred Gratien** nv ⑤
- **Charles Heidsieck** nv ⑤
- **Henriot** nv ⑤
- **Jacquart** nv ⑤
- **Lanson** nv ⑤
- **Louis Roederer** nv ⑤
- **Pol Roger** nv ⑤
- **Veuve Clicquot** nv ⑤

Chalk is all important in the Champagne region both above ground and below. In the vineyards the chalky soil plays a vital role in drainage and in reflecting the sun's heat back onto the vines and the cool dark subterranean chalk pits originally excavated by the Romans are used by the Champagne houses to mature their wines. These cellars belong to the Champagne house Taittinger in Reims and are well worth a visit.

The Rhône Valley

If you want spicy, warm-hearted wines of remarkable depth and complexity, this is where you come. At least, this is where you come in France, because the Rhône Valley is the French home of the Syrah grape, which produces rich flavours of herbs and smoke. The grape's other home is Australia, where it is known as Shiraz, so if you want to get a full picture of the grape's flavours, compare a good Rhône red with a softer, more obviously fruity Barossa Valley Shiraz. It's the difference between Old World and New World styles encapsulated in a single grape variety.

There's a division in the Rhône, however, between north and south. On the map it's shaped a bit like an upturned funnel: narrow at the top, then abruptly widening at the base. Well, the narrow bit is the North, where Syrah is the only red grape planted. Where it widens is the south, and a whole range of grapes is planted here – 12 red varieties are allowed for the various appellations. Wines from the south don't have the minerally, smoky austerity of the northern wines. Instead they're broader and more generous – mostly because the soft, juicy Grenache grape is part of the blend. And of course there's far more wine made in the south. That has two effects for us: first, prices are generally higher in the north. Secondly, quality is more variable in the south.

That's the red wines. When it comes to whites, the Rhône starts springing surprises. With the Viognier grape it produces some of the most aromatic whites in the world, with a flavour of apricots mingled with spring flowers and the richness of crème fraîche. Viognier's traditional home is in a couple of tiny, high-priced appellations in the northern Rhône: Condrieu and Château-Grillet.

The good news is that growers in the southern Rhône have caught on to the fact that we all love Viognier, or would if we could afford it, and they're busy planting it, so some cheaper versions are appearing. They're not, I have to admit, quite as magical as a top Condrieu, but they do show the grape's astonishing flavours.

The other white grapes of the northern Rhône are Marsanne and Roussanne. This duo is responsible for the dry whites of Hermitage, Crozes-Hermitage, St-Joseph and St-Péray – and they go from austerely herbal, through floral to fat and unctuous. The dry whites of the south vary according to the cocktail of grapes used, from Châteauneuf-du-Pape with its citrussy mineral freshness to soft, scented styles of Côtes du Rhône, frequently flecked with the perfume of wild herbs.

The south has one more trick to pull yet. It's the Muscat grape, making golden, sweet wines that pack a head-reeling punch of crunchy, grapy flavours, laced with rose petals and orange spice, and yet manage to be elegant with it. These wines pack quite a punch of alcohol too, because they're fortified with grape spirit. Muscat de Beaumes de Venise is the most famous and the best, but if you'll permit me to venture beyond the confines of the Rhône for a moment, I'll introduce you to some others scattered around the South of France – Muscat de Frontignan, Muscat de Mireval, Muscat de Rivesaltes and Muscat de St-Jean-de-Minervois.

Do regions matter?

There are differences between north and the south, but the reds are basically all spicy and warm-hearted and the whites, with the exception of aromatic Viognier, are honeysuckle or herb-scented wherever they come from.

Do vintages matter?

People talk about a given vintage being better in the north than in the south, or vice versa. But don't get too hung up on Rhône vintages – they're rarely bad. See the Quick Guide on page 121.

The view from the top of the famous Hermitage hill looking down towards the Rhône flowing southwards.

When do I drink them?

It's a question of mood, as well as food. The reds are cold-weather wines; they're a bit too robust for a summer's day. You can almost feel warmth flowing out of the bottle. They're happiest with strongly flavoured food: a rich casserole, a peppered steak or a slice of saucisson.

Viognier will go with some foods, but it's so hedonistic in flavour that you might enjoy it best on its own. As for the other dry whites, well, drink them for the sake of trying a flavour you won't find elsewhere. They're quite versatile partners for food. You can drink the sweet fortified Muscats as apéritifs – that's what the French do – but they're also a rare match for chocolaty puddings.

Can I afford them?

The top wines, like top wines everywhere, are expensive and rising. Hermitage and Côte-Rôtie in the north and Châteauneuf-du-Pape in the south are the priciest appellations for reds. Viognier from Condrieu and Château-Grillet is astronomically expensive. But there

are lots of tasty wines at the middle and lower end which are very affordable. Crozes-Hermitage is the north's best-value appellation.

The south isn't uniform in quality – it's too big for that – and the all-inclusive Côtes du Rhône appellation covers everything from rich, concentrated wines to thin, dilute ones. So shun the very lowest priced examples and pay more for a single-domaine wine from a serious producer: you'll get far better flavours for your money. Côtes du Rhône-Villages and the village appellations of Gigondas and Vacqueyras, as well as Costières de Nîmes, are the best bets in the south.

QUICK GUIDE ▷ *The Rhône Valley*

Location The Rhône Valley is in south-east France. The vineyards are split into two regions with separate identities: the steep slopes of the north and the hot plains of the south.

Grapes Syrah is the red grape of the north, making smoky, minerally wines; southern reds are made from a cocktail of grapes, including Syrah and juicy Grenache, for softer, broader flavours. All Rhône reds are variants of the spicy, warm-hearted style. Viognier is a highly aromatic white grape, while Marsanne and Roussanne deliver herb and honeysuckle flavours. Muscat is used in the southern Rhône for fortified golden, sweet wines.

Syrah-dominated appellations (all in the north) Cornas, Côte-Rôtie, Crozes-Hermitage, Hermitage, St-Joseph.

Appellations where reds are mostly blends (all in the south) Châteauneuf-du-Pape, Costières de Nîmes, Coteaux du Tricastin, Côtes du Rhône, Côtes du Rhône-Villages, Gigondas, Lirac, Lubéron, Vacqueyras, Ventoux.

Viognier appellations Château-Grillet, Condrieu.

Vintages to look for 2009, anything between 2007 and 2004, 2001, 1999, 1998 and 1995.

Vintages to avoid 2008 and 2002.

NORTHERN RHÔNE

SOUTHERN RHÔNE

• Marseille

Ten to try
RED
• **Allemand** Cornas ❺
• **Chapoutier** Côtes du Rhône-Villages ❷
• **Cuilleron** St-Joseph ❺
• **Graillot** Crozes-Hermitage ❹
• **Domaine Santa Duc** Gigondas, Cuvée Tradition ❹
• **Domaine du Vieux Télégraphe** Châteauneuf-du-Pape, Télégramme ❻

WHITE
• **Gaillard** Côtes du Rhône Viognier ❸
• **Guigal** Côtes du Rhône ❷
• **Perret** Condrieu, Coteau de Chéry ❺

SWEET WHITE
• **Domaine de Durban** Muscat de Beaumes-de-Venise ❸

The Loire Valley

The Loire Valley is the place for classically French flavours that aren't much imitated elsewhere in the world. Both whites and reds are great with food and very popular as lunchtime wines in the restaurants of nearby Paris.

Internationally, the whites are far better known than the reds. There are four main grape varieties, of which the white Sauvignon Blanc and Chenin Blanc are the most exciting.

Sauvignon Blanc is the easier to get to grips with. You will probably have encountered the almost shockingly intense fruity Sauvignons from New Zealand or South Africa – well, the Loire Valley is where Sauvignon comes from. The flavours here aren't quite so vivid as in those New World examples, but that's no bad thing because, especially in Sancerre, Pouilly-Fumé and Touraine, they have a palate-tingling green apple, gooseberry and blackcurrant leaf taste that's as refreshing as a wine can get.

Chenin Blanc is less easy to understand because it comes in a whole range of styles, dry, sweet and sparkling. And unless it is fully ripe it makes lean and sullen wines. All this changes when the sun shines and it then displays fascinating flavours. Dry styles run the gamut from steely and austere through to honeyed wines laced with quince and angelica. Vouvray and Savennières need several years' aging. Saumur and Anjou Blanc are better young.

Thrilling sweet Chenins come from grapes affected by noble rot – labelled Vouvray *moelleux*, Quarts de Chaume, Bonnezeaux and Coteaux du Layon. These need 10 to 20 years to transform their youthful high acidity and piercing sweetness into a marvellous mellow maturity of honeycomb and quince.

The other two major grapes are red – Pinot Noir (producing delicate reds and rosés, especially in the upper Loire and Sancerre) and Cabernet Franc (producing superb, tinglingly leafy-fresh, raspberry-rich reds in Saumur, Chinon and Bourgueil.) One more important grape is Muscadet, grown around Nantes at the mouth of the Loire and used for the neutral-tasting dry wine of the same name.

WINE TERMS
Know your Pouillys

Pouilly-Fumé is the Loire's famous crisp, refreshing wine made from Sauvignon Blanc. It has a slight smoky edge that earns it the 'Fumé' tag. Don't confuse this with **Pouilly-sur-Loire**, an unmemorable wine made in the same area from a grape called Chasselas. And don't mix it up with **Pouilly-Fuissé**, **Pouilly-Loché** or **Pouilly-Vinzelles**. These are rich, fruity Chardonnay wines and they come from Burgundy.

Location A large region stretching the length of the River Loire from central France to the west coast.

Grapes Sauvignon Blanc and Chenin Blanc make green, tangy whites; Chenin also makes sweet wine. Muscadet is bone dry and neutral. Cabernet Franc and Pinot Noir make light raspberryish or strawberry-scented reds; Gamay is simple and light.

Sauvignon Blanc appellations Menetou-Salon, Quincy, Reuilly, Pouilly-Fumé, Sancerre, Touraine.

Dry Chenin Blanc appellations Anjou Blanc, Montlouis, Saumur Blanc, Savennières, Vouvray.

Sweet Chenin Blanc appellations Bonnezeaux, Coteaux de l'Aubance, Coteaux du Layon, Montlouis, Quarts de Chaume, Vouvray.

Local jargon *Sec* – dry. *Moelleux* – sweet. *Liquoreux* – very sweet. *Sur lie* – aged on lees. *Crémant* – traditional-method fizz. *Mousseux* – sparkling.

Vintages to look for 2008 (not sweet), 2007, 2006 (not sweet), 2005, 2003 (not Sancerre), 2002 (not Sancerre); (for sweet) 1997, 1996, 1995, 1990, 1989, 1988, 1985, 1983, 1976.

Nantes   Tours   Loire

① Muscadet
② Anjou-Saumur
③ Touraine
④ Sancerre and Pouilly-Fumé

Ten to try
RED
- **Frédéric Mabileau** St-Nicolas-de-Bourgueil ③
- **Château de Villeneuve** Saumur-Champigny ③

DRY WHITE
- **Domaine des Aubuisières** Vouvray ③
- **Henri Bourgeois** Sancerre ③
- **André-Michel Brégeon** Muscadet de Sèvre-et-Maine Sur Lie ②
- **Jacky Marteau** Sauvignon de Touraine ②
- **Domaine Richou** Anjou Blanc ②

SWEET WHITE
- **Baumard** Quarts de Chaume ⑤
- **Huet** Vouvray Moelleux ⑤

SPARKLING WHITE
- **Langlois-Château** Crémant de Loire ②

Facing page: The river Loire meanders across open countryside at les Loges in the heart of the Pouilly-Fumé appellation, the Loire Valley's famous white wine from Sauvignon Blanc.

The Loire also produces fairly sharp sparkling wines made in the same way as Champagne. The whites have a more appley fruit than Champagne and there are a few strawberryish sparkling rosés, too. Ah, yes, rosé. The Loire rather lets itself down with sweetish, cloddish still Anjou Rosé, which is seldom much fun. Cabernet d'Anjou is usually drier, tastier and much more refreshing.

Do regions matter?

Different regions grow different grapes, so yes. Sancerre and Pouilly-Fumé in the east grow Sauvignon Blanc and Pinot Noir; Anjou and Touraine in the middle grow mostly Chenin Blanc and Cabernet Franc, though the best Touraine whites are Sauvignon Blanc; and the Pays Nantais in the west grows Muscadet.

Do vintages matter?

They do, and it's a complicated picture. Chenin Blanc and the red grapes do best in the warmest years; but if it's too warm the Sauvignon Blanc gets flabby. The great sweet wines are only made in years when conditions are favourable. See the Quick Guide (left).

When do I drink them?

Sauvignon is delicious enough to enjoy anytime, with or without food, but Chenin Blanc and the reds really cry out for it – their balance, their subtlety are brilliant as part of a meal. The reds, in particular, are perfect for drinking in the summer, slightly chilled if you like, but they're good enough for quite grand dinner parties too. Muscadet comes into its own with a plate of seafood.

Can I afford them?

Chenin Blanc is great value, the reds are good value and Sancerre and Pouilly-Fumé are on the pricy side: other wines made from Sauvignon Blanc are cheaper. Muscadet makes fairly priced, refreshing drinking.

Alsace

When it comes to aromatic white wines, no region in the world can match Alsace. These wines all share a rich, dry spiciness, a fatness quite unlike anything from the rest of France, or anywhere else in the world.

Gewurztraminer is the spiciest, most fragrant grape of the lot – it's the benchmark for the aromatic white wine style – but even a grape like Pinot Blanc, which everywhere else makes a rather well-behaved, sober sort of wine, becomes lush in Alsace. Sylvaner, too, normally a light, dry and rather earthy individual, here has a touch of spice. Even lean, citrussy Riesling, which takes on a limy, toasty character in Australia, and in Germany is minerally or smoky and peachy, often runs to a bit of spice here. And Pinot Gris is second only to Gewurztraminer in its richness, though it tends to be smoky, earthy and honeyed rather than rose- and lychee-scented like Gewurz.

The exception to the rich, spicy rule is the tiny amount of dry Muscat made in Alsace, but it wins through with a heavenly floral, grapy aroma which, in its own way, is almost as intense as that of Gewurztraminer.

And these wines are all dry. Well, dryish at least; that spiciness makes them seem richer. That means they go well with food, particularly spicy foods, or foods that mix sweet and savoury flavours.

There are sweet whites, too. The richest are made from noble-rotted grapes, but they're rare and expensive. The locals drink them with foie gras. There's also some light red, made from Pinot Noir, but it's

Alsace is a wine tourist's and gourmet's paradise. This is the medieval town of Riquewihr.

generally little more than dark rosé – attractively perfumed, but not up to the quality of the whites.

Do regions matter?

No, all the wines are in the uniquely Alsatian style.

Do vintages matter?

The wonderful sweet wines are made only in the best years, and the reds need warm summers. But otherwise don't worry too much about vintages.

When do I drink them?

At any time. They're good restaurant choices because they'll go with a whole range of different foods around the table, and I've never met anyone who didn't like them. They're also unusual enough to impress at special occasions. Riesling is the best all-round food wine; Gewurztraminer and Pinot Gris are especially good with Chinese and other Asian foods. They are delicious on their own, too, and Muscat is a pure delight by itself.

Can I afford them?

Yes, certainly. They're never the cheapest wines in any shop, and the best ones are pretty pricy, but they can be bought with confidence at every level. Even the simplest wines will be good buys.

Southern France

This is where the excitement is in France right now, where the Old World meets the New. In the vin de pays regions, particularly Vin de Pays d'Oc, Australian and Australian-trained winemakers, lured by the tremendous potential of the vineyards, have been moving in to produce wines with typically New World upfront fruit, sometimes tempered with creamy new oak. Initially they favoured the international varieties like Cabernet, Merlot and Chardonnay, but they're now also discovering the joys of the blends of traditional grape varieties used by the producers in the AC regions. They use Syrah as well, and some Viognier. Anything, in other words, with the potential for bags of quality and bags of flavour.

This influence is also being felt in the traditional AC wines of the South-West, Languedoc-Roussillon and Provence. More and more producers are using improved techniques to get the best out of the many local grape varieties found throughout these regions, although the wines still taste resolutely Old World. Flavours in much of the South-West are influenced by Bordeaux. But as you get further from Bordeaux you'll find highly individual wines that are often robust and wildly herby, but which are increasingly showing the benefits of modern freshness. I love the dusty fruit of the traditional wines, when they're well-made; but I also love the sheer verve of the new vin de pays styles.

Do regions matter?

Yes, very much, because of the division between Old World and New World styles. In Bergerac and Côtes de Duras in the South-West you get red and white Bordeaux lookalikes. A little further from Bordeaux, you'll find wild, spicy, brawny and tannic reds in Cahors and Madiran.

In Languedoc-Roussillon the reds are spicy and often herb-scented, sometimes with a dry austerity as well.

You'll find these flavours in the wines of Fitou, Minervois, Corbières, Faugères, St-Chinian, Coteaux du Languedoc and Côtes du Roussillon.

Provence, with the appellations of Bandol, Côtes de Provence, Coteaux d'Aix en Provence and Les Baux-de-Provence, makes both spicy, warm-hearted and intense, blackcurrant reds, plus a great many good rosés. The dominant grape often determines the style: Cinsaut makes the palest rosé; Syrah the tastiest rosé and red.

Vins de pays from Oc and elsewhere in the south should be juicier, more directly fruity interpretations of these red and rosé styles, and they also add white wines in the ripe, nutty and aromatic styles to the repertoire.

Traditional whites range from bone dry and neutral to those with a tang of wild herbs; Jurançon can be delightfully perfumed. Rosés are strawberryish and, again, have a whiff of herbs. Sparkling Blanquette de Limoux is sharp, refreshing and appley. There are some sweet, golden fortified Muscats, too, from Frontignan, Mireval, Rivesaltes and St-Jean-de-Minervois, and, next door to Bordeaux, the sweet Sauternes-lookalikes of Monbazillac.

Do vintages matter?
Not really, but even here there are occasional aces.

When do I drink them?
Whenever you feel like it. The reds can be a bit assertive for hot weather, but the whites and rosés are perfect.

Can I afford them?
With the exception of a few cult wines, yes.

Facing page: The village of Caramany is just one of several in the northern Roussillon producing exciting reds from their mountainous vineyards.

QUICK GUIDE ▷ *Southern France*

Location The vineyards are in three regions: the South-West, Languedoc-Roussillon and Provence.

Grapes In the South-West Cabernet Sauvignon, Cabernet Franc and Merlot are widely grown reds. Malbec has its moment of glory in Cahors. Tannat and Négrette are intriguing local varieties. Whites are often Sémillon and Sauvignon Blanc, but there is also a host of local grapes. Carignan is the traditional Languedoc-Roussillon red, but the better-quality Rhône reds, Grenache, Syrah, Mourvèdre and Cinsaut, are widely grown, too. International favourites, both white and red, are commonly found. Provence has the same red varieties; its best white is Rolle.

Ten to try
RED
- **Domaine Alquier** Faugères ③
- **Château l'Hospitalet** Coteaux du Languedoc, La Clape ③
- **Château de Pibarnon** Bandol ⑤
- **Domaine Gauby** Côtes du Roussillon-Villages ④
- **Prieuré de St-Jean-de-Bébian** Coteaux du Languedoc ④
- **Château Ste-Eulalie** Minervois ②
- **Château La Voulte-Gasparets** Corbières ③

DRY WHITE
- **Domaine de Cauhapé** Jurançon ③
- **Domaine du Tariquet** Vin de Pays des Côtes de Gascogne ②

SWEET WHITE
- **Domaine Cazes** Muscat de Rivesaltes ③

① Bergerac
② Cahors
③ Minervois
④ Corbières
⑤ Fitou
⑥ Bandol

italy

Italy has its own grape varieties and its own way of doing things; and it's now doing them better than ever. Famous names like Soave, Valpolicella and Chianti are restoring the shine to their tarnished reputations, while the south is re-establishing itself with inexpensive wines, brimful of character, that every wine shop wants on its shelves.

Facing page: Vineyards near the town of Montalcino in southern Tuscany. The powerful wine from here, Brunello di Montalcino, is now one of Italy's most famous reds.

Below: I can tell you from experience that grape-picking is really hard, messy work but these pickers in Campania, southern Italy, still seem remarkably cheerful.

Italy doesn't really make the sorts of wines that other countries do. Even when Italian producers use international grapes like Cabernet or Chardonnay or modern techniques like aging the wine in new oak, they give the wines a distinctive Italian twist. So when do you opt for a bit of Italian style? When you're staring at a plate of food, that's when. The reds are full of sweet-sour cherryish fruit that sets your mouth watering, and the bone-dry, neutral, but increasingly herb-scented whites are so well behaved they'll accompany even the most delicate dish. The whites make terrific apéritifs, but the reds need food.

ITALIAN CLASSIFICATIONS

The Italian system is loosely based on the French model. DOC is the equivalent of France's AC.

Denominazione di Origine Controllata e Garantita (DOCG) In theory the classic wines, limited to a few regions and with tight restrictions on yields and production methods. But it's still a completely mixed bag.

Denominazione di Origine Controllata (DOC) These are the major appellations, similar to the AC regions of France. Grape varieties, yields, vineyard sites and production methods are all regulated.

Indicazione Geografica Tipica (IGT) Wines with a regional identity, similar to the French vin de pays. This classification is also widely used by producers of high-quality wines that do not comply with the DOC or DOCG regulations.

Vino da tavola In general the most basic wines, with little regulation and no information on the label about where the wine was made or the vintage. Once used for maverick high-quality wines, but most of these have now converted to IGT (above).

Piedmont and the North-West

If you like powerful, scented reds that mature majestically, this is your region. Nebbiolo is the grape and Barolo, if you're feeling rich, is the summit of your ambition. The colour is rarely dark, but the flavours are impressive.

Barolo is a blockbuster of a red wine. Think of the scents of chocolate and cherries, of prunes and tobacco, of tar and of roses. Whirl them all together and you've got an idea of what mature Barolo tastes like. It used to be a wine that took years and years to age, but a new generation of modernizing producers is making wines that are approachable far younger, and are less tannic and forbidding. But Nebbiolo *is* a tannic grape and Barolo, ancient or modern, is a tannic wine. Barbaresco is similar but lighter. Other Nebbiolo wines – Langhe, Nebbiolo d'Alba, Carema and Gattinara – range from ripe and juicy to rough and ready.

But Nebbiolo doesn't dominate the vineyards. That role is left to Barbera, which crops up everywhere. High acidity and low tannin are its keynotes, together with flavours of slightly unripe plums and raisins; the best age well, but most can be drunk young. The third main red grape is Dolcetto, which is juicier and fruitier than the other two, but still has that typical Italian sweet-sour tang, and often a good streak of tannin as well.

Whites are not a big deal round here, with the exception of deliciously grapy, sweet Asti and other sparkling wines made from the Muscat, or Moscato, grape. There's some aromatic Arneis and refreshing but overpriced Gavi, made from Cortese grapes, but overall it's reds that rule.

Do regions matter?

Yes, because styles vary. Barolo is the biggest, grandest Nebbiolo, followed by Barbaresco, followed by the others I mentioned above. Dolcetto d'Asti and Dolcetto d'Acqui tend to be lighter than Dolcetto d'Alba. Barbera d'Alba and Barbera d'Asti are the best Barbera wines.

Do vintages matter?

Yes, for the better reds. See the Quick Guide (right).

When do I drink them?

With food. In the case of the reds, they simply demand food like almost no other wines. They're powerful, expressive, impressive, but not easy to understand. Asti and the other sweet Moscato whites are perfect for summer drinking, or with rich desserts.

Can I afford them?

Top Barolo and Barbaresco are fantastically expensive. Go for a fairly simple Nebbiolo from a good producer – though it still won't be cheap. Barbera and Dolcetto are less costly; Asti is inexpensive and fun.

QUICK GUIDE ▷ North-west Italy

Location Piedmont is the most significant wine region of north-west Italy.

Aromas Nebbiolo, Barbera and Dolcetto make reds in the mouthwatering sweet-sour style, with Nebbiolo being the weightiest and most perfumed. Of the whites, Arneis is fairly aromatic; Moscato (the Italian name for Muscat) is very aromatic and used for sweet and sparkling wines; and Cortese is dry and lean.

Nebbiolo-dominated regions Barbaresco, Barolo, Carema, Gattinara, Langhe, Nebbiolo d'Alba.

Barbera-dominated regions Barbera is grown everywhere in north-west Italy. DOCs include Barbera d'Alba and Barbera d'Asti where the top estates can produce stunning wines.

Dolcetto-dominated regions DOCs include Dolcetto d'Acqui, Dolcetto d'Alba and Dolcetto d'Asti.

Local jargon *Bricco* – a prime hilltop vineyard. *Sorì* – a south-facing hillside vineyard (i.e. one that catches the best of the sun). *Riserva* – wine given extra aging before it goes on sale. *Spumante* – sparkling. *Spanna* – a nickname for Nebbiolo.

① Barolo and Barbaresco
② Asti

Vintages to look for Anything between 2009 and 1995, except 2002.

Vintages to avoid 2002, 1994, 1992 and 1991.

Ten to try
RED
- **Elio Altare** Dolcetto d'Alba ③
- **Domenico Clerico** Barolo, Ciabot Mentin Ginestra ⑤
- **Aldo Conterno** Barbera d'Alba, Conca Tre Pile ⑤
- **Pio Cesare** Barbaresco ⑤
- **Prunotto** Barolo ⑤
- **Albino Rocca** Dolcetto d'Alba ③
- **Vajra** Langhe ③
- **Vietti** Barbera d'Asti ④

WHITE
- **Bruno Giacosa** Roero Arneis ③
- **La Spinetta** Moscato d'Asti ③

Facing page: Truffle hunting with dogs is a serious pastime in the hills around Alba in Piedmont.

Right: The village of Barolo, one of the most famous names in Italian wine.

North-east Italy

This is mostly white wine country. The wines range in style from light and mountain-fresh up in the high Alto Adige to riper and fuller further south and east in the Veneto and Friuli. But bear in mind that Italian penchant for neutrality in white wines. Even with aromatic grapes like Sauvignon Blanc, you won't find anything like the pungency that you'll get from New Zealand. Pinot Grigio is generally light and dry: quite different from Pinot Gris in Alsace. Gewürztraminer is floral but delicate. Sparkling Prosecco is fresh, bouncy and light. Many wines are made from single grape varieties, and named by the grape, which makes it easy to guess the flavour. Soave is the major exception. It's made from Garganega and Trebbiano grapes and is a typically Italian bone-dry, neutral white. Some is pretty classy, with an ability to age, but most are merely light, uncomplicated and, so long as you buy Soave Classico from the heartland of the region, enjoyable. The wines of Alto Adige, Trentino and Friuli will usually offer more flavour and personality.

Reds, including Valpolicella and Bardolino from the Veneto, are mostly light, but can have an attractive bitter-cherry twist. International grapes like Merlot are almost always much lighter than versions from other countries. However, if you see a Valpolicella labelled Recioto, it will be sweet, rich and probably wonderful. Buy it. (There's a white Recioto from Soave, too, which is just as good.) Amarone is like Recioto della Valpolicella, but dry: it's a fascinating, bitter-sour, heavyweight red.

Do regions matter?

Yes, hugely, since each region has its own style. Alto Adige makes the lightest, tangiest wines; Trentino's are slightly fuller; Friuli's the most intense. Valpolicella, Bardolino and Soave from the Veneto are the most famous. Quality here has been compromised by overproduction, but plenty of producers make the kind of wine that earned these regions their fame in the first place. Stick to wines labelled Classico and you are less likely to be disappointed.

Facing page: Alto Adige is a spectacular mountain region.

Above: Drying grapes for Valpolicella Amarone, one of the greatest but most unusual red wines in the world.

Do vintages matter?

They do vary, but they're not worth worrying about unless you're buying Reciotos and Amarones or the most expensive whites. See the Quick Guide, right.

When do I drink them?

The whites are good as apéritifs, or as partners for light food. The light reds are for simple meals like pizza and pasta. Reciotos and Amarones are for feasts. The latter demand aging in bottle – up to ten years if you can wait.

Can I afford them?

Not all the wines are brilliant value. Friuli is expensive for the quality; Alto Adige relatively so. The Veneto, if you choose well, is not so expensive, especially for Valpolicella, Soave Classico and lemony white Lugana.

QUICK GUIDE ▷ *North-east Italy*

Location The Veneto and Friuli-Venezia Giulia are located around Venice. Valpolicella and Soave are near Verona. Trentino-Alto Adige extends north into the Austrian Alps.

Grapes Garganega and Trebbiano are the grapes of Soave. Red Corvina is the main grape of Valpolicella and Bardolino. Alto Adige, Trentino and Friuli have a number of local varieties, such as white Friulano and red Teroldego, but are dominated by international grapes. Whites include Pinot Bianco, Pinot Grigio, Gewürztraminer, Chardonnay and Sauvignon Blanc; reds include Merlot, Pinot Noir and Cabernet Sauvignon.

Local jargon *Classico* – the central heartland, and therefore the best part, of a region. *Recioto* – sweet Soave or Valpolicella made from semi-dried grapes. *Amarone* – Recioto, but fermented out to dryness. *Ripasso* – ordinary wine passed over the lees of Amarone to add a bitter-sweet flavour and increase the alcohol level.

Vintages to look for
(Amarone) 2009, 2008, 2006, 2004, 2003, 2000, 1997.

Vintages to avoid
(Amarone) 2007, 2005, 2002.

① Bardolino
② Valpolicella
③ Soave

Ten to try
RED
- **Allegrini** Amarone della Valpolicella Classico ⑥
- **Foradori** Teroldego Rotaliano ③
- **Tedeschi** Valpolicella Classico Superiore ②
- **Villa Russiz** Collio Merlot, Graf de la Tour ⑤
- **Zenato** Valpolicella Superiore Ripasso ③

WHITE
- **Andriano** Alto Adige Gewürztraminer ③
- **Anselmi** I Capitelli ③
- **Pieropan** Soave Classico ③
- **Schiopetto** Collio Tocai Friulano ④

SPARKLING
- **Villa Sandi** Prosecco di Valdobbiadene ③

Tuscany and central Italy

Chianti is far and away the most famous wine of this part of Italy – in fact it's probably the most famous wine of Italy, period. It's the essence of the sweet-sour cherryish style that dominates Italian reds, but there's a twist of tea leaves in there as well, if you're lucky – a tomato savouriness if you're less lucky – a whiff of violets, and a good backbone of tannin. And quality, you'll be glad to hear, has been surging upwards since the late 1990s.

The key to most of the reds in this part of Italy, including Chianti, is the Sangiovese grape. It's at its lightest in the inexpensive vini da tavola you'll find in every Tuscan supermarket, and at its richest and most expensive in two DOCGs, Brunello di Montalcino and Vino Nobile di Montepulciano. Both these wines need some serious aging to allow their acidity and tannin to soften, but there are sort of 'junior' versions, Rosso di Montalcino and Rosso di Montepulciano, which are fruitier and can be drunk younger. Morellino di Scansano and the other wines from the Tuscan coastal area called the Maremma are riper and juicier in style, although Bolgheri is home to some dark, dense superstars like Sassicaia. Carmignano near Florence is austere but good.

Apple-fresh, plum-rich Montepulciano (the grape, not the town that makes Vino Nobile mentioned above) is the other major red variety and is the main player on the east side of the Apennines. Montepulciano d'Abruzzo is good, gutsy stuff at its best. Tasty Rosso Conero and Rosso Piceno from Marche blend it with Sangiovese.

Whites are light, dry and generally neutral: Vernaccia di San Gimignano, Verdicchio, Frascati and Orvieto are the best known. They can all be very attractive, but apart from the top wines, you can treat them interchangeably. Lambrusco is light, fizzy white or red. The best is purple and dry with a lipsmacking sharp bite, but most exported Lambrusco is sweetened, and pretty insipid.

Do regions matter?

With the exception of the Super-Tuscans and 'designer' wines (see right), Tuscany has one basic style of red. There is a theoretical hierarchy of regions, with Brunello di Montalcino as top dog, but it would be snobbish to insist on it. Vino Nobile di Montepulciano and the best Chianti Classicos are serious contenders. Other Chiantis are less serious (and dare I say easier to enjoy), while Bolgheri and

A tranquil scene near Panzano in the heart of the Chianti Classico area.

WINE TERMS **Vin santo**

Traditionally a Tuscan speciality but made all over Italy, **vin santo** (holy wine) is produced from dried Trebbiano, Malvasia and other grapes. It can be dry or sweet, depending on whether it is intended as an apéritif or a dessert wine. The best truly are divine – sweet wines with a taste of nuts, dried apricots and crystallized orange peel.

WINE TERMS Super-Tuscans and modern 'designer' wines

There was once an Italian wine law which, among other absurdities, forced Tuscan producers to add white grapes to their Chianti. Top producers couldn't stand it and they started a rebellion. They made no effort to comply with the rules and instead experimented with grape varieties that were forbidden for DOC wines, like Cabernet Sauvignon, and techniques like aging wine in new oak barrels, which was also forbidden. They classified the wines as simple vini da tavola, gave them fancy names, like Sassicaia or Tignanello, and charged a fortune for them. The wines became known as **Super-Tuscans** or **Super Vini da Tavola**. Now, the law has changed and most of them have become DOC or, more commonly, IGT. But those top producers have never stopped experimenting and are famed for both traditional wines like Chianti and highly fashionable ones made from international grapes, including Cabernet, Syrah, Merlot, Pinot Noir, Chardonnay and Viognier.

Scansano in the Maremma region are making increasingly exciting wines. Montepulciano-based reds taste different: richer, but coarser with it. The whites are mostly neutral, with some shining exceptions among Verdicchios and Orvietos.

Do vintages matter?
Yes, for the better reds. See the Quick Guide, right.

When do I drink them?
Whites are best as everyday wines. Drink the reds with robust food – it's what they were made for. Really good reds demand a few years' bottle age.

Can I afford them?
Yes and no. Top quality reds hit the investment market. Less expensive wines are good value.

Location These are the wine regions forming the calf and knee of Italy's boot shape. Tuscany is the most significant.

Grapes Principally Sangiovese for the reds. Montepulciano is grown in Marche and Abruzzo. Trebbiano, Verdicchio and Vernaccia are the main whites. Cabernet Sauvignon and Chardonnay are well established international varieties and producers are experimenting with other such as Sauvignon.

Local jargon *Riserva* wine with extra aging before release. *Classico* – the central, best part of a region. *Rufina* – the best Chianti sub-zone after Chianti Classico. Other Chianti zones are Colli Aretini, Colli Fiorentini, Colli Senesi, Colline Pisane, Montalbano, Montespertoli.

Vintages to look for 2009, 2008, 2007, 2006, 2004, 2003, 2001 and 1999.

Vintages to avoid 2002.

① Chianti
② Verdicchio
③ Orvieto

Ten to try
RED
- **Antinori** Brunello di Montalcino, Pian delle Vigne ⑤
- **Avignonesi** Vino Nobile di Montepulciano ④
- **Casanova di Neri** Rosso di Montalcino ③
- **Isole e Olena** Cepparello ⑤
- **Marramiero** Montepulciano d'Abruzzo ⑤
- **Selvapiana** Chianti Rufina ③
- **Umani Ronchi** Rosso Conero, Cúmaro ⑤
- **Villa Cafaggio** Chianti Classico Riserva ③

WHITE
- **Antinori** Cervaro della Sala ②
- **La Carraia** Orvieto ②

Location Puglia, Molise, Campania, Basilicata and Calabria, which make up the toe and heel of Italy's boot, plus the islands of Sicily, Sardinia, Pantelleria and Lipari.

Grapes Almondy Aglianico, dark, glowering Negroamaro and scented Nero d'Avola are the most exciting reds, followed by burly, peppery Primitivo. Cannonau is a Sardinian relative of Grenache. Local whites include Greco, Fiano, Falanghina, Nuragus, Vermentino, Vernaccia, Grillo and Catarratto. Muscat produces delicious sweet wines.

Fortified wines Marsala, Moscato di Pantelleria.

Ten to try

RED
- **Caggiano** Taurasi ⑤
- **Candido** Salice Salentino ②
- **D'Angelo** Aglianico del Vulture ③
- **Duca di Salaparuta** Duca Enrico ⑤
- **Felline** Primitivo di Manduria ②
- **Planeta** Santa Cecilia ④
- **Santadi** Antigua, Monica di Sardegna ②

WHITE
- **De Bartoli** Vecchio Samperi ⑤
- **Feudi di San Gregorio** Fiano di Avellino ③
- **Sella e Mosca** Vermentino di Sardegna, La Cala ②

① Fiano di Avellino
② Taurasi
③ Aglianico del Vulture
④ Primitivo di Manduria
⑤ Salice Salentino
⑥ Copertino
⑦ Marsala

Southern Italy

I think I love this part of Italy most of all. The wines are just so good. They're not expensive, but they're stuffed with flavour, unrestrained and slightly wild. They couldn't taste more Italian if they tried.

In other words, it's an up-and-coming region, and it's coming up so fast I can hardly keep pace with it. Mostly it's the reds that excite me: they're sturdy, spicy and chocolaty, with a touch of prunes and raisins and roast coffee beans. Puglia led the way with Salice Salentino and Copertino but now Sicily and Campania are striding ahead with some brilliant wines and Sardinia is racing to catch up.

Southern Italy has loads of exciting and individual red grape varieties, like Aglianico, Nero d'Avola, Nerello

Mascalese and Frappato. Puglia is the home of Primitivo, the grape that is generally agreed to be the European ancestor of California's Zinfandel. In some places there are terrific whites, too: Puglia generally makes them from international grapes like Chardonnay, but elsewhere in the south you'll find fascinating fragrant, herb-scented native varieties like Fiano, Falanghina, Catarratto, Grillo, Greco and Vermentino. I'm also fond of fortified Marsala, for its brown-sugar sweetness and its tingling acidity, but dry versions are even tastier.

Do regions matter?
Not that much: you'll get southern Italian character pretty much whatever you buy.

Do vintages matter?
Ditto.

When do I drink them?
These are relaxed, informal wines, but they still repay attention. It's a waste to knock them back too carelessly. Cook some good rustic Italian food for them.

Can I afford them?
Yes, yes, yes. There are loads of brilliant-value budget wines, and the expensive ones are seriously classy.

Along with Puglia and Sicily, the mountainous region of Campania is leading the wine revolution in Italy's south.

spain

Spain could now justifiably claim to be Europe's trendiest country when it comes to eating and drinking. Spanish cuisine is buzzing with imagination and irresistible raw materials. And Spanish wine has leapt to the fore with a whole array of flavours and styles, ancient and modern. I love the freshness, the brightness that modern methods and ideas have brought to wine. But I'd hate to lose the great traditional flavours of wines like Rioja or sherry – and luckily, in Spain, the old and the new exist successfully side by side.

Rioja, sherry and Cava fizz used to be pretty much the only Spanish wines you'd see under their own names. That's all changed. Areas that used to simply despatch their wines to vast blending vats around the world – La Mancha, Valdepeñas, Valencia, Campo de Borja, Jumilla – are all discovering what they do best, and offering us very individual flavours at very fair prices, with their names on the

Above: The Spaniards always know how to throw a good party. This is Jerez's Festival of the Grape in the far south of Andalucia.

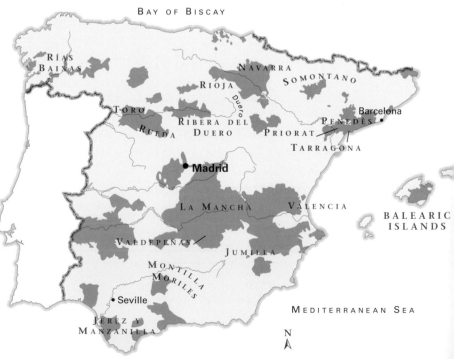

label. Old vineyards, modern methods – that's the key here – resulting in easy-drinking reds packed with the flavours of strawberries and damsons and scented with the swish of herbs, dry, gutsy pink wines and light, refreshing, citrussy whites.

The more serious flavours haven't disappeared – indeed there are more spicy, warm-hearted vanilla-scented reds aged in oak barrels than ever before. There are still creamy, oak-aged whites. And the flavours of great sherry haven't changed for generations.

Cava

All Spanish fizz made by creating a second fermentation in the bottle – this is how they do it in Champagne – is called Cava. Nearly all of it comes from Penedès, near Barcelona. Cavas used to be recognizable for their rustic, earthy flavours, but since they were cheap, no one worried too much.

Nowadays the vineyards and production methods have greatly improved, and most Cava is fresh, lemony, clean and invigorating. The grapes normally used are Parellada, Macabeo and Xarel-lo – all quite neutral – but you will often find some Chardonnay added to give a creamy sheen to the wine.

For some spectacular scenery head inland from Barcelona to the region of Priorat, where rugged mountains form a backdrop to the small terraced vineyards interspersed with olive and almond trees.

SPANISH CLASSIFICATIONS

The Spanish system, like all EU systems, has layers of quality. And like Italy, Spain has an extra, top tier.

Denominación de Origen Calificada (DOCa) This is the top category reserved for wines with a long tradition of high quality. So far only Rioja and Priorat have been awarded the accolade.

Denominación de Origen (DO) The standard designation for quality wine applies to over 60 regions, with fairly strict regulations regarding grape varieties, yields and the like.

Vino de pago A category for single-estate DO wines. So far there are three in Navarra and five in La Mancha.

Vino de la tierra These 'country' regions are akin to the French vin de pays regions for wines that should have regional character. Many have ambitions to be promoted to DO status.

Vino de mesa As in other European countries the most basic wines are known as table wine.

North-west Spain

A very diverse offering, with wines ranging from light, fresh whites to Spain's biggest, burliest dry reds. The most famous – and most expensive – is Ribera del Duero (see page 141) – but there are lots of more affordable wines to try. Let's look at whites first.

Rueda, south of Valladolid, is one of Spain's leading white wine regions. Flavours are green and tangy; quality reliable. You might think, from a quick taste, that they're all made from Sauvignon Blanc: there is some Sauvignon here, though the major grape is Verdejo. Some are aged in oak for a more butter-and-toast flavour.

Rías Baixas, in the wet, cool, northwestern corner of the country, is Spain's other leading candidate for the title of most refreshing white. These aromatic, citrussy wines generally come from the Albariño grape. Not all have the sort of elegance and lightness that I expect – and they're expensive. Similar wines from Valdeorras, Ribeiro and Ribeira Sacra can be cheaper and more fragrant, with the perfumed Godello grape at work.

For red wines, the leading contender after Ribera del Duero is Toro. This can be thought of as a sort of country cousin Ribera del Duero in flavour: plummier, more robust, perhaps without quite the focused flavour, but still a hell of a mouthful of palate-blasting fruit. Toro is quite good value, though prices have risen.

There are light, fresh reds in Ribeiro and Ribeira Sacra, and the wines get fuller further inland with warmer, drier conditions in Valdeorras and, especially, Bierzo where the local Mencía grape is producing exciting modern reds. Cigales is famous for *rosado* (pink), but is making increasingly good reds.

Do regions matter?
Only as above.

Do vintages matter?
In almost all cases, drink the youngest. Toro reds have significant aging potential.

When do I drink them?
Pinks and whites make lovely apéritifs and Rías Baixas is excellent with fish and seafood and Toro with red meat.

Can I afford them?
Rueda is affordable, Rías Baixas just a bit more expensive. Toro is getting more expensive, as is Bierzo.

QUICK GUIDE ▷ *North-west Spain*

Location The cool, wet, northwestern corner of Spain and warmer, drier vineyards along the River Duero.

Grapes Reds – Tempranillo (Tinta de Toro), Mencía; whites – Albariño, Godello, Sauvignon Blanc, Verdejo.

Local jargon Red wines with extra aging before release may be labelled *Reserva*.

Ten to try

RED
• Descendientes de José Palacios Bierzo, Pétalos ③
• Frutos Villar Toro, Muruve ②
• Luna Beberide Bierzo, Mencía ②
• Elias Mora Toro ③
• Fariña Toro, Gran Colegiata ③

WHITE
• Adegas Galegas Rías Baixas ③
• Belondrade y Lurton Rueda ⑤
• Godeval Valdeorras ③
• Marqués de Riscal Rueda ②
• Pazo de Señorans Rías Baixas ③

BAY OF BISCAY

① Rías Baixas
② Ribeiro
③ Ribeira Sacra
④ Valdeorras
⑤ Bierzo
⑥ Toro
⑦ Cigales
⑧ Rueda
⑨ Ribera del Duero

• Valladolid

Ribera del Duero

If I were the king of Spain I'd expect to be able to get my hands on pretty much any Spanish wine I wanted at the flick of my fingers. I'd pay, of course, but what's the point of being king if you're told, you'll have to wait your turn, just like everybody else. Well, that's allegedly what happened when King Juan Carlos tried to buy some Vega Sicilia red without getting on the waiting list. At the time – in the early 1990s – Vega Sicilia, from Ribera del Duero, was Spain's most famous single wine. Although Vega Sicilia has been going since 1864, Ribera del Duero only began to receive recognition – and then adoration and obsession – in the 1980s.

The grape used is a version of Tempranillo (Rioja's grape), which they call Tinto del País or Tinto Fino, and growers can also use non-Spanish grapes such as Cabernet Sauvignon and Merlot. The remarkably focused flavours of black fruit, especially blackcurrant, are possible because of limestone-dominated vineyards on the slopes of the Duero Valley that are sometimes so white they seem to be coated in snow.

Well, they might be, because these vineyards are very high – up to 850 metres. This is dangerous – there are only 125 days a year when there is no frost risk – but that short summer period brings very high daytime and very low nighttime temperatures. That temperature difference, with the limestone, creates the gorgeous pinging black fruit of Ribera del Duero. When the wine is aged in vanilla-ey oak barrels, the result is sublimely good. But these wines have become the darlings of wealthy wine lovers the world over, and prices are high.

Do regions matter?
The region stretches east to west for 100km, with correspondingly different conditions, but the Ribera del Duero DO covers the entire zone.

Do vintages matter?
Yes. Sometimes the autumn rains come early, as do frosts. But in less good years the cheaper/younger *joven* or *crianza* wines can be very good because no top end *Reservas* are made – all the grapes are blended together.

When do I drink them?
These are impressive wines, often oaky, often tannic, but with a magnicefent core of dark sweet fruit. Drink them with your best cuts of lamb or beef.

Can I afford them?
They're never cheap, but the *crianza* and non-*crianza* wines (less special grapes, less oak aging) may be affordable. Top examples are some of Spain's most expensive wines.

Rioja

Rioja is an area in transition and all the better for it. If you like the traditional flavours of Spain – the soft vanilla and strawberries, the leathery maturity of the reds and the powerfully dry and nutty whites – you can still find them here. But there are plenty of juicy, unoaked or lightly oaked young reds being made in Rioja, too, and there's been an upsurge in oaky, dark and dense single-estate wines, too. Many producers now make white Rioja in a modern tangy, lemon-zesty style. The best examples become vegetal and creamy, not unlike mature white Burgundy, but with a pungent sour-cream finish.

Muga is the only bodega in Rioja still using oak for every stage of their red winemaking.

Do regions matter?

Rioja Alta and Rioja Alavesa are the best sub-regions, but most wines are a blend of grapes from all over Rioja.

Do vintages matter?

They do for the top wines. But don't worry about vintages for the young wines.

When do I drink them?

They're tasty enough for any occasion, though the finer red Riojas deserve good food and a reflective mood. Really top traditional white Rioja might come as a shock the first time you try it. Persevere. The light young *joven* reds are great for summer glugging.

Can I afford them?

Usually, although the top wines (often labelled Gran Reserva or with a fancy title from a single estate) will be pretty expensive. Simple young Riojas no longer offer the same value as reds from elsewhere in Spain, but the lightly oaked *criadera* styles (reds and whites) can be very tasty. Young rosés are usually dry, appetizing and affordable.

North-east Spain

There could hardly be a better overview than this of what's been happening to Spanish wine in recent years. Navarra, once Rioja's understudy, is a hotbed of experimentation and there's no one single style. There are young juicy, fruity reds and oak-aged, mature wines; there are varietal wines and there are blends; there are traditional Spanish grapes like Garnacha and Tempranillo, and international ones like Cabernet and Chardonnay. There are plenty of crisp whites and strawberryish *rosados* (the Spanish term for rosé), too.

Penedès was the first region in Spain to plant international varieties like Chardonnay and Cabernet Sauvignon. Whites come in both the ripe and toasty, and green and tangy styles; reds are intense and blackcurrant or spicy and brawny. Some are varietals; others are blends of international and Spanish grapes. Penedès, like Navarra, has struggled to create an identity outside Cataluña, but there is a different reason here. Torres. This great family company is so well-known throughout the world that its name overshadows that of the region. Its enormous fame may be a mixed blessing, but Miguel Torres has done more to modernize Spanish wine practices and flavours than anyone else.

If Navarra and Penedès have led the modernizing wave, two smaller areas have taken full advantage. Somontano, squeezed up against the Pyrenees foothills, is a cool green oasis that produces delightful fresh, sometimes aromatic, whites and lean but tasty reds. Costers del Segre, inland from Penedès, makes modern reds and whites. Coastal Alella produces attractive fresh whites, most of which go to satisfy local thirsts. And in Mallorca, it is, at last, worth sampling the local wines.

The most fashionable area of the North-East is Priorat, a wild, mountainous region where tiny yields of mostly black grapes (95%) produce dense, raisined,

sun-drenched reds that I sometimes find a bit much, but which have developed cult status in Spain and the USA. The neighbouring area of Montsant produces milder examples at a much lower price.

Relatively unfashionable are the inland areas of Campo de Borja, Calatayud and Cariñena, near Zaragoza. Vast plantations of old bush vines – mostly Garnacha, backed up by Tempranillo – produce juicy, herb-strewn reds, some of Spain's best-value wines.

QUICK GUIDE ▷ North-east Spain

Location Navarra is Rioja's neighbour (see page 142). Somontano is cooler, the regions to the south – Campo de Borja, Cariñena and Calatayud – are warmer. Penedès and Priorat are the best-known wine regions of Cataluña in the east.

Grapes For the reds, Tempranillo (under various names) and Garnacha (some from very old vines), as well as Cariñena (Spanish for Carignan), and international varieties such as Cabernet Sauvignon. For the whites you'll find Moscatel (Muscat), Parellada, Xarel-lo (aka Pansa Blanca) and Macabeo (aka Viura), plus international varieties such as Chardonnay and Gewurztraminer.

Local Jargon Much the same as in Rioja (see page 142).

Vintages to look for (Priorat) 2005, 2004, 2001, 2000.

BAY OF BISCAY

MEDITERRANEAN SEA

① Rioja
② Navarra
③ Campo de Borja
④ Calatayud
⑤ Cariñena
⑥ Somontano
⑦ Alella
⑧ Penedès
⑨ Priorat

Ten to try
RED
- **Borsao** Campo de Borja ②
- **Capçanes** Montsant, Mas Collet ②
- **Chivite** Navarra, Gran Feudo Crianza ②
- **Guelbenzu** Azul ③
- **Joan d'Anguera** Montsant, Finca L'Argatà ④
- **Tomàs Cusiné** Costers del Segre, Vilosell ③

WHITE
- **Marqués de Alella** Alella ③
- **Pirineos** Somontano, Mesache Blanco ②
- **Torres** Penedès, Fransola ④
- **Torres** Penedès, Viña Sol ②

Do regions matter?

Only as above.

Do vintages matter?

Not a lot for fizz and whites, but Navarra reds differ quite a bit and Priorats reflect vintage conditions.

When do I drink them?

I wouldn't choose the cult wines of Priorat unless I was being treated to dinner by a well-heeled enthusiast. Otherwise these are wines for pretty well any occasion.

Can I afford them?

Definitely. However, top Penedès and Navarra wines are expensive, and as for the top Priorats, well, I expect you've got the message by now: they're not cheap, and Montsant wines give you most of the flavour for a lot less money.

Central & South-east Spain

The different regions here are at last making a name for themselves, either for good quality at a low price or, in some cases, for very high quality at a high price (as in Manchuela). The vast vineyard region south of Madrid is the home of fresh, bright – and cheap – reds, pinks and whites, led by La Mancha and Valdepeñas. The Levant, the hot but fertile strip along the Mediterranean, is famous for its fruit and veg, but Valencia, Utiel-Requena, Alicante, Yecla and Jumilla are now producing good-quality red, pink and white wines at low prices

Do regions matter?

Only as above.

Do vintages matter?

Rarely. It's very hot every year.

When do I drink them?

Mostly easy-going everyday wines, though the red wines from the Levant can be pretty beefy.

Can I afford them?

Easily. Except for the occasional boutique winery in Manchuela and Dominio de Valdepusa near Toledo.

Location The vast central region of Castilla-La Mancha lies to the west of the Levant.

Grapes Monastrell (aka Mourvèdre), Tempranillo (aka Cencibel), alone or blended with Syrah or Cabernet Sauvignon; Bobal for rosés and reds. Airén for neutral but increasingly modern whites. Sweet whites – either light or rich – from Moscatel (aka Muscat).

Ten to try
RED
• **Carchelo** Jumilla ②
• **Casa de la Viña** Vino de la Tierra de Castilla ②
• **Dominio de Valdepusa** Petit Verdot ⑤
• **Finca Antigua** La Mancha, Syrah ②
• **Juan Gil** Jumilla ②
• **Mustiguillo** Mestizaje ②
• **Piqueras** Almansa, Valcanto ②
WHITE
• **Ercavio** Blanco ②
SWEET WHITE
• **Gutiérrez de la Vega** Casta Diva Cosecha Miel ④
• **Vicente Gandia** Valencia, Fusta Nova ②

① La Mancha ⑤ Valencia
② Valdepeñas ⑥ Alicante
③ Manchuela ⑦ Yecla
④ Utiel- ⑧ Jumilla
　Requena

Madrid •

• Valencia

Sherry

I've got news for you: sherry doesn't have to taste a bit like that sweetish brown concoction we've all endured at some time. That was sherry dumbed down for export. Sherry as the Spanish drinks it is altogether different. For one thing, it's bone dry. For another, it's intensely aromatic, smelling of bread yeast and apple cores, nuts and prunes, coffee and toast. It's one of the great fortified wines of the world.

Dry sherry can be light and pale (*fino* or *manzanilla*), browner and wonderfully nutty (*amontillado*) or even more brown and fantastically concentrated (*oloroso*).

Good sweet sherries do exist. The Pedro Ximénez grape makes intensely grapy, scented wine that is almost black in colour. The Spanish drink this with dessert, or pour it over ice cream. Other good sweet sherries will have the Spanish word *dulce* on the label, or *muy dulce*, meaning very sweet. Spanish words like this – *muy viejo* for very old, or *seco* for dry – are a good sign: they indicate that the same wine is sold on the Spanish market, to people who are serious about the quality of their sherry.

Nearby Montilla makes wine similar in style and flavour, though it seldom has the bite of good sherry.

Málaga is a sweet fortified wine and the best are intensely nutty, raisiny and caramelly.

Do regions matter?
Get to grips with styles before you worry about regions.

Do vintages matter?
Virtually all sherry is non-vintage. It is produced by the solera system, which basically means that you have a series of barrels of wine at different stages of maturity. You bottle wine from the most mature barrel, but you take only a proportion of the barrel. You top up the barrel from the next most mature barrel, and so on until

QUICK GUIDE ▷ *Sherry*

Location In the far south of Spain. The region's official name is Jerez y Manzanilla. See the map on page 138.

Grapes Most sherry is made from Palomino, which makes incredibly boring unfortified wine. But turned into sherry it's fabulous. The other grape (and the main one in Montilla) is Pedro Ximénez (or PX), which makes wonderfully grapy sweet sherry.

Local jargon *Dulce* – sweet. *Muy dulce* – very sweet. *Muy viejo* – very old. *Seco* – dry. *Almacenista* – small-scale producer with just a few barrels of high-quality sherry. The company of Emilio Lustau makes a speciality of bottling these.

Ten to try
FINO AND MANZANILLA
• **Barbadillo** Solear ❷
• **Gonzalez Byass** Tio Pepe ❷
• **Hidalgo** La Gitana ❷
• **Valdespino** Inocente ❶
AMONTILLADO
• **Barbadillo** Principe ❸
• **González Byass** Del Duque ❺
• **Hidalgo** Napoleon ❸
OLOROSO
• **Williams & Humbert** Dos Cortados ❸
• **González Byass** Matusalem (sweet) ❸
• **Osborne** Solera India ❸

you reach the youngest, which you top up with new wine. Every bottle of sherry is therefore a blend of wine of almost all ages.

When do I drink it?
Fino and *manzanilla* are perfect apéritifs, and ideal with tapas. Dry *amontillado* makes a good winter apéritif, when it seems a bit dark and cold for *fino*. Intense, dry *olorosos* are wonderful winter warmers before or after a meal, and really good sweet sherries are excellent after dinner. *Fino* needs to be fresh: ideally, buy half bottles and polish them off in one go.

Can I afford them?
Good sherry is terrifically cheap for the quality.

portugal

Portugal is just discovering itself, in wine terms. Yes, port and Madeira are among the world's great sweet fortified wines, but the table wines, red and white, are only now finding their feet. And they have flavours, especially in the reds, that you'll find nowhere else: of chocolate, cherries, damson and vanilla; soft and juicy, yet slightly sour.

Below: Port is Portugal's most famous wine, but is drunk much more outside Portugal than in it. There are several styles of port, but my favourite has to be a glass of the vintage stuff – dark, powerful and serious with a good few years of aging. You really should age it for 20 years, and ideally more. I've had stuff from the 19th century which was absolutely astonishing.

Right: Inland from Lisbon the huge Alentejo region is now producing some of Portugal's most exciting modern red wines.

Table wines

Good reds are now being made in Portugal, from the far north to the deep sandy south of the Algarve. Red Vinho Verde is an acquired taste in the north, thin and pungent, but a little further south, the Douro river, home of port, is now making some of Portugal's best and most expensive reds. Deciding whether to use their top grapes for Douro table wine or for port has become much harder for the producers. Bairrada, Beiras and Dão make austere but increasingly good wines while the Ribatejo, Alentejo, Estremadura and even the Algarve make numerous juicy, sun-ripened reds.

Portugal has less of a white tradition. White Vinho Verde can be excellent if it's the real thing – snappy, sharp, tasting of laurel and apricot skins – but much of the exported wine is sweetened up. There are serious whites made in all Portugal's wine areas – sometimes from international grapes such as Chardonnay – but more often from Portugal's own honeyed, lanoliny varieties. And pink Portuguese isn't just Mateus. There's lots of tasty dry stuff as well.

Do regions matter?
Northern regions like Douro, Dão and Bairrada are noticeably different from the southern regions of Ribatejo and Alentejo.

Do vintages matter?
Only rarely, and mostly in the north. Most Douro vintages are good but Dão and Bairrada vary a lot.

When do I drink them?
The reds mostly need food – they're full of flavour and reasonably assertive. White Vinho Verde is excellent with seafood and lovely as a tangy apéritif. The dry rosés are anytime quaffers.

The Baga grape is one of Portugal's many wonderful, unique varieties, making dark tannic wines in the Bairrada region.

Can I afford them?
Yes, yes, yes. Most Portuguese wines are cheap for the quality they offer. Their unfamiliarity keeps the prices down, but the lack of demand fuels a determination to succeed among the producers. Unfamiliar names and grape varieties also help the price/quality ratio. Douro table wines can be pricier but the quality can be superb.

Port and Madeira

Both these famous wines are fortified, but they are totally different. Port is sweet and nutty, and vintage port is full of black fruits, pepper and spice; Madeira is tangy and pungent with a dry finish, even when it's sweet.

Port styles are basically divided between vintage and non-vintage ports. **Vintage** port comes from a single year, and only in the best years do the producers 'declare' a vintage. The wines should be matured in bottle for ten or 15 years before being opened. **Single-quinta vintage** ports are a variation on this theme: they come from the best estate owned by the producer, but are made in the second-best years. They are ready to drink at about ten years old. **LBV**, or **Late-Bottled Vintage**, is rather different. Yes, it's wine from a single year, but it's usually over-processed. 'Traditional' unfiltered LBV, however, is a lovely, perfumed drink that can be enjoyed as soon as you buy it.

Crusted is a non-vintage blend that is usually an excellent budget substitute for vintage port; **vintage character** is mostly undistinguished. **Tawny** is the most wonderful of the non-vintage styles. 10-Year-Old tawny combines maturity with freshness; 20-Year-Old is nuttier and more mature; and 40-Year-Old is very nutty, smooth and rare. Then there are the ports that simply have a proprietary name, like His Excellency's Frightfully Old Port. Some of these are good, but many are just glorified cheap rubies and tawnies. Read the back label carefully for clues. If it says **Ruby**, it's the simplest and youngest of ports, and nothing will ever turn it into anything better.

Madeira is classified quite differently. Here levels of sweetness are the key. **Sercial** is the lightest and driest; **Verdelho** is slightly weightier and off-dry. **Bual** is fairly sweet and rich, and **Malmsey** is very sweet. All get their pungent, smoky tang from they way they are heat-treated, so that the wine gently oxidizes. It's not a flavour you'd welcome in other wines, but in Madeira it's essential.

Do regions matter?
No.

Do vintages matter?
Only for vintage port. Most Madeira is non-vintage.

When do I drink them?
At the end of the day, unless you want to fall asleep. The Portuguese drink tawny as an apéritif; dry Madeira is also a good apéritif. Vintage port deserves serious treatment, not to mention a lie-in the next morning.

Can I afford them?
Good ports and Madeiras aren't cheap, and poor ones aren't worth the hangover. Having said that, if you are looking for a classic mature wine to celebrate a birthday or anniversary, there are still examples around and they are much cheaper than an equivalent Bordeaux or Burgundy and much more likely to be a lovely drink.

Location Vinho Verde, port, Dão and Bairrada are from the north, but the upcoming regions are further south in Ribatejo, Alentejo and Estremadura. Madeira is an island west of Morocco.

Grapes The secret of Portugal's flavours is its abundance of indigenous grapes found nowhere else. Few of these grapes' names appear on labels, but Touriga Nacional, Baga and Tinta Roriz (Tempranillo) are good red grapes whose names you might see. The main Madeira grapes are Sercial, Verdelho, Bual and Malmsey: each of the different styles is made from the grape of that name.

Local jargon *Quinta* – estate. *5/10/20/40-Year-Old* – Age statements refer to the average age of the wine in the blend, not to any particular vintage. The age is an indicator of style for tawny port. Only buy Madeira with an age statement, preferably 10-Year-Old, or you won't get the full character.

Vintages to look for (port) 2008, 2007, 2005, 2004, 2003, 2000, 1997, 1994, 1985, 1983, 1980.

Ten to try
RED
- **Bacalhôa** Alentejo, Tinta da Anfora ❷
- **Quinta do Crasto** Douro ❷
- **Esporão** Reserva ❷
- **Luís Pato** Beiras, Vinha Pan ❸
- **Casa Santos Lima** Alenquer, Quinta das Setencostas ❷
- **Tagus Creek** Ribatejo ❷

PORT
- **Ramos Pinto** Quinta de Ervamoira 10-Year-Old Tawny ❺
- **Taylor** Quinta de Vargellas (single-quinta vintage) ❺

MADEIRA
- **Blandy's** 10-Year-Old Verdelho (dry) ❸
- **Henriques & Henriques** 10-Year-Old Malmsey (sweet) ❸

Facing page: The vines for port are planted on steep terraces along the Douro Valley.

Left: The grapes for the finest vintage port are sometimes still trodden in shallow tanks or lagares in the traditional way. (That's me, second left.)

germany

Tell me your attitude to German wine, and I'll tell you whether you're a wine snob or not.

Seriously. You see, Germany produces some sensationally good white wines – some of the best in

the world. They have elegance, refinement, concentration and they live for decades, maturing to a

fascinating honeyed richness. But these vinous wonders have been horribly overshadowed by the

fact that Germany also makes some of the worst wines in the world. They're cheap, sugary and the

worst of it is, they are made in a style that apes that of the very best wines.

*The river Mosel twists and turns as it
makes its way from Luxembourg to
Koblenz on the Rhine and I never tire
of its great beauty. This view is at
Trittenheim.*

Anybody who has tasted good German wine and fallen in love with
it – and the two processes are usually simultaneous – could not
possibly mistake the two styles. But several generations of wine
drinkers have been brought up to despise German wines because all
they've ever tasted is the dross.

The fact that you're reading this chapter indicates that you're
prepared to look beyond the received opinions of wine snobs. Read a
bit further and I'll tell you how to find those sensationally good wines.

Riesling

The best and simplest guide to quality is the word Riesling on the label. Riesling is the classic white grape of Germany, and it's too costly to grow to be used for the worst wines. Riesling is *never* used for sugared-up cheap wines like Liebfraumilch. Riesling's characteristic flavour in Germany is tangy, though not particularly green; grapy and flowery, sometimes peachy, sometimes appley, sometimes smoky when young, and there's usually some sweetness in the wine to balance the grape's high acidity. That's important, because these are light wines with low levels of alcohol, and the acidity has to be balanced by something.

Looking at it the other way round, don't be put off by a touch of sweetness in a good Riesling: the acidity makes it delicious rather than cloying. That's the basic flavour. The picture is complicated by the German system of classification, which grades wines according to the ripeness and natural sweetness of the grapes. The highest grades of wines are invariably very sweet. The lower grades can be dry or off-dry. Most of the wines drunk in Germany itself are made dry, but in good examples a little perfumed fruitiness always peeps out.

Certain regions, mostly in the south, are producing increasing amounts of red wine, and as global warming kicks in they can be surprisingly ripe and good; but, to me, Germany is still fundamentally a white-wine country.

Do regions matter?
They do, very much, but above all stick to good grape varieties. The best wines usually come from the Mosel (lighter, tangier, smokier wines); the Rheingau (weightier, riper); the Rheinhessen (softer, and with only a small proportion of its vineyards dedicated to good quality); and the Pfalz (big ripe wines, often from Pinot Blanc, Pinot Noir and others as well as Riesling). Baden wines, white or red, should be good – the Pinot family is more important here than Riesling – and Franken has impressive dry Silvaner and good Müller-Thurgau.

Do vintages matter?
Yes and no. There is certainly great vintage variation, but the system of classification of wines by grape ripeness means that the better grades are only produced when the grapes are ripe enough – so in poor vintages only simple wines will be made, but they're often delightful, since the grapes from the best vineyards will end up in the cheaper wine.

When do I drink them?
The lighter wines – QbAs (see page 150), Kabinetts, Spätleses – make lovely apéritifs, but also go well with foods like trout or salmon or crab, with pâté, or with gently spicy Chinese or South-East Asian food. Keep the very sweet wines for puddings or preferably for drinking on their own after dinner. But remember that Riesling needs bottle age. Even a light Kabinett will improve for four years or so after the vintage, and the higher grades need longer.

Can I afford them?
Luckily, yes. Prices for top producers are high because demand is high in Germany, but it's still possible to buy a very good quality Kabinett or Spätlese from a less trendy producer or village for a much lower price than you would pay for a comparable wine from many other countries. And you'll often find good merchants selling mature Kabinetts or Spätleses for surprisingly low prices – because nobody wanted them.

German red wines

Most people think of Germany as a white wine country. Well, it is – just. About 60 per cent of the wines are white, but that leaves a remarkable 40 per cent that are red. I say 'remarkable' because Germany is the coolest, the furthest north of all Europe's great wine countries, and all its most famous wines over the centuries have been white and usually sweet. Global warming and an ambitious bunch of young winemakers are changing all that.

Yet the area with the greatest percentage of red vines has traditionally been the Ahr Valley – most northerly of the vineyards clustered along the Rhine Valley, and only beaten in the latitude stakes by the old East German areas of Sachsen and Saale-Unstrut, almost on the 52nd parallel – that's nearly as far north as London. Even they have 20 per cent red varieties.

The Mosel Valley actually used to ban red varieties but now has 10 per cent, including, amazingly, some Cabernet Sauvignon. The areas along the Rhine have always made some red wine, especially at Assmannshausen near Rüdesheim, but as we follow the river south past Mainz and down towards Switzerland and the Bodensee, more and more red vines are planted. The Pfalz has 40 per cent red grapes and is a hotbed of experimentation. Baden has even more with 44 per cent and Württemberg a whopping 70 per cent. Much of this is Pinot Noir (also called Spätburgunder), as well as modern, 'created' varieties like Dornfelder and Regent, but Cabernet and Merlot also crop up, and I wouldn't be surprised to be tasting German Syrah some time soon. After all, the Swiss have been making Syrah for years.

Assmannshausen's beautiful vineyards sloping down to the river Rhine are unusual for the Rheingau region in that they are best known for their excellent red wines from Pinot Noir.

GERMAN CLASSIFICATIONS

Germany's classification system is based on the ripeness of the grapes and therefore their potential alcohol level.

Tafelwein and **Landwein** are the most basic and not worth bothering with. **Qualitätswein bestimmter Anbaugebiete** (QbA) wines come from one of 13 wine regions. They can be okay – and there's some good QbA Chardonnay and Pinot Noir – but the infamous Liebfraumilch is a QbA, so beware. The next grade up and the one to look for is **Prädikatswein** and there are six levels, in ascending order of ripeness: Kabinett, Spätlese, Auslese, Beerenauslese, Eiswein and Trockenbeerenauslese.

The kind of area a wine comes from also has a bearing on its likely quality. Single vineyards, or **Einzellagen**, are the ones to go for. On the label you'll see the name of the village with the suffix **-er** (for example, Bernkasteler from the village of Bernkastel), followed by the name of the vineyard. An increasing number of top estates are using single-vineyard names on their top wines only.

Grosslagen are bigger areas without the same specific character. Grosslagen are very difficult to spot on labels, because they have invented names for themselves that sound just like single vineyards. For example, Niersteiner Gutes Domtal is a Grosslage and Niersteiner Pettenthal is a top vineyard. A **Bereich** is larger than a Grosslage, but again it can be very confusing. For example, Bernkastel is a top village and produces excellent wine; but the Bereich Bernkastel extends much further and includes some decidedly inferior vineyards.

QUICK GUIDE ▷ *Germany*

Location The wine regions are mostly in the south-west of the country, gathered around the river Rhine and its tributaries.

Grapes Riesling makes the best wines, in a tangy though not green style; Scheurebe is fragrant and grapefruity; Pinot Blanc (or Weissburgunder) is less tangy and more nutty; Pinot Gris (Grauburgunder or Ruländer) is honeyed and smoky; Silvaner is dry and neutral. Traminer (Gewürztraminer) is floral, Müller-Thurgau is generally undistinguished. The best red is Pinot Noir (Spätburgunder).

Local jargon *Trocken* – dry. *Halbtrocken* – off-dry. *VDP* – an organization of quality wine estates. *Sekt* – sparkling wine.

Vintages to look for 2009, 2007, 2005, 2004, 2003, 2002, 2001, 1990.

Vintages to avoid 2000.

Ten to try
All these producers make a range of wines from various individual estates in their region. Prices begin at ❶ for a Kabinett wine, ❷ for a Spätlese. The best and rarest wines are ❺.
- **Dönnhoff** Nahe
- **Gunderloch** Rheinhessen
- **Fritz Haag** Mosel
- **Karl H Johner** Baden
- **Toni Jost** Mittelrhein
- **Juliusspital** Franken
- **Franz Künstler** Rheingau
- **J Leitz** Rheingau
- **Dr Loosen** Mosel
- **Müller-Catoir** Pfalz

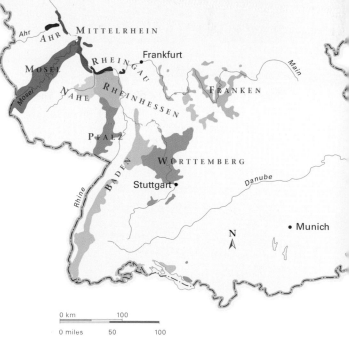

austria

I can't think of a European nation where the wine culture has changed so dramatically over a generation as it has in Austria. Austria still makes great sweet wines, but a new order based on medium- and full-bodied dry whites and increasingly fine reds has emerged.

Above: Lake Neusiedl on the border with Hungary is a paradise for water birds, holiday makers and noble rot, a type of fungus that attacks the grapes at harvest time and what the best sweet wines need.

Facing page: In the Wachau region west of Vienna the vineyards rising up above the Danube produce some of Austria's top dry Rieslings.

Austria may classify its wines in much the same way as Germany (with one or two differences), but the basic style of Austrian wine is not the same. Many wines in Germany are light and low in alcohol, and may be dry or medium depending on the producer. Austrian wines are basically dry, but riper and weightier, and noticeably higher in alcohol. Whites can be neutral, green and tangy, or intense and nutty; the peppery, bay-leaf scented Grüner Veltliner is a fascinating speciality. Reds are mostly juicy and peppery, though the more serious of them discard that instant juiciness in favour of greater structure concealed beneath velvet fruit. And when Austria makes wines sweet, they are very sweet: rich, honeyed, complex and concentrated.

All of Austria's vineyards lie along the warmer and drier eastern edge of the country, from the border with the Czech Republic and Slovakia in the

AUSTRIAN CLASSIFICATIONS

Wine categories are similar to those in Germany, beginning with **Tafelwein** (table wine) and **Landwein** (country wine). **Qualitätswein** wines must come from one of 16 main wine regions. Like German wines, Austrian quality wines may additionally have a special category (in ascending order of ripeness, sweetness and price): Kabinett, Spätlese, Auslese, Beerenauslese, Ausbruch and Trockenbeerenauslese. Most Austrian wines are either dry or nobly sweet.

Over recent years Austria has developed its own geographic appellation system, called DAC, but it comes with stylistic constraints.

QUICK GUIDE ▷ Austria

Location The wine regions are all in the far east of the country, running north and south of Vienna.

Grapes Riesling makes the best white wines, more in the style of Alsace than Germany. Grüner Veltliner is Austria's speciality, making very individual dry whites with a peppery tang. Reds are mainly Blauer Portugieser, Zweigelt, St Laurent and Blaufränkisch.

Local jargon *Trocken* – dry. *Halbtrocken* – off-dry. In the Wachau, Steinfeder wines are made for early drinking,

Federspiel wines can last for three years or so and the most powerful wines are known as Smaragd.

Vintages to look for
There hasn't really been a bad vintage since 1999, though 2003 is atypical.

Five to try
- **Bründlmayer** Riesling Alte Reben ④
- **Franz Hirtzberger** Grüner Veltliner ④
- **Alois Kracher** Grande Cuvée ⑤
- **Nikolaihof** Riesling ④
- **Franz X Pichler** Riesling ④

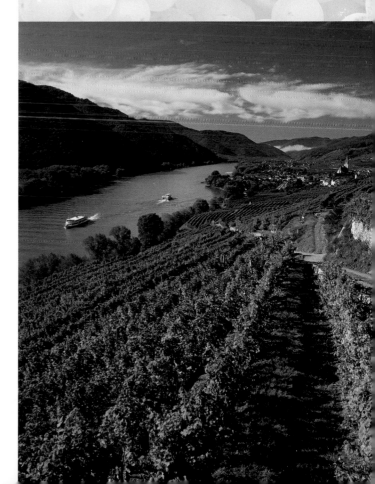

north, running past Vienna, south to Slovenia and Hungary. It is the climate here that makes viticulture feasible and only in the Wachau and Kremstal is the benign influence of the river Danube really necessary.

Different regions have different styles. The best, fruitiest, most velvety reds, as well as the darkest and oakiest, come from Burgenland and the Neusiedlersee on the border with Hungary, as do the intense sweet wines, some of which are truly world class. The best areas for dry whites are either on or near the river Danube in the Niederösterreich region to the west of Vienna. Greatest of these areas is the Wachau, home of superlative Rieslings and fine Grüner Veltliners. Almost as good are the Kremstal and Kamptal areas where Grüner Veltliner is transformed into spectacular savoury yet rich whites as good as any in Europe. The Weinviertel, in the north-east, produces large quantities of decent reds and Grüner Veltliner whites. The Steiermark region in the far south makes pale and steely whites, especially from Chardonnay, Pinot Gris and Sauvignon, which have achieved cult status in the country.

other european countries

This is where we get into unfamiliar grape varieties, and flavours which, without being strident, manage to be quite unlike any others. Vineyards crop up across the continent from the eastern border of Germany right across to the shores of the Black Sea and well beyond. And to the north, an increasing number of spots in England and Wales have what it takes to grow excellent grapes.

England and Wales

This is a great time to be an English wine enthusiast. A mixture of global warming, talented winemakers and some business-savvy owners has brought English wine to a place in the sun. Vineyards are now flourishing as far north as Yorkshire and west into Wales and Cornwall, though most are still in the south. Kent, East and West Sussex are the most heavily planted areas, and hundreds of acres of brand new vineyards are now taking advantage of growing conditions on the chalky Downs that are extremely similar to those in Champagne (just across the Channel). Sparkling wines have made huge strides in the last decade and the best, led by Nyetimber, Ridgeview and Camel, can easily stand up to French competition. White wines have developed a delightful delicate elderflower-scented style based on Bacchus and Siegerrebe. Rondo and Regent are producing gutsy dark reds while Pinot Noir and Dornfelder make lighter reds and gorgeous pinks.

Switzerland

There are three basic styles of Swiss wine: French, German and Italian. The best wines are nearly all French-style, made in the French-speaking cantons. The main white grape is the neutral Chasselas: reds are mostly light, jammy Gamay or Pinot Noir, or often a blend of the two, such as Dôle. They don't taste as good as Burgundy or Beaujolais, but they cost as much.

Well, Chasselas whites can be tasty and zesty if drunk young. Or, try to find some of Switzerland's speciality grapes, such as Petite Arvine, Amigne and Humagne Blanc. These produce rich, dry wines – sometimes sweet ones, too. The beautiful Valais region also manages some good Chardonnay and Syrah. Whites from German-speaking Switzerland are mostly made from the dull Müller-Thurgau (Riesling-Sylvaner). The southern Italian-speaking canton of Ticino makes light, easy-going Merlots, but a new wave of producers is now making deep, ripe, oaky reds of real interest.

Facing page far left: Vineyards in Kent, the 'garden of England'.

Facing page left: The Valais is the most important wine region in Switzerland.

Greece

Greece has grape varieties grown nowhere else. And many are pretty good: you'll see names like Assyrtiko, Robola, Roditis and Moschofilero on the labels of the whites; Xynomavro, Limnio or Agiorgitiko on the reds. The whites are green and tangy, with a crisp lemony flavour and good acidity and weight, though Moschofilero is aromatic and Muscat is usually sweet. The reds are spicy, sometimes herby, full-bodied and assertive, often unnervingly but satisfyingly dry.

Above right: Bottles of Tokaji aging in the cellars. Don't worry about that mould – it's been in the Tokaj cellars for centuries and never done any harm. In fact, it protects the wine, if anything.

QUICK GUIDE ▷ *Greece*

Location Greek vineyards are scattered from Makedonia in the north to the islands of Rhodes and Crete in the south.

Grapes Many of the best Greek wines today successfully combine traditional native varieties such as the red Agiorgitiko, Limnio and Xynomavro, and white Assyrtiko, Moschofilero and Roditis with international varieties such as Cabernet, Chardonnay and Semillon. Muscat is used for the famous sweet whites of Samos and Patras.

Five to try
RED
• **Gerovassiliou** red ➍
WHITE
• **Antonopoulos** Chardonnay ➎
• **Domaine Costa Lazaridi** Amethystos white ➌
• **Mediterra** Vilana ➋
• **Samos co-op** Anthemis (sweet) ➌

Eastern Europe

The countries of Eastern Europe produce both modern, New World-influenced wines and traditional styles from indigenous grapes – and while at the moment the reliable New World flavours are probably the best value, we ought to see more and more exciting native styles as they get their vineyards and their winemaking sorted following the fall of Communism.

Bulgaria has good-value copies of classic French styles, using Cabernet Sauvignon, Merlot and some passable Chardonnay; Mavrud, Gamza and Melnik are also good varieties for slightly jammy, juicy reds. Quality used to be more reliable during communist times, but the handful of private estates shows what is possible.

Hungary has the rose-scented white Irsai Olivér and red Kadarka and Kékfrankos. There are also more and more excellent examples of international grapes like Sauvignon Blanc, Chardonnay and Pinot Gris. At the moment these are just attractive, everyday gluggers, but Hungary's long-term potential is enormous. Tokaji, Hungary's fabulous sweet wine, has been famous for centuries and is still leading the way.

Romania could be great, but suffers from uneven quality and low prices; reds can be soft and jammy, whites balanced and nutty at their best. Very good

WINE TERMS **Tokaji**

Hungary's delicious sweet wine is uniquely tangy and smoky. It is made using grapes with a high level of natural sugar (usually the result of noble rot, the fungus that concentrates the sugar in grapes) which are known as **Aszú**. These wines are labelled **Tokaji Aszú** and the sweetness is measured in **puttonyos**. A 3-puttonyos Tokaji is sweet, 6-puttonyos is concentrated and rich. **Aszú Eszencia** is sweeter still and very intense. **Szamorodni** contains only a small proportion of Aszú grapes and ranges from dry to medium-sweet.

sweet wines come from the Tămîioasă grape, other good grapes include the aromatic Fetească. The Czech Republic and Slovakia both have light, gently spicy whites. Both Croatia and Moldova have exciting potential, and Slovenia has good, weighty whites from Laski Rizling and Pinot Blanc, tangy Sauvignon Blanc and some juicy reds.

Do regions matter?
Most regions only have one major winery, but the growing number of private estates will bring certain regions to the fore.

Do vintages matter?
Freshness can be a problem, so in general stick to the most recent vintage you can find.

When do I drink them?
Mostly they're everyday wines. Tokaji is for special occasions and after dinner.

Can I afford them?
Good Tokaji is expensive. Prices are relatively high in Slovenia, but the rest of Eastern Europe has loads of good wine at low prices.

QUICK GUIDE ▷ *Eastern Europe*

Location Bulgaria, Hungary and Romania are the main exporters. Moldova, the Czech and Slovak Republics and Slovenia also have good wine.

Grapes Bulgaria has lots of Cabernet Sauvignon, Merlot, Gamza, Mavrud and Melnik for blackcurranty reds of fair intensity or for juicy, fruity styles. Whites are patchier in quality; there's a fair bit of Chardonnay. Hungary has Furmint and Hárslevelü for Tokaji; Irsai Olivér, Kékfrankos, Kékoporto and others for aromatic whites and soft reds; it has international grapes, too. Romania has Pinot Noir, Chardonnay and others, plus the indigenous Fetească and Tămîioasă; Slovenia has Laski Rizling, Pinot Blanc, Sauvignon Blanc and others.

Ten to try
BULGARIAN RED
- **Bessa Valley** Enira red ❷
- **Sliven** Merlot ❶
- **Telish** Cabernet Sauvignon ❷

HUNGARIAN RED
- **Weninger & Gere** Cabernet Franc ❺

HUNGARIAN WHITE
- **Hilltop Neszmély** Irsai Olivér ❷
- **Royal Tokaji Wine Company** Tokaji Aszú, 5 Puttonyos (sweet) ❹
- **Istvan Szepsy** Tokaji Aszú, 6 Puttonyos (sweet) ❺

ROMANIAN WHITE
- **Cotnari** Grasa (sweet) ❶

SLOVENIAN WHITE
- **Movia** Veliko Bianco ❹
- **Verus** Furmint ❷

united states

The US is where the modern wine revolution began – the movement that has delivered clean, fresh, fruity-flavoured wine from all around the globe at affordable prices. It began, to be precise, in California, where the warm, dry climate is worlds away from that of the classic European regions. But late-20th-century technology provided the key, and the local viticultural centre, the University of California at Davis, provided the know-how and a stream of highly trained winemakers.

The result has been wines that in the 1970s challenged the domination of Europe, in the 1980s led the charge for change and which now confidently set their own agenda. Wine is produced in many other states, foremost among them Washington, Oregon and New York. But in terms of both quality and quantity, California is way out in the lead.

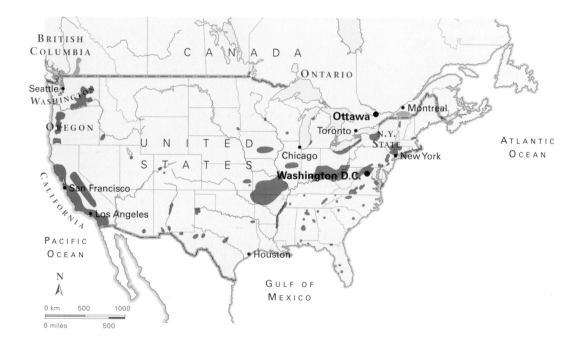

California

The wines here are generally big, ripe and ultra-modern in style. They can be simple and mass produced, or rich, complex and made in artisan quantities. Well-made, interesting wines abound in all but the cheapest price brackets, but they are generally more expensive than an equivalent from Chile or Australia. And be aware that by forking out for the most expensive cult reds you may be paying as much for the ego of the winemaker as for the quality of the wine: California is a place where you can produce a supposedly world-class super-premium wine simply by saying you will, and by charging a world-class, super-premium price. For wines that are genuinely world-class (and affordable) – and California has plenty – start by looking for a track record of quality.

Cabernet Sauvignon, Merlot and California's speciality grape, Zinfandel, rule for reds, often in the intense, blackcurranty or spicy, warm-hearted styles; and Pinot Noir makes good silky, strawberryish wines in selected spots such as the Russian River Valley and Santa Maria Valley. Ripe, toasty Chardonnay accounts for most of the best whites; Riesling and Sauvignon Blanc are also widely grown, though they tend to be less tangy than their counterparts elsewhere. Sauvignon, in particular, may be aged in new oak for a softer, spicier taste. These wines can be labelled Fumé Blanc.

The range of flavours is currently expanding, as more and more producers become interested in the grapes of Italy and the Rhône Valley: Sangiovese is fashionable, as are Syrah, Grenache, Mourvèdre and others. These are big spicy, attention-grabbing reds. The aromatic Rhône white variety Viognier is increasingly popular. Sparkling wines have fallen strongly under the influence of Champagne, partly because so many Champagne houses have set up shop here, and the best match Champagne for quality. A few Sauternes-style sweet Sémillons and sweet fortified Muscats have ultra-ripe fruity flavours.

Zinfandel deserves special consideration because it is thought of as California's own grape. In fact, it is the same as Primitivo from southern Italy. But Zinfandel has achieved renown in a way that Primitivo never did. At its best it makes warming, heavyweight, berry-flavoured reds with soft, ripe tannins; but it is the most amenable of grapes and can make any style you fancy, from soft, juicy gluggers to sweetish pink wine that is usually labelled as 'blush' or White Zinfandel, right up to the burliest of beefy reds and even heady 'port' styles.

Do regions matter?

AVAs (American Viticultural Areas) on the whole don't matter in the way French AC or Italian DOC regions do. AVAs are delimited appellations, but often based on political boundaries rathern than soil or climate. They don't tell you what grapes you can grow, or what style of wine you must make. This is winemaker heaven: you can make what you want, where you want – just as long as nature will let you and you reckon you can sell it.

Nevertheless, some places are particularly well suited to individual grapes or styles. Napa Valley is California's most famous area. It's where many of the most

---

US CLASSIFICATIONS

The first **American Viticultural Areas (AVAs)** were introduced in 1983 to impose some degree of classification on the rapidly developing US wine industry. They indicate only the area of origin of a wine and impose no regulations on its quality. They also require honest labelling of grape varieties. In general, the name of the producer is a surer guide to both style and quality when you are buying wine.

renowned wineries are based and its red wines, in particular its Cabernet Sauvignons and Merlots, have long been regarded as California classics. Stags Leap, Oakville and Rutherford are outstanding sub-regions for Cabernet Sauvignon.

Sonoma County is right next to Napa and is home to excellent whites and reds. The reds are generally a little softer and rounder than those from Napa. Two sub-regions – Dry Creek Valley and Russian River Valley – produce exciting Chardonnay and inspired Zinfandel and Pinot Noir. Sonoma Coast is proving inspirational for Pinot Noir. To the south of Napa and Sonoma, straddling both regions, is Carneros, a cool, foggy region famous for Chardonnay, Pinot Noir and sparkling wine.

South of San Francisco there are vineyard regions sprinkled right down the coast to Los Angeles. Most important of these are Monterey, San Luis Obispo and, in particular, Santa Barbara, including Santa Ynez and Santa Maria Valley, where some of California's finest Pinot Noir and Chardonnay are grown.

Further inland, the Sierra Foothills produce tub-thumping Zinfandel while the Central Valley is a vast agro-industrial area making the bulk of California's everyday wine, but with the good sub-regions of Lodi

Autumnal vineyards in northern Sonoma near Healdsburg.

and Clarksburg. If the label says North Coast, it means the general region north of San Francisco right up to Mendocino. Central Coast wines come from south of San Francisco.

Do vintages matter?

Only really for the finest wines and the coolest areas. Vintage variation is never as drastic as in, say, Bordeaux.

When do I drink them?

Nearly all California wines can be drunk young: only the very best will age. Since the very best are startlingly expensive, treat them with the respect due to a hefty outlay of cash and save them for a special occasion.

Can I afford them?

They're not cheap, compared to what's available from some other countries, particularly at the lower level. There's upwards pressure on price at the premium level, with producers seemingly competing to make the most expensive Cabernet or Chardonnay. Pinot Noir is about the price of its Burgundian equivalent; top Cabernet does not aim to be cheaper than top Bordeaux.

WINE TERMS **Meritage**

California producers introduced this marketing term to describe wines made from the same grape varieties as the classic wines of Bordeaux in France. It can apply to both red wines blended from **Cabernet Sauvignon, Merlot** and **Cabernet Franc** and to white **Sauvignon Blanc/Semillon** blends. However, it's rare to see the term on the wine label: as most meritage wines are sold instead under a suitably dignified proprietary name. If a California wine is called anything like Tapestry, Anthology, Elevage, Hommage or Affinity, chances are it's a meritage blend.

QUICK GUIDE ▷ *California*

Location The West Coast of the US.

Aromas intense, blackcurranty reds come from Cabernet Sauvignon, sometimes blended with Merlot, or from Merlot on its own. There's good Pinot Noir in the cool spots. Zinfandel comes in many styles: the best are spicy and rumbustious. The spicy style also belongs to blends of Syrah, Mourvèdre and Grenache. Sangiovese and other Italian grapes tend to be spicy, too. Whites are most often ripe and toasty from Chardonnay, Sauvignon Blanc, Viognier and Riesling, which tends to be soft and fruity rather than tangy.

Vintages to look for 2008 to 2001, 1999.

Twenty to try
RED
- **Au Bon Climat** Santa Barbara County Pinot Noir ③
- **Bonny Doon** Le Cigare Volant ④
- **Cline Cellars** Bridgehead Zinfandel ④
- **Laurel Glen** Cabernet Sauvignon ⑤
- **Long Meadow Ranch** Cabernet Sauvignon ⑤
- **Ravenswood** Sonoma County Zinfandel ③
- **Ridge** Zinfandel ④
- **Saintsbury** Pinot Noir ⑤
- **Shafer Vineyards** One Point Five Cabernet Sauvignon ⑤
- **Spottswoode** Cabernet Sauvignon ⑤
- **Sean Thackrey** Orion ⑤
- **Truchard** Syrah ④
- **Viader** Cabernet Sauvignon ⑤

WHITE
- **Calera** Viognier ④
- **Marimar Estate** Chardonnay ⑤
- **Newton Unfiltered** Chardonnay ⑤
- **Ramey** Chardonnay ⑤

SPARKLING
- **Roederer Estate** Anderson Valley Brut ⑤
- **Schramsberg** ⑤

SWEET FORTIFIED
- **Quady** Elysium Black Muscat ②

Ten for starters
Exciting California wine is expensive. These less costly wines give an idea of the styles, but don't expect the thrills of the main selection.
RED
- **Cycles Gladiator** Cabernet Sauvignon ②
- **Delicato** Shiraz ②
- **Kenwood** Russian River Valley Pinot Noir ②
- **Pedroncelli** Dry Creek Valley Zinfandel ②
- **Ravenswood** Lodi Zinfandel ②

WHITE
- **Beringer** Knights Valley Alluvium ②
- **Bonterra** Viognier ②
- **Dry Creek** Dry Creek Valley Sauvignon Blanc ②
- **Edna Valley** Chardonnay, Paragon ②
- **St-Supéry** Sauvignon Blanc ②

Right: Ballooning above the Napa Valley. These early morning fogs blanket the valley floor and play a crucial part in cooling the vineyards.

Washington

The states of Washington, Oregon and Idaho are known collectively as the Pacific Northwest. They are newer wine regions than California, but have gained a reputation precisely because they make wines in a non-Californian style.

Most of Washington's vineyards are in the Columbia Valley, east of the Cascade Mountains, in what are virtually desert conditions. It's very sunny, very dry, but there's plenty of water for irrigation. Subregions within the Columbia Valley include Walla Walla, Red Mountain, Wahluke Slope, Horse Heaven Hills and Yakima Valley.

The most popular red wines are intense, blackcurranty Cabernet Sauvignon and Merlot and good, warming Syrah. Riesling – in a range of styles, from dry to sweet – and Chardonnay – usually ripe and toasty – vie for position as most widely planted white grape. Semillon and fairly tangy Sauvignon Blanc are worth a look, too. And whereas Oregon has some real stars and a lot of wannabes, Washington State is more reliably good all round.

Do regions matter?
Not really. Most vineyards are in the Columbia Valley or one of its subregions.

Do vintages matter?
Not really.

When do I drink them?
Any time. Washington reds are good food wines.

Can I afford them?
Washington can produce great flavours at a fair price. However, some of the top producers' wines are almost impossible to get hold of – at any price.

QUICK GUIDE ▷ Washington

Location Most of Washington's vineyards are east of the Cascade Mountains, in the dry Columbia Valley region.

Grapes Cabernet Sauvignon, Merlot and Syrah are the main Washington reds; white grapes are Chardonnay, Riesling, Semillon and Sauvignon Blanc.

Vintages to look for The vineyards in eastern Washington enjoy modest weather fluctuations and the reds are consistently good.

Ten to try

With a few exceptions, Washington wines are difficult to find outside the US.

① Columbia Valley
② Yakima Valley
③ Red Mountain
④ Walla Walla Valley

RED
- **Chateau Ste Michelle** Indian Wells Cabernet Sauvignon ③
- **Col Solare** ⑤
- **Columbia Crest** H3 Horse Heaven Hills Merlot ②
- **Hedges** CMS ②
- **K Vintners** Syrah ④
- **Long Shadows** reds (Pedestal Merlot, Sequel Syrah, Feather Cabernet Sauvignon) ⑤

WHITE
- **Eroica** Riesling ③
- **L'Ecole No 41** Semillon ③
- **Chateau Ste Michelle** Columbia Valley Chardonnay ②
- **Poet's Leap** Riesling ③

Above: Mount Rainier looms over the Yakima Valley in eastern Washington State.

Oregon

Oregon Pinot Noir gained international recognition in the early 1980s thanks to the stunning wines made by handful of pioneering winemakers who planted vines in the Willamette Valley in the late 1960s and early 1970s. This long, wide valley lies between the Cascade Mountains to the east and the Coast Range to the west; it's cooler and wetter than California, but has an extra hour of sunlight a day, and there is a huge difference in temperature between the warm days and cool nights, all of which go to produce wines with bright fresh fruit flavours. That's the theory, anyway. Oregon wines are generally light, with Pinot Noir in the silky, strawberryish style, understated, nutty Chardonnay, spicy Pinot Gris and the odd good Riesling.

Oregon's wine industry is mainly in the hands of small, family-run wineries that focus on quality over quantity, so the wines tend to be expensive.

Do regions matter?
Not to most wine-drinkers. The Dundee Hills (a sub-region of the Willamette Valley with ancient red volcanic soils) is usually considered to be the star region, but Willamette winemakers are exploring the many different types of soil in the valley.

Do vintages matter?
They matter most for Pinot Noir (see Quick Guide).

When do I drink them?
Any time. Oregon Pinot Noirs and Chardonnays are food-friendly wines.

Can I afford them?
Oregon wines can never be cheap – conditions just aren't conducive to bulk production.

① Finger Lakes ② Long Island

Location New York State is the leading East Coast state for wine production.

Grapes The best European vines are Merlot and Pinot Noir for reds; Chardonnay and Riesling for whites. American or hybrid vines have very different flavours. They include Concord, Baco Noir, Chambourcin, Norton, Seyval Blanc and Vidal.

Vintages to look for
Nearly all the wines are made to be drunk young.

Ten to try
New York wines are difficult to find outside the state.

RED
- **Bedell** Reserve Merlot ⑤
- **Paumanok** Assemblage ③
- **Pellegrini** Cabernet Franc ②
- **Wölffer** Reserve Merlot ③

WHITE
- **Fox Run** Reserve Chardonnay ②
- **Dr Konstantin Frank** Dry Riesling ③
- **Glenora** Chardonnay ②
- **Heron Hill** Reserve Riesling ④
- **Lamoreaux Landing** Dry Riesling ②
- **Hermann J Wiemer** Dry Riesling ③

New York State

The best wines here come from European vines like Merlot, Pinot Noir, Chardonnay and Riesling, but New York State has a long history of making wines using native vines and hybrids (crosses between American and European varieties), which can cope better with the harsh climate. The native vines belong to a different vine species from European varieties and have quite different flavours: strawberryish, but with an intense floral perfume. Quality from the European vines is pretty good, and improving. Chardonnay is quite light and toasty; Riesling citrussy and flowery; and Gewürztraminer fragrant. Merlot tends to a grassy version of the juicy, fruity style rather than anything much more intense, but Pinot Noir is succulent and silky at best.

Do regions matter?
The Finger Lakes region is the largest and the most important. Long Island's boom seems to have fizzled somewhat but there are still good reds, especially from the North Fork. The Hudson River Region and the shores of Lake Erie have several good producers each.

Do vintages matter?
The erratic weather patterns of the East Coast mean that there is vintage variation between the regions.

When do I drink them?
Ideally, when holidaying in the Hamptons or in the beautiful Finger Lakes. Failing that, anytime will do.

Can I afford them?
Yes, but don't expect them to be bargain basement wines. Top wines are pricy and rare.

The Finger Lakes is New York State's most important wine region.

Other East Coast states

Virginia and Pennsylvania each have well over 100 wineries, and the wines are improving year by year. Wines made from European grapes are beginning to make their mark, especially in Virginia, where Cabernet Franc and Bordeaux-style red blends and Chardonnay and Viognier whites are establishing Virginia's identity among 'serious' wine enthusiasts. Italian varieties such as Sangiovese and Pinot Grigio thrive in south-eastern Pennsylvania. Native American vines such as Virginia's Norton, and hybrids such as Chambourcin, can make pretty nice wine, and the white hybrid Seyval Blanc makes a delicious accompaniment to the East Coast's famous seafood. Maryland has fewer wineries than its larger neighbours, but all three states offer a very wide range of wines, including good sparkling.

North Carolina has a subtropical climate, but has wineries throughout the state. Maine, farther north than Montreal, *can* ripen grapes, although its handful of wineries are best known for their fruit wines.

Below: In the heart of Virginia wine country near the Blue Ridge Mountains Barboursville Vineyards has links with Thomas Jefferson who designed the original estate mansion.

Midwest

The Midwest has a history of growing grapes and making wine dating back to the 1850s; in the late 19th century Ohio and Missouri rivalled California and New York as the major wine-producing states, but Prohibition brought this to an abrupt end. Freezing winters and hot summers are best suited to hardy native American grapes such as Catawba, Concord and Norton, as well as newer hybrids such as Vidal, Vignoles and Seyval Blanc for white wines, Chambourcin and Foch for reds; these grapes are also ideal for the semi-sweet and sweet wines preferred by many Midwesterners.

Classic European grape varieties are gaining ground in Ohio. One of the most promising regions is along the southern shore of Lake Erie, in the north of the state, which is producing a diverse range of wines; whites such as Chardonnay, Pinot Grigio, Gewürztraminer and Riesling are successful here, along with reds from Cabernet Sauvignon, Cabernet Franc and Pinot Noir. Icewines are another speciality.

Missouri's leading grape variety is Norton, for red wines ranging from dry to sweetish. Whites from hybrid grapes are also popular. Cold, snowy, old Michigan is positively throbbing with vineyards and wineries. Old Mission Peninsula and Leelanau Peninsula that jut out into Lake Michigan near Traverse City benefit from warm air from the lake and produce bright fresh Riesling, Gewürztraminer, Pinot Grigio, Pinot Blanc and good sparkling wine. Wisconsin's revival began in the 1970s; it has been most successful with the hybrid Foch, for red wine in a variety of styles. Illinois' fast-growing wine industry is based on hybrids such as Chambourcin (red) and Chardonel (white).

Left: Hermann is a historic town in the heart of Missouri wine country.

QUICK GUIDE ▷ Midwest

Location The Midwestern states of Ohio, Missouri and Michigan produce only a tiny percentage of US wines, but winemaking is undergoing a revival and there are now nearly 100 wineries in each of these states.

Grapes The best European vines are Cabernet Sauvignon, Cabernet Franc and Pinot Noir for reds; Chardonnay, Riesling, Pinot Grigio and Gewürztraminer for whites. Native American and hybrid vines have very different flavours. They include Chambourcin, Concord, Foch and Norton for red wines, Seyval Blanc and Vidal for whites.

Five to try
Few of these wines are sold outside their home state.
RED
• **Debonné Vineyards** Cabernet Franc, Ohio ❷
• **Stone Hill** Norton, Missouri ❸
• **Wollersheim** Domaine du Sac, Wisconsin ❷

WHITE
• **Firelands** Gewürztraminer, Ohio ❷

SPARKLING
• **L Mawby** Blanc de Blancs, Michigan ❺

Texas

Texas took its first steps into the modern world of wine in the late 1970s, with the usual suspects – Cabernet Sauvignon and Merlot – but grapes better suited to the Texan heat, such as Sangiovese, Syrah, Tempranillo, Grenache and Viognier, have gradually risen in favour. Unfortunately for Texan winemakers, no grape variety can withstand the occasional devastating hailstorms, which can destroy crops within minutes. Storms permitting, vintages are fairly consistent.

Since 2000 the number of wineries has increased dramatically, from 40 to more than 180, but many of these are small producers. Texas can't grow enough grapes to meet demand, so grapes are often bought in from California and elsewhere.

Other US wine regions

It's when I find that North and South Dakota have vineyards and a handful of wineries; that Minnesota has over 150 acres of vines and that even Alaska and Hawaii have wineries that I realize I need to get out and about more. Many of these states make their wines from native American grape varieties like Concord, which gives floral-scented wines, or newer French-American hybrids such as Minnesota's Frontenac or Hawaii's Symphony, bred to cope with challenging conditions. But wherever they can, winemakers are using the classic varieties – Riesling, Chardonnay, Cabernet, Merlot and Pinot Noir. Colorado, in particular, is making some top Merlot, Syrah, Riesling and Chardonnay wines from high-altitude vineyards in the west of the state.

Most of these wines never leave their state, some hardly make it to their nearest town – but if you're visiting, well, there isn't a single state now that can't offer a glass of something proudly homegrown.

QUICK GUIDE ▷ *Texas and other US wine regions*

Location Every state in the Union now boasts wineries, and with the gradual loosening of inter-state shipping regulations there has been a huge explosion in the last decade or so. California produces over 90% of US wine, followed far behind by Washington, New York and Oregon. States such as Texas are becoming serious players, too.

Grapes In Texas there are reds from Cabernet Sauvignon, Syrah, Sangiovese and Tempranillo, plus whites from Sauvignon Blanc, Chenin and Chardonnay. Elsewhere it's a mixed bag: some states are too cold, too wet, too dry or too humid to grow anything but hybrid varieties – although many have a go with Chardonnay and/or Riesling for whites and Cabernet Sauvignon for reds.

Five to try
Few of these wines are sold outside their home state.
RED
• **Boulder Creek** Syrah, Colorado ❸
• **Flat Creek** Super Texan, Texas ❸
• **McPherson** Tre Coloré, Texas
WHITE
• **Llano Estacado** Chardonnay Cellar Reserve, Texas ❸
SPARKLING
• **Gruet** Gilbert Grande Reserve, New Mexico ❺

Above: Barren moonscape cliffs tower over the vineyards in western Colorado.

canada

Icewine is the wine that made Canada famous – sweet white made from grapes picked when the temperature plummets and freezes them on the vines. They are picked and pressed before they defrost, with the result that the water content stays behind in the press, and just the stickily sweet juice oozes out. It's a remarkable wine, made in tiny quantities from Riesling or Vidal grapes.

The Okanagan Valley is British Columbia's most important wine region. The large lakes help moderate the climate and also provide a spectacular backdrop for the tourists.

But of course it's not a wine you can drink every day. To make up for that, Canadian producers have been busy improving the quality of their dry wines, and they're now producing light, elegant and sometimes positively intense flavours from classic cool-climate grapes. Pinot Noir and Merlot make pleasant, juicy reds; Chardonnays are nutty, Pinot Gris mild but spicy and Riesling crisp and citrussy. There are plenty of hybrid vines grown as well, for simple, perfumed, jammy reds and off-dry whites, but the best wines come from European vines.

Do regions matter?

British Columbia and Ontario produce 98 per cent of Canada's premium wine. The two major regions are the Niagara Peninsula in southern Ontario and Okanagan in British Columbia. Quebec and Nova Scotia both have a small but keen wine industry. One enthusiast in Prince Edward Island produces wine from grapes grown under glass; and the remaining provinces make fruit wines.

With its long sunny days and ice-cold nights Okanagan looks set to become a region of considerable diversity, suited to delicate whites in the north and some substantial Syrah and Bordeaux blends in the south down by Lake Osoyoos on the US border. Here the weather can get so dry you need to irrigate the vines. Ontario's vineyards rely on being between two vast bodies of water – the cool Lake Ontario and the warmer Lake Erie – which moderates what would otherwise be a very harsh climate and allows excellent ripening of whites like Riesling and Chardonnay, but also Pinot Noir, Merlot, Cabernet and Syrah, in particular on the limestone slopes and benches above Lake Ontario.

Do vintages matter?

They vary, but the wines are made to be drunk young. Red grapes don't always ripen; white grapes usually do.

When do I drink them?

The dry wines are good, light, all-purpose wines. Icewine should be savoured more slowly.

Can I afford them?

None of these wines are cheap and the best are snapped up by Vancouver and Toronto locals for high prices; icewines are expensive but luscious.

Picking grapes for icewine, Canada's speciality and a perfect example of how to turn a difficult climate to good effect.

QUICK GUIDE ▷ *Canada*

Location The vineyards are in the south, hugging the shores of the Great Lakes in Ontario, near the Atlantic Coast in Quebec and Nova Scotia, and near the Pacific Coast in British Columbia. See the map on page 160.

Grapes Pinot Noir, Merlot, Cabernet and Syrah for reds; Chardonnay, Pinot Gris, Riesling and Gewürztraminer for whites; Riesling and Vidal for whites and icewine.

Local jargon *VQA* – the letters stand for *Vintners Quality Alliance*, an organization which enforces high quality standards.

Ten to try
Apart from icewine, Canadian wines are difficult to find outside the country.
WHITE
• **Burrowing Owl** Pinot Gris ⓤ
• **Cedar Creek** Estate Select Syrah ④
• **Jackson-Triggs** Chardonnay ②
• **Mission Hill** Chardonnay ②
• **Southbrook** Chardonnay ③
• **Sumac Ridge** Gewürztraminer ②
• **Thirty Bench** Riesling ③
ICEWINE
• **Inniskillin** ⑤
RED
• **Henry of Pelham** Cabernet-Merlot ②
• **Quails' Gate** Pinot Noir ③

south america

The great revolution in wine – the emergence of ripe, fruity reds and whites at prices everyone could afford – began in California in the 1970s and really took hold in Australia in the 1980s. But as the 20th century galloped to a close, South America had begun to mount a very serious challenge and was laying claim to becoming the most consumer-friendly region of the wine-producing world. The reasons were simple: fruit, flavour and value.

South American wine is the epitome of the modern New World style: flavours are soft and juicy for reds; clean, tangy or toasty for whites. Experimentation is the order of the day in the two major wine-exporting countries, Chile and Argentina, and some extremely serious wines are emerging alongside the excellent everyday bottles. Brazil can produce some lovely fizz, decent whites and reds and together with Uruguay and its beefy, throbbing Tannat reds could yet provide a South American second division, but right now, for flavour and value, Chile and Argentina are a wine drinker's new best friends.

The Vale do São Francisco in northern Brazil is hot and arid and produces two harvests of grapes a year.

Brazil

Brazil is South America's major wine producer after Argentina and Chile (see pages 174-177). Traditionally most vineyards have been in the very beautiful and marching Rio Grande do Sul, where high humidity and summer rains make ripening reds difficult. However, several new areas are now being developed in the drier conditions towards Uruguay and in the sub-equatorial north at São Francisco Valley where the vines produce two vintages a year. Reds have improved recently and there is a refreshing lack of oak and lowish alcohol in many of them, but sparkling, both dry and grapily sweet, are Brazil's best wines so far.

Uruguay

Most of the vineyards are on clay soils spread around the capital, Montevideo. Cooled and dampened by the Atlantic gales, ripening isn't easy, and the Tannat grape, from South-West France – a traditional late ripener – struggles a bit. But it is the national grape and can make good, tough but scented reds. The 'international' reds and whites make up most of the rest of the vines. Dry hot vineyards on the Brazilian border show promise.

Peru and **Bolivia** make Pisco brandy from most of their grapes, but there are a few wines made in other countries, for example in **Venezuela**.

Mexico

This Central American country suffers dry and fierce heat and has more a beer and brandy than a wine culture. With the aid of irrigation Baja California in the north and high-altitude vineyards further south make good sites for heat-loving red grapes: varieties like Petite Sirah, Zinfandel, Nebbiolo and Cabernet do well. Whites struggle for freshness.

The vineyards of Chile and Argentina are some of the most spectacular in the world: these ones are in Chile's Aconcagua Valley just north of Santiago.

Chile

This is a country on the fast track to stardom. Chile has the good fortune to possess vast disease-free vineyards, stuffed full of classic grape varieties and blessed with endless sunshine due to the rain shadow of the Andes – and endless supplies of irrigation water from these mountains. Add all that to new-found political and economic stability and the 1990s were ripe for Chilean wine to burst onto the international stage.

Soft, juicy Merlot, Cabernet Sauvignon and Carmenère are what Chile is best known for in red wine, and toasty, tropically fruited Chardonnay and crisp, tangy Sauvignon Blanc in whites. But all sorts of other grape varieties are popping up, too. Reds share a basic style of ripe fruit and lots of it; whites are fresh and generally have good acidity, while aromatic grapes like Gewürztraminer and Viognier can be very highly perfumed. There's also dark rosé, with a strong,

strawberryish taste. Quality is reliable. A few mega-priced reds have been launched: some are genuinely excellent, while others rely more on smart marketing.

So let's take a look at this pencil-thin country that stretches for 4300 kilometres/2700 miles from the Atacama desert (the world's driest place) in the north to the frozen wastes of Patagonia in the south. There are some amazing wines coming from the far north, from the valleys of Elqui, Limarí and Choapa in Coquimbo. It should be too hot up there, but there is an icy off-shore ocean current called the Humboldt Current which runs up from the Antarctic and literally freezes the west coast of South America. Each day as the sun rises in the wide sky, bone-chilling cold winds get dragged up these river valleys from the sea. Brilliant sunshine and ice-cold winds create fantastic conditions for the grapes, resulting in full, fruity ripeness balanced by refreshing

The Maipo Valley south of Santiago.

acidity. Look for these valley names on some of Chile's best and newest reds and whites. The Humboldt Current continues to exercise its chilly charm further south in Aconcagua; you'll find increasing numbers of wines – particularly whites, with Sauvignon in the lead – sporting the names Aconcagua, Casablanca and Leyda, all very sunny spots cooled by icy blasts off the ocean.

Chile's traditional vineyard areas are further inland in the Central Valley. Maipo, just south of Santiago, is famous for reds, particularly Cabernet. Cachapoal and Colchagua make round, smooth reds and whites, though the Apalta subregion is known for dark dense reds. Curicó and Maule are fairly warm and produce much of Chile's cheaper stuff, often labelled Valle Central. In the far south, things turn cool again and, frequently, damp, as Patagonia creeps closer. Ripening is more difficult, but lovely, fragrant wines are coming from the regions of Itata, Bío Bío and Malleco, with Pinot Noir, Riesling and Gewürztraminer leading the way.

Do regions matter?
Yes. Styles are very different from north to south. Cheaper blends will probably be labelled Valle Central or Central Valley.

Do vintages matter?
Not much. There are vintage variations, but the wines are never less than good.

When do I drink them?
Chilean reds and whites are great all-rounders, with enough bright fruit to drink by themselves, yet enough weight and structure to accompany all foods.

Can I afford them?
Yes, 99 per cent of the time. There are a few absurdly priced 'icon' wines – but you don't have to buy them.

QUICK GUIDE ▷ Chile

Location The vineyards are mainly in the Central Valley and its sub-regions Maipo, Rapel, Curicó and Maule. To the west of Santiago are the important Casablanca Valley and San Antonio, with its cool sub-zone of Leyda. To the north is Aconcagua and the exciting cool regions of Limarí and Elqui. To the south, below Maule, are the cool, damp Itata and Bío-Bío sub-regions.

Grapes Chile grows the whole range of international grapes. Merlot, Cabernet Sauvignon, Carmenère and Syrah are the main reds; Chardonnay and Sauvignon Blanc the major whites. More than half of what was thought to be Merlot in Chile turned out to be Carmenère, a fantastic traditional Bordeaux grape variety thought to be extinct, which gives rich yet savoury wines in its own right and blends brilliantly with Merlot and Cabernet.

- Coquimbo
- Aconcagua
- Central Valley
- Southern Region

• Santiago

Ten to try
RED
- **Carmen** Nativa Cabernet Sauvignon ❷
- **Concha y Toro** Don Melchor Cabernet Sauvignon ❺
- **Errázuriz** Merlot ❷
- **Montes** Alpha Syrah ❸
- **Viña Falernia** Carmenère ❷
- **Viña Leyda** Pinot Noir ❷
- **Tabalí** Syrah ❷

WHITE
- **Cono Sur** 20 Barrels Chardonnay ❷
- **Santa Rita** Floresta, Leyda Sauvignon Blanc ❷
ROSÉ
- **Torres** Santa Digna Cabernet Sauvignon ❷

Argentina

Both Chile and Argentina manage to make wines with a real national identity which are nonetheless international in their appeal. As yet Chile's offerings are a bit more focused and individual, but that is partly because she has found it much easier to identify and develop her cooler-than-average vineyards along the chilly Pacific coast.

Argentina's main vineyard area is Mendoza, tucked up against the Andes and a very long way from any cooling sea breezes. Ah, but the Andes have foothills and valleys and it is up there that the vineyards are climbing. The higher the vineyard, the cooler the conditions, yet the sun shines relentlessly, so Argentina's general style is always going to be rich and round and ripe. This is fine for the reds, especially the Malbec – which is Argentina's calling card and excellent for rich, juicy flavours – as well as Cabernet, Syrah, Merlot and another Argentine speciality, Bonarda. Whites are not so good, but the local Torrontés grape provides delightful, musky flavours, Chardonnay is quite chubby and Sauvignon only occasionally works.

However, there has been an influx of investment and enthusiasm both from Europe and the Americas, convinced that Argentina can make some of the world's great wines. Most of the incomers have focused on Mendoza, and this has created a far greater awareness of the subregions of this vast vineyard area. South of the city of Mendoza, altitudes rise from about 850 metres to 1060m and the higher vineyards do give a fresher, juicier quality, especially to Malbec. Look for names of top zones like Las Compuertas, Luján de Cuyo, Perdriel, Agrelo and Ugarteche on the label. The Uco Valley, climbing up into the Andes, has long been identified as having the best cool conditions in Mendoza, but there are big differences between Tupungato, at an altitude of up to 1500 metres, and San Carlos, whose vineyards are nearer 900m high.

Mendoza no longer has a monopoly on quality. To the north, the areas of San Juan, La Rioja and Catamarca used to be dismissed as hot, dusty, bulk wine regions, but all are now showing some style and even producing

Lujan de Cuyo's high-altitude vineyards produce beefy red wines, primarily from well-established Malbec vines.

fragrant whites. Argentina's most perfumed whites come from Cafayate, even further north, in Salta, where the Torrontés grape balances succulence with heady floral scent. Altitudes of over 1700 metres and clear skies create perfect conditions for intense reds and whites.

There's also a load of wine activity way south of Mendoza in Patagonia. At present most of the action is along the fast-flowing Río Negro, the black river, so called because it runs deep and clear while most of Argentina's Andean rivers look more like milky tea. The Río Negro region is well-established, while the Neuquén region, just outside Neuquen city, is newer. Both offer reds and whites of intensity and focused flavours. And there are even a few hardy souls planting vines a good deal farther south.

Do regions matter?
Yes. They're very different, north to south. And within Mendoza and the Uco Valley, subregions give quite distinct flavours.

Do vintages matter?
Argentina has very few bad vintages – too much sun is more likely to be the problem. Vintages are more important in the south and the north.

When do I drink them?
Reds are mostly fairly full and ripe, but young ones can be fresh and fruity. They mostly demand sturdy food. Scented Torrontés white can be a delight on its own.

Can I afford them?
Yes, although there are some pricey 'boutique' estates and 'icon' wines, particularly reds..

Right: Summer hailstorms are a real problem for Argentina's grape growers. The hailstones can be as big as golf balls and wreak havoc in the vineyards. This is the high Uco Valley.

australia

Australia, as you might expect from a land built by pioneers, is a wine pioneer as well. A nation that has had to make its own rules from the word go was never likely to be happy conforming to the norms of classic wine styles. And so it invented its own: upfront fruit, opulent texture and new oak – all at an affordable price. And it works equally well for reds and whites. European wines were the starting point, and the grapes (since Australia has no indigenous vines) are mainly the classic ones of Cabernet Sauvignon, Shiraz (France's Syrah), Chardonnay, Semillon and Riesling. Nowadays, many of Australia's wine styles are copied around the world, and Australian winemakers and vineyard experts have influenced wine production on every continent.

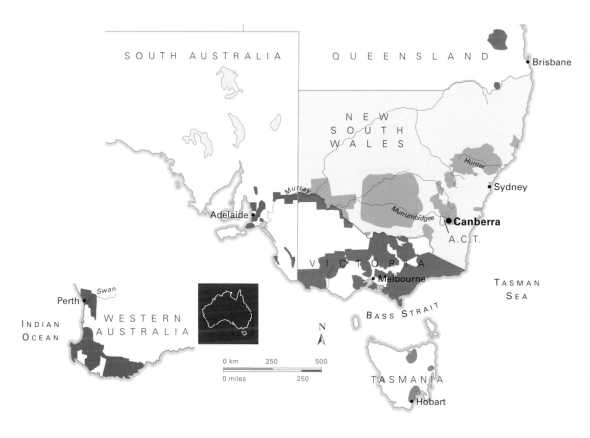

fruity wine in even the hottest, driest, most unpromising conditions – the sort of conditions that in Europe would in the past have been written off as incapable of making wine worth drinking. Australia changed all that with the introduction of refrigerated fermentation, for both whites and reds – the 20th century's single most important advance in winemaking technology. Arguably the world leader now in technology, it's almost impossible to overstate Australia's influence on the flavour of the wine we drink.

These sweet-looking roos are a real menace for the growers as they nibble the juicy ripe grapes just before harvest time.

Because Australia is so different from Europe in the way it organizes its wine industry, let's take a few moments to look at how it works. For one thing, every winemaking state in Australia makes almost every wine style. If you want a cool climate you go up into the hills, and further south; if you want a warm climate you go north, and stay nearer the plain. That way you can control whether your wines taste ripe, very ripe, or very ripe indeed. There's an increasing move to cool climates and more subtle wines; but Aussie wines never lose that ripeness. It's the single most important key to the national style.

Wines can come from a single vineyard, or they can be blended from every state in the country – or anything in between. Look at the distance involved – and then think of grapes being trucked perhaps from the Hunter Valley north of Sydney to the Barossa Valley near Adelaide, and arriving in perfect condition, ready to be made into ripe, fresh-tasting wines. That's the sort of technical know-how that Australia takes for granted. Its winemakers are trained to produce tasty, clean,

South Australia

South Australia produces huge quantities of wine. It
makes more than any other Australian state – everything
from light wines to lush ones, from everyday cheapies to
seriously expensive reds and whites, and even ports.
How to generalize? Impossible. Pick a style: chances are
somebody's making it. Yes, there's the ubiquitous toasty
Chardonnay, but South Australia has classic, unique
styles, as well.

Barossa Valley Shiraz – often from very old vines,
even a century or more old – is extraordinarily dense,
spicy wine, oozing sun-baked fruit: you'll taste ripe
tannins and flavours redolent of old leather, spices,
earth, blackberries. McLaren Vale Shiraz is similar. And
Grenache, again from very old vines, can be a riot of
herbal scent and rich strawberry fruit.

Rieslings from the Clare and Eden Valleys have
established a new benchmark style. They're not a bit like
either German or Alsace Rieslings: instead, they start
lean and citrussy then develop an amazing taste of toast
and limes. You can't believe it until you try it.

Coonawarra Cabernet is probably what all Cabernet
Sauvignon would taste like if it could: intense and
blackcurranty, yes, but with a vivid brightness of fruit
that is hard to find elsewhere, and a glorious minty
edge. These are just the main areas, but from the
Limestone Coast in the south, to Langhorne Creek,
Fleurieu and Adelaide Hills near Adelaide, right up to the
baking Flinders Ranges in the north, you'll find people
producing wine packed with individuality.

Do regions matter?

They do, but it's a complex picture since there are suble
and not so subtle differences inside all the regions. Wines
from the Adelaide Hills are generally cool-climate and
pinging with fruit; Barossa wines are bigger and beefier;

*The Barossa Valley in South Australia is one of my favourite
Australian landscapes, the green vines and gums standing like
oases in the middle of the parched acres.*

and Coonawarra, Clare and Eden go for intensity
without brawn. Other regions, including bulk-producer
Riverland, usually deliver big, ultra-ripe flavours.

Do vintages matter?

In Adelaide Hills, yes; in Coonawarra, yes; otherwise, not
really. Poor in South Australia would be good elsewhere.

When do I drink them?

Drink Coonawarra Cabernets with lamb roasted with
garlic and rosemary. Hefty Barossa Shiraz is more of a
winter evening wine. Clare and Eden Rieslings are ideal
for quenching your thirst as the sun goes down. As for
the Grenache, drink it to put you in wild party mood.

Can I afford them?

Absolutely. There are lots of inexpensive, tasty wines. The
best aren't cheap, but they are classics. Drink them once
in a while to remind yourself how amazing wine can be.

QUICK GUIDE ▷ *South Australia*

Location High-quality wines come from Barossa, Eden and Clare Valleys, Adelaide Hills, McLaren Vale, Coonawarra and Limestone Coast. Riverland is the bulk-wine region.

Grapes Anything and everything. Classics are Shiraz, Cabernet Sauvignon, Chardonnay and Riesling.

Local jargon Don't confuse South Australia with the more general South-Eastern Australia appellation.

① Clare Valley
② Barossa & Eden Valleys
③ Riverland
④ McLaren Vale
⑤ Coonawarra

Twenty to try

RED

- **Tim Adams** Shiraz ②
- **Balnaves** Cabernet Sauvignon ⑤
- **D'Arenberg** The Custodian Grenache ②
- **Eldredge** Sangiovese ③
- **Henschke** Mount Edelstone Shiraz ⑤
- **Majella** The Musician Cabernet Sauvignon-Shiraz ②
- **Nottage Hill** Shiraz ②
- **S C Pannell** Shiraz/Grenache ④
- **Parker Coonawarra Estate** First Growth Cabernet ⑤
- **Primo Estate** Joseph Cabernet Sauvignon-Merlot Moda ④
- **Rockford** Basket Press Shiraz ⑤
- **Skillogalee** Shiraz ③

WHITE

- **Tim Adams** Semillon ②
- **Grosset** Polish Hill Riesling ④
- **Jacob's Creek** Reeves Point Chardonnay ③
- **Peter Lehmann** Eden Valley Riesling ②
- **Mount Horrocks** Watervale Riesling ③
- **Petaluma** Chardonnay ③
- **Shaw & Smith** Sauvignon Blanc ②
- **Yalumba** Eden Valley Viognier ②

The Murray river is the lifeline for New South Wales, Victoria and especially South Australia, providing essential irrigation and, in Adelaide's case, largely keeping the city watered. Years of overuse and national drought have brought this great river to its knees, reducing water flow by up to 90%. Many of Australia's bulk producing vineyards may have to go out of business if the drought continues.

Victoria

Victoria has more small isolated wine regions than any other state, some boasting only a couple of wineries, some up and coming, some old and just hanging on. The styles range from pale and delicate to pungent and impressive, red, white and sparkling. Many are world class, but there are two styles that no one in the world does better – the fortified Liqueur Muscats and Tokays of North-East Victoria. These are explosively sweet, with a concentrated grapiness and an intense perfume of coffee and toffee, raisins and nuts, and sometimes rose petals, that is almost shocking in its richness.

Victoria does cool-climate wines, too. It produces some of the country's tastiest Pinot Noir, from the Yarra Valley and Mornington Peninsula. The best are a match for good Burgundy. Yarra Valley fizz is also excellent.

Other wines range from the inexpensive bulk wines from Murray Darling up to elegant reds and whites with well-defined flavours from the cooler areas near the coast or special little pockets inland. There are a few big, fat wines, but not as many as in New South Wales.

Do regions matter?

Yarra Valley has elegant wines with finely focused flavours: Chardonnay from here is more intense and nutty than rich and toasty. There are various small regions scattered around Melbourne. Mornington Peninsula and Geelong are fairly cool, but the climate gets warmer as you head north and the wines are correspondingly richer and beefier in the Goulburn Valley, Bendigo, Beechworth or Heathcote. Rutherglen and Glenrowan are the places for the fortified wines.

Do vintages matter?

In the Yarra and around Melbourne, yes. Elsewhere, not that much. See the Quick Guide, above.

Location Yarra Valley, Mornington Peninsula, Bendigo and Heathcote, Rutherglen and Glenrowan are significant for quality, Murray Darling for quantity.

Grapes The stars are sweet fortified Muscat and Muscadelle (Tokay), subtle Pinot Noir, scented Shiraz and Chardonnay.

Local jargon Rutherglen Muscats come in four quality grades. In ascending order, they are: Rutherglen, Classic, Grand and Rare.

Vintages to look for (Yarra) 2006 to 2002, 2000, 1998.

Ten to try
RED
- **De Bortoli** Pinot Noir ③
- **Kooyong** Pinot Noir ④
- **Mount Langi Ghiran** Shiraz ⑤
- **Tyrrell's** Rufus Stone Shiraz ③

① Bendigo
② Heathcote
③ Rutherglen and Glenrowan
④ Yarra Valley
⑤ Mornington Peninsula

WHITE
- **Stonier** Chardonnay ③
- **Tahbilk** Marsanne ②
- **Tarrawarra** Chardonnay ⑤

SPARKLING
- **Green Point** ③
- **Seppelt** Show Sparkling Shiraz (red) ③

FORTIFIED
- **Chambers** Grand Rutherglen Muscat ⑤

When do I drink them?

Premium Yarra Valley reds and whites deserve a special occasion. The fortified Muscats are a match for chocolate and Christmas pudding, but you could also put them with – or on – ice cream, or just tuck into them on their own.

Can I afford them?

The best Yarra Valley Pinot Noirs are pretty expensive and suffer from vintage variations just as red Burgundies, their European counterparts, do. Fortified Muscats are quite expensive, especially the oldest ones, but they're certainly not overpriced.

New South Wales

Well, this is where I started in Australia. There was a time when I thought virtually the whole world of wine revolved around the Hunter Valley, two hours' drive north of Sydney (or rather more if you stopped off at Wollombi for a snifter of Dr Jurd's Jungle Juice).

The rich, ripe, utterly un-European flavours were a revelation then – and Hunter Valley reds and whites are still some of Australia's most individual: Chardonnay is fat and full of tropical fruit and toast, tasting reassuringly old-fashioned; Shiraz is rich, berried and leathery-tasting – spicy and warm-hearted on a big scale from the top Hunter vineyards; and Semillon, usually unoaked, can be tart and raw when young but ages to a wonderful toastiness, allied to waxy, leathery, lanolin richness and a flicker of custardy sweetness – one of the wine world's greatest and most unexpected transformations.

Nearby, the small region of Mudgee, with marginally cooler temperatures, makes good blackcurrant reds and Cowra is famous for rich, fat Chardonnay. If you see Orange, Hilltops, Tumbarumba or Canberra District on the label, the wine will be from high, cool vineyards and should have a thrilling, if lean, intensity of fruit. Riverina is New South Wales's bulk wine area. Flavours here are generally simple, ripe and juicy, but there are oakier, more concentrated wines as well, and several world-class golden, super-sweet ones.

Do regions matter?

They do, but the producer usually matters more. Even so, Hunter Valley wines are quite unlike any others in Australia, coming from virtually subtropical vineyards and with a tricky climate. The regions of Orange, Hilltops and Canberra are quite different – the vineyards here are high altitude and cool.

Do vintages matter?

They matter a lot in the Hunter Valley where rainstorms often occur just before harvest – reds and whites can often have totally different results.

When do I drink them?

Hunter Valley wines for whenever you feel like fat, lush flavours. They can nearly all be drunk young; unoaked Semillon needs to age. Cool-climate wines are ready to drink when bottled, but they will age too.

Can I afford them?

Given that Sydney is near by, most wines are quite expensive, though Riverina is better value.

QUICK GUIDE ▷ *New South Wales*

Location The major quality regions are Hunter Valley, Cowra, Mudgee, Orange, Hilltops and Canberra. The largest regions are Riverina and Murray Darling, Swan Hill and Perricoota on the Murray River.

Grapes Semillon and ripe, toasty Chardonnay are the main whites; leading reds are spicy, full-on Shiraz and blackcurranty Cabernet.

Ten to try
RED
• **Brokenwood** Graveyard Shiraz ❺
• **Clonakilla** Shiraz-Viognier ❺
• **Hope Estate** Shiraz ❷
• **Tyrrell's** Vat 9 Shiraz ❹
WHITE
• **Allandale** Chardonnay ❷
• **Brokenwood** Semillon ❸
• **McWilliam's** Mount Pleasant Semillon ❷

• **Philip Shaw** No 19 Sauvignon Blanc ❸
• **Tyrrell's** Vat 47 Chardonnay ❹
SWEET WHITE
• **De Bortoli** Noble One Botrytis Semillon ❺

① Riverina   ④ Mudgee
② Cowra   ⑤ Hunter Valley
③ Orange

Western Australia

The thing is, Western Australia is so far away from the rest of Australia. It's about 4000 kilometres west–east from Perth to Sydney and most of that's desert. Basically 'Australia' has come to mean the states of the east and south-east and Western Australia was left to develop as best as it could an awful long way from the rest of the country. But with global warming threatening much of South Eastern Australia, the whole south-western corner of Western Australia where it's very cool and mostly undeveloped could be in a for a further bonanza as the world turns away from super-ripe styles of wine.

By far the most important area is Margaret River, a knob of land butting out into the sea just where the warm Indian Ocean and the cold Southern Ocean meet. This creates breezes that cool the vines down and give beautiful, tangy fresh whites and deep-flavoured serious reds that really do match the French classics of red and white Bordeaux and white Burgundy. Sauvignon, Semillon (often blended as in Bordeaux) and Chardonnay are the best whites; Cabernet, Merlot (again often blended as in Bordeaux) and Shiraz are the

best reds. South of Margaret River the Manjimup and Pemberton both produce good cool-climate flavours, and the large Great Southern area right down near the Southern Ocean is brilliant for tangy whites and tasty reds. North of Margaret River there are good vineyards in Geographe, Peel and Perth Hills while the original area of Swan Valley is still well planted with vines. But it's hot here and the wines are rich and round. It would make wonderful Aussie 'ports' and 'sherries' but no-one seems to want them nowadays.

Do regions matter?
Yes, there are big variations in style.

Do vintages matter?
Yes, the wines are always good, but cooler areas may not fully ripen their grapes in wet or cold vintages.

When do I drink them?
Great Southern whites, especially Riesling, are lovely just by themselves, as are Margaret River Sauvignons. The reds are brilliant food wines.

Can I afford them?
Only Swan Valley wines are cheap. But Great Southern isn't expensive, and Margaret River, while never cheap, has lots of affordable labels.

The gums in Western Australia are some of the tallest and most beautiful in the nation.

QUICK GUIDE ▷ *Western Australia*

Location The best regions are Margaret River, Great Southern and Pemberton. Swan District near Perth is the bulk region.

Grapes Cabernet Sauvignon and Shiraz for the reds; whites from Chardonnay, Riesling and Sauvignon Blanc, plus Chenin Blanc and Verdelho.

Five to try
RED
• **Cullen** Cabernet-Merlot ❺
• **Pierro** Pinot Noir ❹
• **Plantagenet** Shiraz ❺
WHITE
• **Cape Mentelle** Semillon-Sauvignon Blanc ❸
• **Voyager** Chardonnay ❸

Tasmania

The island state of Tasmania sits well south of the bottom tip of Victoria across the cold and stormy Bass Strait and for most of its history experts have said it's too cold for vines: why not grow apples? Well, most of Tassie is too cold or wet, but there are sheltered stretches of land often huddled together on river banks or along estuaries where the winds die and warmth is reflected off the water, where brilliant flavours can be created. Cool conditions are also exactly what you want for sparkling wine and Tasmania provides the fruit for most of Australia's best fizz.

In the north the vineyards are mostly on the Tamar Valley above Launceston or Pipers River. The East Coast is surprisingly warm and can make lush Pinot Noir and Chardonnay. And in the south, along the Coal, Derwent and Huon Valleys near Hobart you may sometimes lose most of your crop to frost, but some delicious wines are made. When choosing wines the producer's name is more important than the region or vintage. They won't be cheap but they should be good.

Queensland

On the face of it Queensland would seem to be getting too hot for growing quality wine grapes, let alone for producing some pretty classy reds and whites – even in the cooler far south along the border with New South Wales there is subtropical rain forest. But when the sun shines mercilessly the only way to get real consistent quality is to head up into the hills as the higher you go the cooler it gets, especially at night.

In Queensland this means the Granite Belt region, especially the vineyards around Stanthorpe on the border with New South Wales. Most of the best grapes either come from here or from South Burnett, north of Brisbane.

QUICK GUIDE ▷ *Tasmania*

Location Tasmania is the centre of cool-climate grape-growing in Australia, but has several diverse growing regions. See the map on page 171.

Grapes Intense, nutty Chardonnay, scented Pinot Gris and fine Riesling whites; silky, strawberryish Pinot Noir reds – but the real star is fabulous premium fizz.

Five to try
Apart from fizz, the wines are hard to find outside Australia.
RED
• Tamar Ridge Devil's Corner Pinot Noir ❷
WHITE
• Moorilla Chardonnay ❸
• Pipers Brook Riesling ❷
SPARKLING
• Arras ❺
• Jansz ❸

QUICK GUIDE ▷ *Queensland*

Location Most vineyards are in the south-eastern corner. See the map on page 171.

Grapes Shiraz is the principal grape. Cabernet Sauvignon, Chardonnay, Viognier and Verdelho also do well.

Five to try
A few larger producers export, but most wines are sold at the cellar door.
RED
• Ballandean Cabernet-Shiraz ❹
• Boireann Shiraz-Viognier ❺
• Robert Channon Verdelho ❸
• Symphony Hill Cabernet Sauvignon Reserve ❺
WHITE
• Sirromet Seven Scenes Chardonnay 25 ❸

Below: Albert River in the Gold Coast hinterland is one of Australia's great wine tourism destinations.

new zealand

This is the home of benchmark New World Sauvignon Blanc, the archetypal green, tangy wine. And it's a pretty recent benchmark, too, because the first Sauvignon Blanc was planted in Marlborough – now a classic region for the grape – in 1973. It became clear almost instantly that this is what Sauvignon Blanc should taste like. Until then the only benchmark for the grape had been Sancerre and the other Sauvignons of the Loire Valley in France. New Zealand Sauvignon is more aggressive, more gooseberryish, more pungent, whereas Sancerre is rounder, more subtle – and more unreliable. Sauvignon Blanc in New Zealand, at whatever level of quality, has that hallmark gooseberry and lime zest fruit that makes it almost irresistibly mouthwatering.

New Zealand is not all Sauvignon Blanc from Marlborough – Sauvignon Blanc does well in other regions, too. In fact, New Zealand grows a variety of other grapes as well as any other country in the southern hemisphere – and its reputation as a white-wine-only place is rapidly changing because of its recent successes with red grapes like Pinot Noir, Merlot and Syrah.

Generally speaking, New Zealand makes cool-climate New World styles that are lighter and more fragrant than Australian wines. It is good at grapes Australia finds more difficult, in particular subtle, mellow Pinot Noir, where New Zealand can be world class and the different regions all show encouragingly different styles. It's the same with Chardonnay. There are superb examples made all the way from up near Auckland, right down to Central Otago in the far south. Riesling is generally floral but can be sharp and thrilling in the deep south. Sparkling wine follows the Champagne model and often equals it in quality. Of the other red grapes, Cabernet Sauvignon struggles to ripen, but can be brilliant in Hawkes Bay and on Waiheke Island. Merlot is outstanding in Hawkes Bay and Syrah, on a part of Hawkes Bay called Gimblett Gravels, is a cool, fragrant revelation.

Do regions matter?

Yes, very much. New Zealand's two islands are very different. Basically the North Island is virtually tropical in the north but cool enough for Pinot Noir at the southern end. The South Island was considered too cold for grapes until the 1970s but is now the centre of the wine industry and boasts wonderful vineyards all the way down to Central Otago in the snowfields of the south. There are some vines north of Auckland but the conditions are warm and humid, as they are around Auckland itself, though Waiheke Island out in the bay opposite Auckland is an outstanding Cabernet and Merlot producer. There are splashes of vineyard as we

How magical is this moonrise over the vineyards of Marlborough? How tranquil can a vineyard seem? But come daylight Marlborough is transformed into the engine-room of New Zealand's wine industry.

head south, but things don't really kick off until we get to Napier on the south-east coast. Gisborne, famous for Chardonnay and Gewürztraminer, and Hawkes Bay, famous for serious reds from Cabernet, Merlot and Syrah, grow a range of superb grapes. Gimblett Gravels is the outstanding area here. Down by Wellington, Wairarapa, especially the area around the town of Martinborough, produce positively Burgundian Pinot Noirs.

Facing Wellington at the tip of South Island is Marlborough, now New Zealand's biggest wine region by far. It's centred in the Wairau Valley but spreads down the east coast through and beyond the Awatere Valley. Famous for Sauvignon, it does other whites very well, and is increasingly good at fizz and Pinot Noir. Nelson, north-west of Marlborough, is another excellent cool region, as is Waipara, heading south to Christchurch and the Canterbury Plains. It's getting very cool by now but Central Otago, in the mountains near Queenstown, provides one more brilliant vineyard region – extreme, continental, desert-like in summer and snow-covered in winter. The Pinot Noirs, Chardonnays and Rieslings reflect the extreme conditions.

Do vintages matter?

They do, but few wines need aging. Buy wines from a recent year and drink them young.

When do I drink them?

Anytime. Cult Sauvignon Blancs like Cloudy Bay will impress your wine buff friends, but you can buy equally good wine for half the price.

Can I afford them?

The wines are never going to be the cheapest to make, and most producers, realizing this, go for quality. It's worth spending a bit more for something extra good. Don't buy suspiciously cheap New Zealand wines.

Location The most southerly of the southern hemisphere wine countries.

Grapes Sauvignon Blanc, Chardonnay, Riesling (sweet and dry) and Gewürztraminer are the grapes for the best whites. Pinot Noir, the Cabernets, Merlot and Syrah are the reds. Styles vary from north to south. Hawkes Bay Sauvignon Blanc is softer than the tangy Marlborough style. Chardonnay is richer in the north. Pinot Noir likes cool Martinborough, Canterbury and Otago, but Cabernet and Merlot are happier in the north, especially Hawkes Bay and Waiheke Island.

① Auckland
② Gisborne
③ Hawke's Bay
④ Wairarapa
⑤ Nelson
⑥ Marlborough
⑦ Canterbury
⑧ Central Otago

NORTH ISLAND
Auckland ①
Gisborne ②
③
Wellington ④
⑤ ⑥
⑦ Christchurch
⑧
SOUTH PACIFIC OCEAN
SOUTH ISLAND
N
0 km   200
0 miles   200

Ten to try

RED
• **Palliser Estate** Pinot Noir ③
• **Vidal** Syrah ②
• **Villa Maria** Reserve Cabernet Sauvignon-Merlot ③

WHITE
• **Astrolabe** Sauvignon Blanc ③
• **Framingham** Riesling ②
• **Kumeu River** Chardonnay ③
• **Montana** 'O' Ormond Gisborne Chardonnay ③

• **Spinyback** Pinot Gris ②
• **Vavasour** Sauvignon Blanc ③

SPARKLING
• **Cloudy Bay** Pelorus ③

NEW ZEALAND CLASSIFICATIONS

Labels guarantee geographic origin. The broadest designation is New Zealand, followed by North or South Island. Next come the 10 or so regions. Labels may also name specific localities and individual vineyards.

south africa

South Africa has been on a steep learning curve since the demise of the apartheid regime in the early 1990s and its subsequent emergence from international isolation. It is rediscovering its past as well as forging an exciting, innovative future. A new generation is taking over vineyards and wineries and the results are dramatic.

South Africa makes all possible styles of wine, from green and tangy whites, through broad-beamed, nutty whites, to rich toasty ones; and reds from light and juicy Cinsauts, through strawberry-soft Pinot Noirs and challenging, blackcurranty Cabernets to spicy, booming Shiraz and Pinotage. There are fortifieds, too, both light and dry sherry-like ones and sweet, dark versions in the style of port.

The range of grapes encompasses all the international favourites – Cabernet Sauvignon, Merlot, Chardonnay, Sauvignon Blanc – and there's Chenin Blanc as well, mostly used for everyday whites. But carefully made Chenin from old vines is good stuff and is a good-value star in the Cape. The country's speciality is the Pinotage grape, which makes both bright, juicy reds and seriously heavyweight ones. It has an unashamed toasted marshmallow and damson flavour that is unique and thrilling at its best.

The local African population have been working in the vineyards for generations. The difference now is that thanks to Fairtrade and Black empowerment schemes they are starting to share in the benefits and profits.

Left: Many of South Africa's vineyards are planted in valleys leading up to awesome mountain ranges. This is Franschhoek, a beautiful long valley barricaded in by steep mountains.
Facing page: This is almost the tip of Africa. New vineyard areas are being planted down towards Walker Bay in Overberg, as producers head south-east through the mountains in search of the coolest growing spots, chilled by the Antarctic Benguela Current.

Quality in South Africa is still uneven compared to Chile or Australia – countries with which it is competing on the international market. But one thing in South Africa's favour is that much of the progress is being led by single-estate wines, not those of vast corporations.

Do regions matter?

Yes, very much. Many of the most exciting wines are coming from newer vineyards in cool, maritime areas like Elim, Cape Point, Constantia, Elgin and Walker Bay in the south, and Tygerberg and Darling in the west. Others are from old bush-vine plantings scattered through the warmer regions such as Swartland in the Coastal Region, Paarl and Franschhoek. Stellenbosch is the traditional centre of South African wine and you'll see that name on a lot of labels.

Do vintages matter?

Most whites should be drunk young. Only the most serious red contenders will benefit from much aging.

When do I drink them?

Anytime, but most reds need food.

Can I afford them?

Almost always, yes. Very few wines are very overpriced, although South Africa is itching to establish some super-premium wines at super-premium prices. Chenin is particularly well priced and there are numerous good-value Sauvignon Blanc, Pinotage and Shiraz wines.

SOUTH AFRICA CLASSIFICATIONS

The Wine of Origin (WO) system divides wine-producing areas into regions, districts, wards, estates and single vineyards. Varietal, vintaged wines for both export and the local market must be made from at least 85% of the named grape and vintage.

QUICK GUIDE ▷ *South Africa*

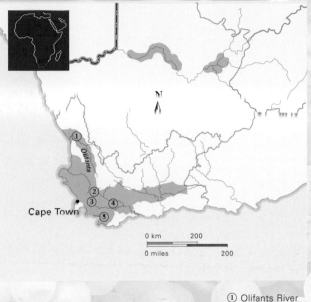

① Olifants River
② Paarl
③ Stellenbosch
④ Robertson
⑤ Overberg

Location Most of the wine regions are clustered around Cape Town. Paarl and Stellenbosch, districts of the vast Coastal Region, are the best established. Robertson is good for whites. Overberg (including Walker Bay) in the far south is good for Pinot Noir. Elim, Cape Point, Tygerberg and Darling are excellent for whites. Olifants River is a bulk wine-producing region.

Grapes Pinotage is South Africa's own red grape. Cabernet Sauvignon and Merlot are popular. Syrah/Shiraz and other Rhône reds, and even California's Zinfandel, are joining the repertoire. Chardonnay and Sauvignon Blanc are both widely grown whites and there's also some Riesling. Chenin Blanc is used for the simplest whites and a few high-quality ones.

Local jargon *Wine of Origin (WO)* – this official statement on the label guarantees the wine's area of origin, grape variety or varieties and vintage. *Estate wine – wine that is grown and made on a registered estate, usually a sign of good quality.*

Ten to try
RED
- **Beyerskloof** Pinotage ②
- **Bouchard Finlayson** Pinot Noir ④
- **Fairview** Shiraz ④
- **Porcupine Ridge** Syrah ②
- **Rustenberg** John X Merriman ③
- **Steenberg** Merlot ③

WHITE
- **Neil Ellis** Groenekloof Sauvignon Blanc ③
- **Ken Forrester** Chenin Blanc ②
- **Hamilton Russell** Chardonnay ④
- **Vergelegen** Sauvignon Blanc ②

other wine countries

The culture of drinking wine is catching on all over the world, especially in Asia, and more and more countries now want to produce their own wine rather than rely on imports from the well-established wine regions in Europe, North and South America and Australia.

Lebanon

Lebanon's finest producers are Chateau Musar, Chateau Ksara and Chateau Kefraya, making world-class spicy, chocolaty reds, but there are some promising new boutique wineries now snapping at their heels. Most wineries are in the Bekaa Valley.

Cyprus

Cyprus has old vines on high sites in the cool Troodos mountains that are beginning to show real quality. Modernization is slow as the vineyards are divided into so many small holdings. There are good reds from the indigenous Maratheftiko grape. Commandaria, a rich, amber wine, has been famous since the Crusades but is currently more of a historical footnote.

Israel

Fine wine is being made in the cooler regions – Upper Galilee, Golan Heights and Judean Hills. Viticulture is technologically advanced and wineries tend to be up-to-date. There are good Bordeaux blends based on Cabernet Sauvignon, dessert wines and, of course, kosher wines. These last are necessary for observant Jews and they are usually suitable for vegans and vegetarians, too.

Turkey

Turkey's enormous potential is yet to be realized. It is the world's fourth largest grape producer but only a tiny percentage ends up as wine because of a Muslim population and a traditional antipathy to wine. Kavaklidere and Doluca are two well-known producers.

North Africa

North African wine is in a transitional stage. The massive growth of the vineyards of Morocco, Tunisia and Algeria in the past was fuelled by the need of France, the colonial power, for cheap, alcoholic reds for its blending market. That market is long gone but recent European investment in Morocco and Tunisia, especially by Castel Frères, is encouraging the development of spicy reds and rosés. The leading producer in Morocco is Celliers de Meknès.

Asia

Indigenous enthusiasm and serious Western investment are the keys to opening up the potential of countries such as China, India, Japan and Thailand.

Right: You might think Lebanon must be a hot place for growing grapes but in fact the Bekaa Valley has long, cold winters.

India

India's climate is generally unsuitable for wine production and only a small percentage of the vines planted are used for wine. However, wine consumption is increasing rapidly among the young urban professionals and the potential for growth is there, aided by high taxes on foreign imports. Chateau Indage with vineyards in the Maharashtra hills east of Mumbai produces still and sparkling wines and Sula Vineyards, using screwcaps on all its wines, is making very attractive fresh, zesty wines. Grover Vineyards, based in the hills near Bangalore, use the famous and ubiquitous Frenchman Michel Rolland as a consultant.

China

China officially promotes wine (especially red, a lucky colour in China) but its potential remains unfulfilled as most Chinese are reluctant to drink it. However, demand is increasing in the cities and homegrown premium wines are emerging, helped by foreign investment. Massive new plantings every year include Chardonnay and Cabernet Sauvignon, along with traditional Chinese, German and Russian varieties. China now has the fourth largest vineyard acreage in the world, though much of the fruit grown is not as yet used for winemaking.

Japan

The Japanese have been interested in wine for a long time but most of the wines are multi-country blends or made from indigenous varieties such as Koshu. Despite humid growing conditions, wine is produced in almost every province.

Thailand

Thailand's high-altitude vineyards are beginning to produce some tasty wines, especially from Shiraz and Chenin. There are also some floating vineyards in the Mekong Delta which make pleasant rosé wines at least.

Below. Wine-drinking in China is a new phenomenon and it is still rare to see women drinking in public. These three seem pretty confident.

appellation decoder

The trouble with buying European wines is that many are named according to where they come from – the appellation – rather than what's in them: the grape variety or varieties. And if you have heard of a wine but aren't sure exactly which region the appellation is in, it can be a hassle to find it in a shop or on a wine list. To help you sort things out this table brings together appellations, their major styles, their regions and their key grape varieties.   KEY   ● Red   ○ White

Name	● / ○	Region	Major Grape Varieties
ALOXE-CORTON	●	Côte de Beaune, Burgundy, France	*Pinot Noir*
ASTI (sweet/sparkling)	○	Piedmont, North-west Italy	*Muscat (called Moscato here)*
BAIRRADA	●	Portugal	*Baga*
BANDOL	●	Provence, France	*Mourvèdre/Grenache/Cinsaut*
BARBARESCO	●	Piedmont, North-west Italy	*Nebbiolo*
BARDOLINO	●	Veneto, North-east Italy	*Corvina*
BAROLO	●	Piedmont, North-west Italy	*Nebbiolo*
BEAUJOLAIS	●	Burgundy, France	*Gamay*
BEAUNE	●	Côte de Beaune, Burgundy, France	*Pinot Noir*
BERGERAC	●/○	South-West France	● *Cabernet Sauvignon & Franc/ Merlot;* ○ *Sémillon/Sauvignon Blanc*
BONNEZEAUX (sweet)	○	Loire Valley, France	*Chenin Blanc*
BOURGUEIL	●	Loire Valley, France	*Cabernet Franc*
BROUILLY/CÔTE DE BROUILLY	●	Beaujolais, Burgundy, France	*Gamay*
BRUNELLO DI MONTALCINO	●	Tuscany, Central Italy	*Sangiovese*
CAHORS	●	South-West France	*Malbec/Merlot/Tannat*
CHABLIS	○	Burgundy, France	*Chardonnay*
CHAMBOLLE-MUSIGNY	●	Côte de Nuits, Burgundy, France	*Pinot Noir*
CHAMPAGNE (sparkling)	○	Champagne, France	*Chardonnay/Pinot Noir/Pinot Meunier*
CHASSAGNE-MONTRACHET	●/○	Côte de Beaune, Burgundy, France	● *Pinot Noir;* ○ *Chardonnay*
CHÂTEAUNEUF-DU-PAPE	●/○	Southern Rhône Valley, France	● *Grenache/Syrah;* ○ *Roussanne*
CHÉNAS	●	Beaujolais, Burgundy, France	*Gamay*
CHIANTI	●	Tuscany, Central Italy	*Sangiovese*
CHIROUBLES	●	Beaujolais, Burgundy, France	*Gamay*
CONDRIEU	○	Northern Rhône Valley, France	*Viognier*
CORBIÈRES	●	Languedoc-Roussillon, France	*Carignan/Grenache/Cinsaut*

Name	●/○	Region	Major Grape Varieties
CORNAS	●	Northern Rhône Valley, France	Syrah
COSTIÈRES DE NÎMES	●	Languedoc-Roussillon, France	Carignan/Grenache/Mourvèdre/Syrah
CÔTE DE NUITS-VILLAGES	●	Côte de Nuits, Burgundy, France	Pinot Noir
CÔTE-RÔTIE	●	Northern Rhône Valley, France	Syrah
COTEAUX DU LANGUEDOC	●	Languedoc-Roussillon, France	Carignan/Grenache
COTEAUX DU LAYON (sweet)	○	Loire Valley, France	Chenin Blanc
CÔTES DU ROUSSILLON	●	Languedoc-Roussillon, France	Carignan/Cinsaut/Grenache
CROZES-HERMITAGE	● / ○	Northern Rhône Valley, France	● Syrah; ○ Marsanne/Roussanne
DÃO	●	Portugal	Touriga Nacional/Tinta Roriz (Tempranillo)
DÔLE	●	Switzerland	Pinot Noir/Gamay
ENTRE-DEUX-MERS	○	Bordeaux, France	Sémillon/Sauvignon Blanc
FAUGÈRES	●	Languedoc-Roussillon, France	Carignan/Grenache/Syrah
FITOU	●	Languedoc-Roussillon, France	Carignan/Cinsaut/Grenache
FLEURIE	●	Beaujolais, Burgundy, France	Gamay
FRASCATI	○	Lazio, Central Italy	Malvasia/Trebbiano
GAVI	○	Piedmont, North-west Italy	Cortese
GEVREY-CHAMBERTIN	●	Côte de Nuits, Burgundy, France	Pinot Noir
GIGONDAS	●	Southern Rhône Valley, France	Grenache
GIVRY	●	Côte Chalonnaise, Burgundy, France	Pinot Noir
GRAVES	● / ○	Bordeaux, France	● Cabernet Sauvignon & Franc/ Merlot; ○ Sémillon/Sauvignon Blanc
HERMITAGE	● / ○	Northern Rhône Valley, France	● Syrah; ○ Marsanne/Roussanne
JULIÉNAS	●	Beaujolais, Burgundy, France	Gamay
LISTRAC	●	Haut-Médoc, Bordeaux, France	Cabernet Sauvignon & Franc/Merlot
MÂCON/MÂCON-VILLAGES	○	Mâconnais, Burgundy, France	Chardonnay
MARGAUX	●	Haut-Médoc, Bordeaux, France	Cabernet Sauvignon & Franc/Merlot
MÉDOC/HAUT-MÉDOC	●	Bordeaux, France	Cabernet Sauvignon & Franc/Merlot
MERCUREY	● / ○	Côte Chalonnaise, Burgundy, France	● Pinot Noir; ○ Chardonnay
MEURSAULT	○	Côte de Beaune, Burgundy, France	Chardonnay
MINERVOIS	●	Languedoc-Roussillon, France	Grenache/Syrah/Mourvèdre
MONTAGNY	○	Côte Chalonnaise, Burgundy, France	Chardonnay
MOREY-ST-DENIS	●	Côte de Nuits, Burgundy, France	Pinot Noir
MORGON	●	Beaujolais, Burgundy, France	Gamay
MOULIN-À-VENT	●	Beaujolais, Burgundy, France	Gamay
MOULIS	●	Haut-Médoc, Bordeaux, France	Cabernet Sauvignon & Franc/Merlot
MUSCADET	○	Loire Valley, France	Muscadet (aka Melon de Bourgogne)
NUITS-ST-GEORGES	●	Côte de Nuits, Burgundy, France	Pinot Noir
ORVIETO	○	Umbria, Central Italy	Trebbiano
PAUILLAC	●	Haut-Médoc, Bordeaux, France	Cabernet Sauvignon & Franc/Merlot
PESSAC-LÉOGNAN	● / ○	Bordeaux, France	● Cabernet Sauvignon & Franc/ Merlot; ○ Sémillon/Sauvignon Blanc

Name	●/○	Region	Major Grape Varieties
POMEROL	●	Bordeaux, France	Merlot/Cabernet Sauvignon & Franc
POMMARD	●	Côte de Beaune, Burgundy, France	Pinot Noir
POUILLY- FUISSÉ	○	Mâconnais, Burgundy, France	Chardonnay
POUILLY-FUMÉ	○	Loire Valley, France	Sauvignon Blanc
POUILLY-SUR-LOIRE	○	Loire Valley, France	Chasselas
PRIORAT	●	Spain	Garnacha (Grenache)
PULIGNY-MONTRACHET	○	Côte de Beaune, Burgundy, France	Chardonnay
QUARTS DE CHAUME (sweet)	○	Loire Valley, France	Chenin Blanc
RÉGNIÉ	●	Beaujolais, Burgundy, France	Gamay
RÍAS BAIXAS	○	Spain	Albariño
RIBERA DEL DUERO	●	Spain	Tempranillo (called Tinto Fino here)
RIOJA	●/○	Spain	● Tempranillo/Garnacha (Grenache); ○ Viura
RULLY	●/○	Côte Chalonnaise, Burgundy, France	● Pinot Noir; ○ Chardonnay
ST-AMOUR	●	Beaujolais, Burgundy, France	Gamay
ST-CHINIAN	●	Languedoc-Roussillon, France	Carignan/Cinsaut/Grenache
ST-ÉMILION	●	Bordeaux, France	Merlot/Cabernet Sauvignon & Franc
ST-ESTÈPHE	●	Haut-Médoc, Bordeaux, France	Cabernet Sauvignon & Franc/Merlot
ST-JOSEPH	●/○	Northern Rhône Valley, France	● Syrah; ○ Marsanne/Roussanne
ST-JULIEN	●	Haut-Médoc, Bordeaux, France	Cabernet Sauvignon & Franc/Merlot
ST-NICOLAS-DE-BOURGUEIL	●	Loire Valley, France	Cabernet Franc
ST-VÉRAN	○	Mâconnais, Burgundy, France	Chardonnay
SANCERRE	●/○	Loire Valley, France	○ Sauvignon Blanc; ● Pinot Noir
SAUMUR-CHAMPIGNY	●	Loire Valley, France	Cabernet Franc & Sauvignon
SAUTERNES (sweet)	○	Bordeaux, France	Sémillon/Sauvignon Blanc
SAVENNIÈRES	○	Loire Valley, France	Chenin Blanc
SOAVE	○	Veneto, North-east Italy	Garganega/Trebbiano
TORO	●	Spain	Tempranillo (called Tinto del Toro here)
VACQUEYRAS	●	Southern Rhône Valley, France	Grenache/Syrah/Mourvèdre
VALPOLICELLA	●	Veneto, North-east Italy	Corvina
VINO NOBILE DI MONTEPULCIANO	●	Tuscany, Central Italy	Sangiovese
VOLNAY	●	Côte de Beaune, Burgundy, France	Pinot Noir
VOSNE-ROMANÉE	●	Côte de Nuits, Burgundy, France	Pinot Noir
VOUGEOT	●	Côte de Nuits, Burgundy, France	Pinot Noir
VOUVRAY	○	Loire Valley, France	Chenin Blanc

the most useful words in wine

Acidity Acid, naturally present in grapes, gives wine its intense and refreshing qualities.

Appellation An officially designated place of origin. In Europe many wines have to be made from a specified grape variety or varieties to qualify for the appellation name.

Barrel aging Time spent maturing in wood, often 225-litre oak barrels called **barriques**. The wine takes on oak flavours from the wood.

Barrel-fermented Describes wine fermented in oak barrels. Like barrel aging, this process gives the wine characteristic oak flavours.

Blend Mixture of wines of different grapes, styles, origin or age. Blending is carried out to improve the balance of the wine, or to maintain a consistent style.

Botrytis or **noble rot** A fungus which sometimes attacks grapes, reducing the water content and concentrating the sugar and acidity, making the grapes ideal for making intense golden, sweet wines such as Sauternes.

Climate A critical influence on the style and quality of wine. Cool climate areas such as Germany, Champagne and Oregon are at the coolest limits for grape ripening and are good for reserved, elegant styles. In warm-climate areas vines ripen easily but often need to be irrigated. Warm-climate wines are rich and high in alcohol. Red grapes generally need a warmer climate than white grapes.

Cold fermentation Long, slow fermentation at low temperature to extract freshness and fruit flavour from the grapes. Crucial for white wines in warm climates.

Corked Term used to describe wine tainted by a contaminated cork. Corked wine has a mouldy, musty smell.

Cru French term meaning 'growth', used to refer to the wine of an individual vineyard and often in conjunction with a quality ranking, such as Premier Cru (First Growth).

Cuvée Literally the contents of a *cuve* or vat. The term refers to a particular blend, either of different grape varieties or of wine from selected barrels and is used to distinguish, for example, a producer's top Chardonnay and everyday Chardonnay.

Domaine A wine estate, particularly in Burgundy.

Dry A wine that is not perceptibly sweet.

Enologist A wine scientist.

Estate-bottled A wine made and bottled by a single property, though this may encompass several different vineyards. Equivalent terms are **mis en bouteille au château/domaine** in French, **azienda agricola** or **imbottigliato all'origine** in Italian and **Erzeugerabfüllung** or **Gutsabfüllung** in German.

Fermentation The process of transforming sugar into alcohol.

Late-harvest or **vendange tardive** (France) Wine made from super-ripe grapes picked after the normal harvest. Late-harvest wines are usually sweet.

Malolactic fermentation A natural process which turns harsh malic acid in a wine into softer-tasting lactic acid. Malolactic fermentation is prevented in many white wines to preserve the refreshing bite.

Négociant French term for a merchant or shipper who buys wine or grapes from growers, then matures, maybe blends and bottles the wine for sale.

New World The non-European wine-producing countries that have come to the world's attention since the 1970s. The United States, Australia, New Zealand, Chile, Argentina and South Africa are all New World countries. By extension, New World is also an attitude of mind that embraces new technology in the attempt to produce fresher, fruitier wines.

Noble rot See botrytis.

Oak The wood used almost exclusively to make barrels for fermenting and aging fine wines. Oak barrels contribute characteristic toasty vanilla flavours and a rounded taste. Oak chips dunked into the wine or even oak flavouring are cheaper alternatives.

Old vines or **vieilles vignes** (France) Mature vines producing grapes with intense flavours. There are no legal definitions of how old a vine has to be to qualify, but the term is a fairly reliable indicator of quality.

Old World The traditional wine-producing countries of Europe, home to most of the world's established wine styles and grape varieties. Old World can also refer to wines from other countries that seek to emulate these styles.

Producer The company that makes the wine and the most important consideration when choosing a wine. In the same region and the same vintage a good producer will make far better wine than a poor one, and the wine won't necessarily be any more expensive.

Reserva (Spain) and **riserva** (Italy) Legally defined terms for wines that receive extra aging either in oak barrels or in bottle (or both) before they go on sale. These terms carry quality connotations. Elsewhere 'reserve' has no legal definition and does not necessarily indicate a higher quality of wine.

Residual sugar Sugar left over in the wine after fermentation is complete. A perceptible level of residual sugar makes the wine taste sweet.

Single-vineyard Wines with real individuality tend to be made using grapes from just one vineyard.

Tannin The bitter, mouth-drying component in red wines, which is harsh when young but adds depth to the flavour and is crucial to a wine's ability to age.

Terroir A French term used to denote the combination of soil, climate and exposure to the sun – that is, the natural physical environment of the vine.

Varietal Wine made from, and named after, a single or dominant grape variety.

Vendange tardive See late-harvest.

Vieilles vignes See old vines.

Vinification The process of turning grapes into wine.

Vintage The year's grape harvest, also used to describe the wine of a particular year.

Viticulture Vine-growing and vineyard management.

Vitis vinifera The species of vine, native to Europe and Central Asia, that all the classic grape varieties belong to.

Winemaker The person responsible for controlling the vinification process.

Yield Perhaps the most important factor in determining the quality of a wine. The lower the quantity of grapes each vine is allowed to produce, the more intense the juice in the grapes and the flavours in the wine will be.